Collision of Wills

COLLISION OF WILLS

HOW AMBIGUITY ABOUT SOCIAL RANK BREEDS CONFLICT

Roger V. Gould

Foreword by Peter Bearman

The University of Chicago Press
Chicago and London

Roger V. Gould was professor of sociology and political science at Yale University and, from 1990 to 2000, taught sociology at the University of Chicago. He wrote *Insurgent Identities: Class, Community, and Protest in Paris from 1848 to the Commune* (1995) and edited *Rational Choice Controversy in Historical Sociology* (2001), both published by the University of Chicago Press.

The University of Chicago Press, Chicago 60637
The University of Chicago Press, Ltd., London
© 2003 by Erin Graves
All rights reserved. Published 2003
Printed in the United States of America
12 11 10 09 08 07 06 05 04 03   1 2 3 4 5

ISBN: 0-226-30548-1 (cloth)
ISBN: 0-226-30550-3 (paper)

Library of Congress Cataloging-in-Publication Data

Gould, Roger V.
    Collision of wills : how ambiguity about social rank breeds conflict / Roger V. Gould ; foreword by Peter Bearman.
        p.   cm.
    Includes bibliographical references and index.
    ISBN 0-226-30548-1 (alk. paper)—ISBN 0-226-30550-3 (pbk. : alk. paper)
    1. Social conflict. 2. Interpersonal conflict. 3. Violence. 4. Social groups. 5. Group identity. 6. Social control. 7. Dominance (Psychology) I. Title.

HM1121 .G68 2003
303.6—dc21
                                                                                        2003005699

[CONTENTS]

For Erin

Roger Gould died at age thirty-nine on April 29, 2002, after a long battle with leukemia. Two weeks before his death he completed this manuscript and submitted it for publication. At submission, the manuscript was missing some elements typically associated with books: a preface, acknowledgments, and a dedication. Roger was a linear thinker who wrote fluidly in first-draft mode. This is the case with this manuscript as well. Everything was completed except the part that sets the stage for the reader, describes the context of the book and the persons whose influences shaped the ideas, and identifies, in retrospect, the scope conditions for the arguments made. For Roger these elements of a manuscript were less important for the review process, perhaps distracting, and often deployed by authors for instrumental reasons, signaling their prior achievements and academic lineage, perhaps to enhance the probability of favorable review. Consequently, he did not write this material. In this brief foreword, I describe the contexts in which this book was written, acknowledge those whose institutional contributions helped shape the final production (as best as I can ascertain), describe the limited role I have taken as midwife for the manuscript, and consider some of the broader issues that this distinguished book raises. Readers may also note that the book does not have a "conclusion" chapter. Because conclusions typically contain little but rehashed versions of previous arguments and findings often stated more clearly in the main text, Roger felt such a chapter unnecessary. I concur, for the central arguments and findings are carefully laid out in the substantive chapters that compose the book.

This book occupied Roger's attention in three distinct settings. This project began when Roger located Corsican feud data at the French National Archives in Paris. Beginning in the summer of 1996 Roger began collecting, translating, and recording the data. Following the data analysis, Roger developed a model and sought to test it with other data sets. He located homicide data from St. Louis, Chicago, Miami, Bhil, and Munda and Oraon. These efforts produced two published articles. Chapters 4 and 5 of the book are significantly modified versions of these articles. Prior to his diagnosis in the summer of 2001, Roger had drafted chapters 1 through 3. During the fall of 2001 he revised the articles, incorporating them into the book. He had been contemplating the contents of chapter 6 for a couple of years and during the last months of his life finally felt he had developed a satisfying conclusion. Consequently, one can consider this a book whose intellectual home was the departments of sociology at the University of Chicago and at Yale University. One could perhaps find influences of each setting in the text, but it is also the case that Roger profoundly influenced the tenor and nature of each department, so that the influences one might imagine could simply be the indirect reflection of Roger's prior influence. This aside, the departments at Chicago and Yale played an important role in Roger's intellectual life and certainly Roger would have acknowledged his colleagues and these institutions for the support they provided. The Russell Sage Foundation provided a supportive environment during the last year, and Roger was greatly appreciative of the support he received from Yale and from Russell Sage while on leave.

Roger was honest with citations and acknowledgments. If he did not use an article, or if someone did not actually do anything helpful, he did not cite or acknowledge them. His was a radical stance in a discipline in which personal connections often appear to matter as much as the quality of ideas. Acknowledgment of the intellectual contributions of Roger's many friends and colleagues in the discipline is impossible. Roger was unusual in that he was the most challenging intellectual critic and best friend of many people. Should I name only the few I know, I would be certain to have pulled the noses of others. But they know that Roger would have gratefully acknowledged their contributions, had they made any, and with equal vigor excised their names had they not. It is better to be cautious and make a global error of omission.

I have edited the manuscript only slightly, correcting the one or two obvious errors discovered during the review process, enhancing the intellectual superstructure (citations) where incomplete, preparing the bibliography, reviewing the index prepared professionally by Margie Towery, adding a few clarifying sentences here and there, and deleting some others that seemed to detract from the central argument. Roger enjoyed intellectual sparring and cared deeply about the state of social science. In this context he often couldn't help but comment that some of his intellectual opponents arrived at the discussion "barefoot and on a donkey"; had he lived, many of these asides would likely have provided wonderful opportunities for all sorts of mutual nose-pulling, perhaps some even in good spirits. These I have retained. Others would have been excised by Roger in revision, and these I have also excised. In any case, readers can have complete confidence that they are reading Roger's work. His style is inimitable.

The work makes a number of claims, and although it is not necessary for me to go over them here—they are better articulated in the book itself—some discussion of the central argument may help the reader navigate through the beautifully written, carefully crafted, yet still dense argumentation. In this I have had the assistance of the reviewers of the manuscript, whose careful reading and comments provided in some cases support for my inchoate ideas and in others wholly new lenses through which to consider the argument.

In this book Gould develops an original framework for making sense of what appears on the surface to be senseless violence between individuals and between small groups. Taken at face value, most accounts of interpersonal violence suggest that violence erupts because of the most trivial things. One idea prevalent in the literature is that violence is about trivial things because all people encounter opportunities for conflict at some time, that most of these opportunities are about silly things, and that some people are simply prone to violence, so in the end, most violence is about things that don't matter much. Gould challenges this idea and shows that interpersonal violence is a property of relations, not persons. The simplest statement of the central argument advanced is that conflicts are more likely to occur (at these small scales) in relatively symmetrical relations in which there is ambiguity between actors concerning relative social rank, that is, asymmetries in perception that could be contested. As implied above, many social relations involve relative asymmetries that are constantly open to (differing) interpretations. These interpretations typically involve actors' willingness to accede to others' deference claims, however subtle they may be. Consequently, conflicts about deference claims occur often, especially among peers in relatively symmetric relations.

Gould shows that these conflicts become both more frequent and more destructive under specific circumstances that heighten ambiguity about relative rank. Specifically, conflict is more likely to occur when previously well-established relations between actors change or when conflicting definitions of the legitimate bases for social status are emerging. The latter argument, prefigured in Gould's earlier work on the Whiskey Rebellion, suggests that conflicts increase under conditions of social and political instability and change because the social and cultural supports for existing status systems that organize the expression of deference in interpersonal relations break down, leading to instability in relations adjacent to or neighboring the focal relation. This is an especially powerful argument from within the structuralist tradition that centers on analysis of relations rather than individuals. This general framework for analyzing individual violence arising from interpersonal interactions is extended with great care and artistry to the group level, where, Gould shows, conflict is likely to erupt when groups fail to credibly signal their solidarity, thereby leading to ambiguity about just how cohesive they really are. Gould shows that if there is uncertainty about relative groups status, conflict is likely to result.

Quite elegant patterns in support of this general argument are found by observation of the symbolic structure of interpersonal conflict. Critical for his argument that conflict is associated with uncertainty about relative position is that symmetric relations are associated with symbolic conflicts, whereas asymmetric relations are associated with substantive conflicts. Evidently, insulting a peer is quite different from insulting a superior or a subordinate. The emphasis on the symbolic structure of conflict—both interpersonal and group—draws heavily on Gould's earlier work and here establishes his legacy as a social scientist deeply engaged in bridging the intellectual divide between those who study culture and those who study structure. Gould considers a wide array of settings in marshaling evidence in support of these claims, from homicide in American cities to vengeance in nineteenth-century Corsica. One is struck by the robustness of the findings, across quite evidently different settings.

One cannot consider Gould's argument as beholden to a simple methodological individualism, or rational choice calculus. In accounting for why conflicts are about trivial things, Gould notes that the surface account—an insult here, a criticism there—is insufficient, because "disputes are not about what they seem—they are disputes about social relationships." The reason that there are conflicts about relationships is that they are sticky. Once locked into a position, one can expect consequences, often for the long term. Consequently, in relations marked by ambiguity, there is often a struggle for coveted roles. And in such struggles, it is the little things as much as the grand that turn out to be critical. As one reviewer noted, if, as Gould argues, "So long as the parties to a relationship base their expectations about future interactions on the dominance patterns established in the present one, arguments about a two-dollar bet can become just as serious as arguments about a two-thousand-dollar loan," the rational actor, concerned about the long-term consequences of losing the minor dispute, might well respond aggressively to protect his or her perceived status position, even if he or she knows that the two dollars is really quite trivial. In relations where ambiguity is intense, where neighboring relations are shifting, and new deference patterns could be established because of the merest slight, forward-looking actors may well (rationally) respond with violence in order to avoid lock-in. The rational actor strives for coveted roles, and Gould would not disagree. But he rejects the idea that all actors have unitary robotic understandings of the world or that they ascribe the same meaning to their past, present, and future selves. On the basis of ordinary observation, Gould reminds us that some people seem much more attached to their past selves than to their present or future selves. Some people will always keep their word, whatever the temptations of the present offer, sacrificing something they might want now for a commitment made earlier. Others are more easy-going, or from the viewpoint of the past-oriented, less responsible. And still others are oriented solely toward the future.

In the final chapter of this book, Gould considers what difference these various orientations toward maintaining their past selves, gratifying their present selves, or insuring their future selves actually make for conflict dynamics. First, he suggests that willingness to sacrifice past and present selves on behalf of future selves encourages people to accept subordination. More strongly, he argues that those whose sense of self is more embedded in the past than devoted to the future are more prone to violence when deference claims are challenged. The first formulation provides a rationale for the association one observes between salvation religions and inequality and brings to mind the problem of theodicy. The second formulation is absolutely novel. And it leaves far behind the more narrow rational choice interpretation of conflict described above. Most interesting is Gould's consideration of the social structural supports for the constitution of individuals within specific networks of relations as past-, present-, or future-oriented. He implies that social formations that consolidate these three orientations, quite independent of individual preferences for one or another investment in the past, present or future, are especially prone to violence.

Two reviewers compared this work to Durkheim's *Suicide*. The comparison is apt. Like *Suicide*, this book does a lot, but of course, it does not do everything, and some consideration of the scope conditions and other issues seems reasonable, in part because these were themes brought up in the review process that under ordinary circumstances an author would have attended to, either in revision of the manuscript or in a foreword such as this. Three major issues appear salient in this context, and I note them here.

First, with respect to scope conditions, although the book touches on large-scale violence, Gould does not, and did not intend to, provide a framework for explaining the emergence of large-scale war or genocide. Nor does this work consider the social processes through which are formed the individuals and organizations that have historically specialized in large-scale collective violence. Armies and militias, mafiosi and enforcers, dictators and inquisitors fall beyond the scope of this work. Some changes in the text were introduced to clarify the scope conditions of this work.

Second, interpretation of the homicide data that Gould provides in support of the contention that violent conflicts are more likely to oc-

cur in symmetric than in asymmetric relations required some care, because these data evidence selection on the dependent variable. The
basic problem is simple. Because there are no data that Gould can observe on the base rate of arguments among peers (those in symmetric
relations) and nonpeers (those in asymmetric relationships), he relies
on homicide data that report the cause of homicide. These data do indeed show that verbal altercations among peers are likely to become
deadly, but it is possible that verbal arguments are considerably more
likely among peers than nonpeers. If such arguments are three times
more likely (19 percent of the homicides between peers stemmed from
arguments, whereas only 6 percent of the homicides between nonpeers stemmed from arguments), then in fact, verbal conflict in symmetrical relations would not be more likely to yield a homicide than
such conflicts in asymmetrical relations. Consequently, the language
used to describe the inferences one can make from these data has been
softened somewhat from the original.

Third, a number of reviewers commented on the relation between
this work and other articles and books that have touched in one way or
another on cognate themes. Collectively these comments suggested
that framing within larger literatures or at least "reaching out" to
works not cited within the body of the text would be helpful and serve
to situate Gould's contributions more clearly. After some consideration, I have not made significant changes to the text in this regard.
First, in a book with as broad a scope as this, the literatures that are relevant are vast and beyond my grasp. Thus, although the work clearly
touches on—and stands on its head—the traditional social exchange
literature, I have not included references to this work not found in the
original. Somewhat differently, works that are clearly relevant to the argument but were not cited in the original have been added. In this class
I include, for example the work of Donald Black on relational distance—the proposition that recourse to law, as opposed to self-help, is
more likely as relational distance increases—which is clearly relevant,
and the brilliant work by Eric Leifer on the dynamics of role acquisition
in contexts of ambiguity. Readers interested in extensions of the Gould
hypothesis may find in these and earlier works evidence that offers
significant support.

Although I noted that I would not try to identify in acknowledgment the specific individuals who helped shape this book, Roger would

have gratefully acknowledged the research assistance of Geneviève Zubryzcki, Ari Adut, and Harris Kim, the outstanding copyediting of Jane Zanichkowsky, and the support of Doug Mitchell and his fantastic editorial group at the University of Chicago Press. Finally, Roger was the first to say that this book could not have been written without the love, support, intellectual companionship, friendship, and caring of his wife, Erin Graves—to whom this book is dedicated.

Peter Bearman

CHAPTER 1

Conflict, Honor, and Hierarchy

One occasionally hears the phrase "senseless violence."
People doubtless mean a range of things when they use these
words, but the phrase almost always suggests the existence of
another kind of violence: the reasonable kind, the kind that
makes sense. Absolute pacifists aside—and there seem to be
very few people who would seriously claim that it is *never* reasonable to cause someone physical harm—it would appear
that some acts of violence are understandable, perhaps even
just, whereas others are condemned as out of bounds, devoid
of sense.

To be sure, people often hold different opinions regarding where to draw the line between reasonable and senseless
violence. At the beginning of the twenty-first century, for instance, there are disagreements about when or whether parents should strike disobedient children, about what constitutes unnecessary use of force by police, and about when
efforts at diplomacy ought to give way to armed intervention.
But there is rarely disagreement about what the dimension is
on which the line is drawn: in general, the higher the stakes
are, the more willing people are to accept that physical violence might be a reasonable response. It seems to make more
sense when urban residents riot after a police killing than
when they riot after their team wins a major game. It is easier

to understand why someone might kill to protect or avenge a family member than it is to understand why someone might kill to keep a mugger from taking the contents of a wallet. It is easier to see why someone might put up a fight when the wallet contains two hundred dollars than when it contains five dollars. And it is easier to explain why two friends might come to blows, or worse, over a dented fender or a romantic rivalry than over a disparaging remark.

At any rate, it seems easier in light of conventional ways of thinking about hostility, anger, and violence. The more intrinsically significant the event—that is, the more someone stands to lose or gain—the more reasonable we tend to think it is if he or she becomes angry, or violent, or deadly. This is not to say that our response is of the form "I too would react that way"; it is simply that we are less likely to feel mystified by the behavior or the emotion it expresses when the stakes seem high. In modern settings, employing physical violence is an extreme measure. It is therefore more readily understood, or at least regarded as understood, when the situation in which violence occurs is itself extreme.

Straightforward though this conventional way of thinking is, it has a hard time with the real world of violence. Specialists in homicide in the United States and other industrialized societies have known for decades that a very large number of killings are "motivated" by apparently insignificant concerns: arguments, verbal insults, small debts, parking spaces, accidental physical contact, and so on. Indeed, one of the first studies to look closely at the details of how and why people kill one another (in Philadelphia, as it happened) set aside a category for "altercations of relatively trivial origin." That rubric or a version of it continues to appear in statistical summaries of homicides all over the United States—and consistently accounts for more than one-third of homicides in American cities.[1] To be more precise, more than one-third of homicides cannot even in principle be attributed to conflict about a serious matter. Because the rest *can* be connected to something serious—such as marital infidelity, property damage, or loss of a job— they have been so classified. But that attribution is often itself guided

<hr/>

1. I am not suggesting that insignificant matters are overrepresented in deadly altercations. It is quite likely that they are underrepresented, inasmuch as small disputes probably outnumber large ones. But the fact that they show up at all raises important questions.

by the conventional wisdom about violence: if one person kills another because of a gambling debt *and* an insult hurled during an argument about the debt, we assume that the murder occurred because of money. By default, the most significant issue, which is to say the issue that has the greatest impact on the disputants' interests, is presumed to be the primary motive for violent behavior. The apparent contribution of "serious" matters to violence, and conversely the amount of violence attributable to serious matters, is thereby maximized by the typical classification procedure.

This interpretive maneuver still leaves an enormous amount of mayhem that by most people's estimation occurs because of trivial matters—"silly stuff," as more than one esteemed social scientist has said in my presence. There appear to be three characteristic responses to this difficulty. The first response amounts to theoretical neglect, although it is typically described in nobler terms. When available theories fail to account for the full range of human behavior, we often attribute the disparity to something like free will—although it is more fashionable for social scientists to say "agency." Never mind that philosophers have struggled for centuries to agree on what the concept of free will refers to, not to mention whether there is such a thing. It is doubly comforting to attribute the mismatch of theory and behavior to a special property of human action: we simultaneously excuse the inadequacy of our models and glorify our status as human beings. There is no need to dwell further on this response—it may turn out to be the best available, but it seems to me that the quest for understanding ends there. In any event, it is rarely invoked in the context of violence, perhaps because it is unpleasant to think that free will manifests itself in wickedness. People like to invoke free will to explain nice surprises, not nasty ones.

The second and more common response is, in essence, to classify as different from ordinary people those who do not conform to established notions about when it is understandable to harm others physically. Non-experts impose such a classification when they refer to anomalous users of violence as "irrational," "crazy," or "evil." Psychologists and others in the therapeutic professions do so when they define the people who engage in anomalous violence as mentally ill. Social scientists—especially sociologists—adopt a similar approach when they construct models of deviance that attribute departures from normative behavior patterns to environmental influences that teach or induce certain people to behave differently from everyone else. A person who shoots a prowler does not require special classification as crazy, ill, or deviant; but a person who shoots someone because the ice cream cone is the wrong flavor does. So violence that does not fit the conventional view is prevented from undermining that view by means of a classification of its perpetrators as unconventional themselves.

Sociologists have made a good deal of progress in identifying the mechanisms that sort people into conventional ways of life, on one hand, and into lives characterized by deviant practices, on the other. In fact, it is one of the unfortunate achievements of the discipline to have made itself unpopular because it appears so often to excuse antisocial behavior. By claiming to locate the sources of such behavior in the social environment rather than in the individual actor, sociological theories of deviance have challenged the self-righteous and punitive stance of law-and-order advocates who believe that people who behave badly are bad people. (Sociologists would likely have had this effect even without the inclusion of the radical perspective, in which the very categories "crime," "deviance," and "antisocial behavior" are denounced as ideological instruments ruling groups use to oppress others.) A large body of evidence suggests that in many people, deviance, including habitual violence toward others, is a response to a life of mistreatment, or thwarted opportunity, or at a minimum neglect and lack of socialization. There is also evidence that people identified as deviant by schools, courts, mental health professionals, and ordinary folk are likely to become more so as a result of this labeling.

Yet we miss an important issue if we approach the matter of violence the way criminologists approach delinquency—that is, as a matter of distinguishing the violent people from the others and then explaining why they differ. Although it is surely the case that some people have a higher propensity than others to inflict serious physical harm, it is also the case that most of those who do harm others do not choose their targets randomly. Not counting warfare, the vast majority of the violence we find out about occurs between people who know each other. It is nearly certain that an even larger proportion of the violence we do not find out about, and of the conflicts that do not end violently, involves people who know each other—principally because violence and conflict between close associates and relatives is much less likely to be reported than violence between acquaintances or strangers. Even people who by any standard have a special penchant for violence do not distribute it evenly: they nearly always direct their rage at specific people or specific categories of people.[2] The same holds more firmly of those whose bouts with physical violence are rare: physical attacks by one-time offenders are particularly likely to concentrate on close associates rather than on bystanders or strangers.

These facts imply that there is something to be gained by thinking about interpersonal violence as a product of social relations, and of the conflict they engender, rather than as an expression of individual personality types. For one thing, it raises the question of whether there are certain kinds of social relations in which conflict is likely to occur, independent of the propensities of the people linked by such relations. It may be that one sort of person might respond to conflict by causing physical harm while another might withdraw or become self-destructive, but there is nonetheless a sense in which harm, when it is the response, might be attributable as much to the relation as to the individual. If it should turn out, for instance, that a disproportionate number of domestic homicides in the United States involve men killing their brothers, we might conclude that there is something about the male sibling relationship that recurrently produces more strife than the brother-sister relationship, the father-son relationship, and so forth. Recalling that many brothers are also fathers, sons, husbands, uncles, and brothers-in-law, we might have to acknowledge that it is *as brothers* that the offenders in such cases committed their acts of violence—in other words, that it was in connection with a specific social relation, and not as a personal disposition, that they were capable of extreme behavior. The idea of deviance conceived as an individual propensity hides this unevenness in the way people interact with others.

It also hides the possibility that violent interactions, occurring as they do within certain kinds of social relations, are emblematic of the less deadly but more frequent battles of will that occur in tens of thou-

2. There is, of course, the issue of opportunity. People spend more time with people they know than with those they do not; consequently, it might turn out that violence *is* distributed randomly once we take account of exposure. I offer evidence in chapter 3 suggesting that differential opportunity does not account for observed patterns in interpersonal violence.

sands of comparable relations every day. If it is true that violence is distributed in systematic ways across types of social relations, then it can offer us lessons about the distribution of conflict in general—lessons we would disregard if we decided that violent behavior is just something violent people engage in.

If only one employee in a thousand responds to being fired or disciplined by returning with a gun, that does not mean that the other 999 employees are not also deeply hurt by the experience; it simply means that their responses attract less attention. Seeing the violent response as an index of how painful employer-employee relations can be, rather than as an indicator of the mental instability of a single person, allows us to learn much more about social conflict in general. Throughout this book I shall view violence—along with data on violence—as a window onto the broader phenomenon of human conflict, not as a lurid expression of deviant personalities.

The third characteristic response to the fact of violence due to apparently trifling matters is to identify a new kind of interest: something called "honor." Someone angered by an insult, rather than by some materially damaging action such as an injury, theft, or legal defeat, can be said to feel dishonored—to feel as if his or her reputation or personal pride has been harmed, even if there is no concrete harm. If honor is important, then defending it by means of violence makes as much sense as defending other important assets. This approach amounts to expanding the range of issues considered significant. It is similar to economists' response to the discovery that people do more of something (such as gardening) than one would expect on the basis of the opportunity costs and the cost of having someone else do it. The anomaly is explained by positing the existence of previously unrecognized rewards of the activity, such as relaxation or a sense of accomplishment. In the context of violence, the corresponding answer to the fact of violence due to apparently trivial matters is to recognize that some people care not only about protecting their material interests but also about preserving honor.[3] Urban youth frequently account for

<hr />

3. A little of this sort of reasoning goes a long way, however. Because it is always possible to infer after the fact that some previously unrecognized interest motivated someone's actions, we should not fool ourselves into thinking that we have thereby explained something. Only if one finds that the concept—whether it is honor, self-esteem, altruism, or something else—can in principle be observed independently of the action it is invoked to explain can one claim to have made sense of social behavior. Otherwise the explanation is tautological.

lethal attacks on others by saying that the victim "disrespected" them. To recognize honor as a valued good is to take such statements seriously as explanations.

As generally understood, then, honor is a resource every bit as important to those who have it as the somewhat more concrete resources of wealth, physical strength, formal and informal authority, social contacts, technical knowledge, and so forth. The key difference is that honor is entirely symbolic: its possession consists in the recognition by others of its possession. To have honor, to be honored, is to be thought honored by others. It makes no sense to say that someone possesses honor even though nobody realizes it, whereas it might make sense to say that someone has power or wealth without others' knowledge. Material resources such as ships, shoes, and horses can be useful to their possessors in a way that is at least partly independent of cultural representations of these resources. Honor, on the other hand, like status, sacredness, legitimacy, and other things predicated on recognition by other people, just *is* a cultural representation. Its value is more profoundly a product of context than is the value of a loaf of bread.[4]

It is therefore no surprise that the study of honor, and of acts of violence driven by considerations of honor, has for decades been seen as a matter of cultural interpretation. To speak of matters of honor as involving symbolic resources is to invoke the notion of meaning systems, of gestures and utterances given significance by their location in a web of other gestures and utterances. Beginning in the 1960s, anthropologists especially—but also historians and the occasional sociologist—have sought to explain honorific violence in terms of the

---

It is comparable to saying "the pill made the patient fall asleep because it was a sleeping pill."

4. There are those who would deny the legitimacy of the distinction I have just made. For such people, the value of any resource—from strawberries to status—is, as the phrase goes, "always already" mediated by systems of meaning. So, although eating lobster flesh may be viewed as a rare treat in some contexts and an act of cruelty to animals in others, in yet others it may be a cheap and distasteful way to nourish prison inmates (e.g., in Maine in the nineteenth century, or so it is said). I would insist, however, that there is a meaningful (that is, consequential) difference between a resource whose value is absolutely a function of the system of social practices that treat it as a resource and one whose value is only partly a function of such practices. If Robinson Crusoe is starving because he does not see the lobster before him as food, it is not the same thing as if he is starving because the only things before him are sand and salt water. He could step outside his cultural horizons (there are many cases of this) and give the lobster a try. We know what would happen if he did the same with the sand.

cultural setting in which it occurs. Scholars writing in this tradition insist that killing someone because of a verbal slight or disrespectful sneer, as alien as it might seem to an outsider, makes sense once one becomes more familiar with the way the people who commit such acts understand social life. Moreover, they point out that a gesture that counts as a slight in one time and place could be a compliment, an expression of gratitude, or a meaningless motion in another context. As a result, explaining acts of violence that cannot be attributed to such obvious concerns as those of property or self-defense depends on interpretation, which in turn demands detailed knowledge of cultural context.

The commitment to culturally sensitive explanation this view demands has produced a remarkably rich body of ethnographic and historical research on "honor societies," from highland New Guinea to Tokugawa Japan on the Pacific rim, from Appalachia to the Andes in the Americas, from Scotland to the Balkans in Europe, and from the Nile valley to the Mediterranean in Africa. We now have a staggering amount of information about the range of ways people think about and display respect, status, shame, integrity, modesty, courage, loyalty, deference, scorn, admiration, and any number of other traits and emotions associated with honor. We know, for instance, that squaring off face-to-face against one's adversary was crucial to being thought honorable at the peak of aristocratic dueling in America and Europe but that ambushing one's enemy—or someone else, for that matter—can be a perfectly honorable way to take revenge among headhunters in the Philippines, feuding families in Sicily and Corsica, and hunter-gatherers in the Amazon.[5] We also know that in Islamic societies a family dishonored by the nonmarital sexual activities of a daughter

---

5. On Europe, see Kevin MacAleer, *Dueling* (Princeton: Princeton University Press, 1994); on America, Bertram Wyatt-Brown, *Southern Honor: Ethics and Behavior in the Old South* (New York: Oxford University Press, 1982); on the Philippines, Michelle Z. Rosaldo, *Knowledge and Passion: Ilongot Notions of Self and Social Life* (Cambridge: Cambridge University Press, 1980), and Renato Rosaldo, *Ilongot Headhunting, 1883–1974* (Stanford: Stanford University Press, 1980); on Sicily, Anton Blok, *The Mafia of a Sicilian Village, 1860–1960: A Study of Violent Peasant Entrepreneurs* (New York: Harper, 1974); Jane Schneider, "Of Vigilance and Virgins: Honor, Shame, and Access to Resources in Mediterranean Societies," *Ethnology* 10 (1971): 1–24; on Corsica, Stephen K. Wilson, *Feuding, Conflict, and Banditry in Nineteenth-Century Corsica* (Cambridge: Cambridge University Press, 1988); on the Amazon, Napoleon Chagnon, *Yanomamo: The Fierce People* (New York: Holt, Rinehart and Winston, 1983).

CONFLICT, HONOR, AND HIERARCHY 9

frequently respond by killing the daughter, whereas in Christian societies it is more common for the aggrieved family to murder the offending man. Ethnographers have found that kin of Nuer murder victims may hold any male member of the killer's lineage accountable, whereas Berber customs extend responsibility only to the ten closest agnates. There is evidence that hospitality has been a central ingredient in the maintenance of honor in Crete, Andalusia, Montenegro, and the American South but was not especially important to the honor of Japan's samurai class or to that of medieval knights in continental Europe.[6]

Anthropologists and historians have also documented wide variation in the kinds of gesture or remark that may give offense. In many honor cultures in the West, one person may gravely insult another with the epithet "coward" or by insinuating something about the sexual habits of the latter's mother. An elite white man in the antebellum southern United States might have insulted a rival, inviting a challenge to a duel, by publicly calling him a liar or by pulling his nose. But for the Tauade in the mountains of Papua New Guinea, it is more common to insult someone with a comment about his (or her) age or white hair or with an invitation to drink the urine of the speaker's spouse. Bedouins can wound each other's pride—to the point of provoking lawsuits—by saying things like "you came here barefoot and on a donkey."[7] If I said that to a neighbor, it would surely provoke more puzzlement than outrage.

In short, recognition that people can arouse anger in others by entirely symbolic means, means that, moreover, vary enormously across

6. See Joseph Ginat, *Blood Disputes among Bedouin and Rural Arabs in Israel: Revenge, Mediation, Outcasts, and Family Honor* (Pittsburgh: University of Pittsburgh Press, 1987); Michael Herzfeld, *The Poetics of Manhood: Contest and Identity in a Cretan Mountain Village* (Princeton: Princeton University Press, 1985); David D. Gilmore, "Honor, Honesty, Shame: Male Status in Contemporary Andalusia," pp. 90–103 in Gilmore, ed., *Honor and Shame and the Unity of the Mediterranean* (Washington, D.C.: American Anthropological Association, 1987); Christopher Boehm, *Blood Revenge: The Enactment and Management of Revenge in Montenegro and Other Tribal Societies* (Philadelphia: University of Pennsylvania Press, 1987); Wyatt-Brown, *Southern Honor;* Frank Henderson Stewart, *Honor* (Chicago: University of Chicago Press, 1994); Eiko Ikegami, *The Taming of the Samurai: Honorific Individualism and the Making of Modern Japan* (Cambridge: Harvard University Press, 1995); Marc Bloch, *Feudal Society* (Chicago: University of Chicago Press, 1961).

7. Kenneth S. Greenberg, "The Nose, the Lie, and the Duel in the Antebellum South," *American Historical Review* 95 (1990): 57–74; Christopher R. Hallpike, *Bloodshed and Vengeance in the Papuan Mountains* (Oxford: Clarendon, 1977), p. 248; Stewart, *Honor,* p. 100.

cultural settings, has pushed many social scientists to focus on the reasons for, or at any rate the occurrence of, such variation. The challenge
is to explain why a man's nose is symbolic of honor in the American
South and in Kabylia but in many other places is not, why hospitality
is essential to honor in Andalusia but not in Crete, or why female
chastity is a key ingredient of family honor in Mediterranean societies
but typically has no such implications among indigenous peoples of
Oceania. Or rather, since most cultural analyses are only implicitly
comparative, the project for each scholar has been to explain why the
set of symbolic resources is what it is in his or her chosen setting. Few
students of cultural systems expect to construct a general theory of
how particular symbols become linked to or detached from honor
across a range of times and places. In fact, the very richness of the observations made of honor and its symbolic contents has led inevitably
to a sense that the general concept is useless. With so many variants of
honor, many writers have become suspicious of the notion that there
is any reason to keep thinking of them as instances of the same thing.[8]
The goal, then, is to represent in as meaningful a way as possible the
experience of those whom the researcher is studying, allowing for
metaphorical connections and perhaps an acknowledgment of family
resemblances across contexts but not for reduction to a common structure. The interpretive tradition, in a sense, does for groups of people
what the notion of free will does for individuals: it exempts each culturally distinct community from the expectation that it will obey strong
regularities by endowing its members with the collective power to live
in a world of their own (collective) making.

It is indeed easy to be enthralled by the spectacular range of ways
human groups build and understand their social world, and more particularly by the creativity with which they produce and react to challenges, insults, and insinuations, on one hand, and gestures of submission, deference, and admiration, on the other. But in concentrating
on variability, one runs the risk of becoming blind to just how much
similarity there is across time and place in the kinds of contests that
lead some people to inflict grievous harm on others. Just as the "deviance" approach to violence obscures the similarities between harm-

---

8. Herzfeld, *Poetics of Manhood*; Unni Wikan, "Shame and Honor: A Contestable Pair,"
Man 19 (1984): 635–52.

less verbal exchanges and those that eventuate in injury or worse, emphasizing the variation in forms of honor obscures the very tangible constants that persist amid such variation. Even as we recognize that moustaches or facial scars may or may not carry significance as indicators of honor, depending on the time and place, we would do well to acknowledge the overwhelming consistency with which certain features are absent from, and others are present in, honor codes.

There are, for instance, no examples (none that I have encountered, at any rate) of social groups that express *greater* admiration for people who choose to ambush their enemies rather than confront them face-to-face, even though the former is often considered the more prudent approach. Although there may be examples of societies in which it is not insulting to spit in someone's face (though, again, I know of none), there are hundreds in which it is. It also appears that the tendency to see vertical placement—high versus low, tall versus short, standing versus kneeling—as a metaphorical representation of status or honor differences is nearly universal.[9]

As observers and interpreters, human beings are typically contrast-seekers: we tend to be better at noticing differences than we are at recognizing uniformity. (If you are an urbanite, think of the last time you tuned out the sound of a car alarm, only to notice it again when it shut off; if you live in a rural setting, think of crickets.) When we look at a range of social contexts, consequently, we often place the ways they seem different in the foreground and relegate their common features to the background—either defining them as uninteresting or forgetting them entirely.[10] Yet it would be a grave mistake not to take seriously the frequency with which certain patterns recur in the context of rivalrous or conflictual social interaction—even as one acknowledges that human groups are also full of surprises. In the first place, the value of broad comparisons is enhanced if one is searching for general patterns (not to say "laws"). If the purpose of examining multiple contexts is primarily to look for differences, the aggregate outcome of thousands of studies may turn out to be little more than a

---

9. Barry Schwartz, *Vertical Classification* (Chicago: University of Chicago Press, 1981).

10. Ruth Benedict made essentially this observation when she wrote, "If deep-sea fish could speak, the last thing they would name is water." It may be arrogant to suppose that we know how fish think, but social scientists are another matter.

catalogue of human variation—a kind of naturalist's guide to the flora and fauna of human lifeways.

If the purpose is to identify regularities, on the other hand, then comparison helps us distinguish what is incidental to a pattern from what is basic. For example, with regard to the matter of honor, the full range of historical and ethnographic research teaches us that, even though the particular manifestations vary—likening someone to a certain species of animal, remarking on physical flaws, calling someone a liar or a coward—verbal insult of some kind is a universal feature of interpersonal conflict. The fact is so obvious that our attention is drawn to the variations in content: Why a pig here and a dog there? Why the chin here, the nose there, and posture somewhere else? But if one were to stand back and look at the whole range, one might decide that it is equally important to understand why it is everywhere the case that people can make each other angry enough to kill just by saying things.

In the second place, and perhaps counterintuitively, the value of detailed, individual case studies is also enhanced if they are seen as tools for generalization rather than items for a catalogue. The way the academic world currently works, authors of case studies (community-level ethnographies, local histories, analyses of a single industry or profession) face a no-win situation. A new study may report the same things earlier studies have observed and thus confirm existing generalizations. In this case, the value of the new study is merely incremental and diminishing with the number of prior studies reporting the same pattern. Or the new study may diverge in some major or minor respect from previously documented patterns, thereby offering a novel finding. But since the divergence is ordinarily seen as refuting or weakening extant generalizations, the impact is in an important sense the same: each new study serves only to reinforce the idea that things differ, that the world is complex, and that generalizations are nearly always wrong.[11] Eventually, there will be no generalizations left to attack. This kind of particularism is self-defeating: once we accept it, we have

---

11. In anthropology, this tendency is often lamented as the "not on Easter Island" phenomenon. But similar patterns can be seen in most of the other human sciences, and even to some degree in the natural sciences. The problem appears to be a standard social dilemma. Collectively, we would all understand the world better if everyone tried to fit his or her work into the cooperative enterprise of building a coherent theoretical edifice. But the rewards to me are greater if everyone *else* does this on the basis of my design. Every other scholar faces

no good reason to examine a new context or revisit an old one unless we have some specific reason for being interested in that particular time and place.

What I am proposing is that additional cases be seen as constraints on generalization, not as adversaries to it. The more we learn about more times and places, the more difficult it becomes for existing general propositions to go unfalsified. One reaction to this fact is to lose faith in the project of generalization, as many social scientists have. But another reaction is to ascribe these recurrent failures to the propositions themselves—not to the practice of formulating and testing them. It is quite possible that the principal flaw of general statements is not that they are general but on the contrary that they are not general enough. To the degree that general theories are extrapolations from what is already known, they are likely to be tainted, as it were, by features particular to the settings on which they are based. When a theory fails to fit new data, the mismatches point to precisely those features.

To shift ground for a moment, take the following example from economic anthropology. Once upon a time, many social scientists believed that markets, surplus production, and division of labor went together: societies in which people produced goods for exchange were thought to be characterized by high levels of occupational specialization and a cash economy, whereas societies in which people produced goods for themselves or for expropriation by social superiors were characterized by low levels of specialization. A few economic anthropologists suggested that the whole range of systems could be accounted for by a general theory presupposing rational, utility-maximizing actors. A variety of findings such as the discovery of large-scale societies with high levels of differentiation but no markets (most of them defunct, like the Maya) contributed to a sharp debate about whether a single model—in this case, formal neoclassical economics—could explain economic behavior across time and place. The issue, of course, was not (or ought not to have been) the semantic one of whether the concept "economy" could be used to refer simultaneously to market capitalism, nonmarket exchange systems, and subsistence production,

---

the same reward scheme. So every new book or article calls for a "fundamental rethinking," which of course never takes place because the next author calls for the same thing. This is one way in which the professional incentive system in academe generates perverse results.

or whether it was properly restricted to the former. The real issue was the theoretical one of whether the same principles could be adduced to explain behavioral patterns in all of these types of economy, despite their superficial differences. "Formalists" argued that, even if explicit monetary exchange did not occur, it was still possible to infer the operation of such principles as cost and profit in the decisions made by producers—and thus to use these principles to explain their behavior. "Substantivists" insisted that inhabitants of different societies produced their means of livelihood according to fundamentally different principles. They therefore derided the effort to construct general models of economic behavior as misguided universalism or—worse yet—as cultural imperialism.[12]

Both sides had a point. The market model exaggerated the degree to which production decisions were determined jointly by price and the desire to maximize returns. In many peasant societies, for instance, cultivators produce "enough" for their families, not "enough" to produce a surplus for reinvestment and expanded production. In many horticultural societies, cultivators do produce a surplus—of yams or shellfish, for instance, or of sumptuary goods—but it is donated to village leaders who redistribute it to gain status and attract political support.[13] Neither pattern looks like the kind of entrepreneurial investment in productive growth that occurs in Western capitalist societies.

12. Much of this debate can be traced in Robbins Burling, "Maximization Theories and the Study of Economic Anthropology," *American Anthropologist* 64 (1962): 802–21; Scott Cook, "The 'Anti-market' Mentality Re-examined: A Further Critique of the Substantive Approach to Economic Anthropology," *Southwest Journal of Anthropology* 25 (1969): 378–406; George Dalton, "Economic Theory and Primitive Society," *American Anthropologist* 63 (1961): 1–25; George Dalton, "Primitive Money," *American Anthropologist* 67 (1965): 44–65; Maurice Godelier, ed., *Un domaine contesté: L'anthropologie économique* (Paris: Mouton, 1974); David Kaplan, "The Formal-Substantive Controversy in Economic Anthropology," *Southwestern Journal of Anthropology* 24 (1968): 228–51; Edward E. LeClair, "Economic Theory and Economic Anthropology," *American Anthropologist* 64 (1962): 1179–1203; Manning Nash, *Primitive and Peasant Economic Systems* (San Francisco: Chandler, 1967); Karl Polanyi, C. M. Arensberg, and H. W. Pearson, eds., *Trade and Market in the Early Empires* (Glencoe, Ill.: Free Press, 1957); Marshall Sahlins, "On the Sociology of Primitive Exchange," pp. 139–236 in M. Banton, ed., *The Relevance of Models for Social Anthropology* (London: Tavistock, 1965); Marshall Sahlins, *Stone-Age Economics* (Chicago: Aldine-Atherton, 1967); B. Voorhies, "Possible Social Factors in the Exchange System of the Prehistoric Maya," *American Antiquarian* 38 (1973): 486–89; Malcolm C. Webb, "Exchange Networks: Prehistory," *Annual Review of Anthropology* 3 (1974): 357–83.

13. Prominent examples of this include Kula exchange in the Trobriand Islands and redistribution by "big men" in New Guinea. See Bronislaw Malinowski, *Argonauts of the Western*

But some substantivist critics of economists went too far in the other direction. The fact that data from a new study fail to confirm a specific prediction stemming from a specific economic theory is no reason to conclude that all economic theories must be wrong. Making such an inference is like concluding that it is impossible to build a flying machine because the first flying machines didn't fly. (Many intelligent people, however, concluded just that.) The more reasonable inference is that certain specific assumptions, such as that of profit maximization, fail to generalize beyond capitalist society, whereas others, such as the importance of travel distance in determining whether a transaction is worthwhile, generalize pretty well. Comparative study helped distinguish what was general in economic behavior from what was culturally specific. Ironically, those who have concluded on the basis of specific failures of general models that models will always fail are guilty of the same charge of overgeneralization they have leveled at the formalists: they have generalized from a particular general theory to all general theories.

I would like to suggest that, as in the case of cross-cultural studies of production and exchange, documenting cultural variation in forms of interpersonal conflict can be immensely useful, but not as a weapon against the project of generalization. There is a difference between showing that a particular generalization fails to match the range of observed behavior and showing that generalization as such is not a worthwhile pursuit. The value of a deep investigation into a specific society is maximized not by invoking the society's unique traits to justify particularism but by obliging general theories to be better—that is, to reformulate their core concepts so as to accommodate a greater range of observed behavior. There is always a danger that general propositions will thereby become so abstract as to be vacuous, but that is in the nature of the enterprise: a good theory consists of propositions abstract enough to hold across a broad array of settings but concrete enough to still say something meaningful.[14] Some abstract claims are empty or

---

Pacific (New York: Waveland, 1994); Godelier, *Un Domaine contesté;* Maurice Godelier, *La Production des grands hommes: Pouvoir et domination masculine chez les Baruya en Nouvelle-Guinée* (Paris: Fayard, 1982).

14. It is always puzzling to me when social scientists object to a general claim by saying that it ignores some detail or other of the cases it covers. For example, I have frequently heard comments like "Your account of revolutionary mobilization in countries A, B, and C

nearly tautological (such as "people do things they want to do," which is meaningful only if wants can be established independent of actions), but many are not.

I have digressed in order to indicate some of the ways in which the problem of identifying general patterns in interpersonal violence amid significant cultural variation is generic rather than peculiar to the problem of violence. But the connection between honor and violence poses certain specific difficulties that make the particularist tendency unusually strong. Above all, the fact that all societies experience some lethal conflict over matters that are (apparently) entirely symbolic has led most scholars to conclude that the contents of "honor" in a given time and place are largely arbitrary. Because the relation between a sign and its meaning is a matter of social convention, it has been difficult to resist the inference that the ways and the extent to which symbolic conflict leads to physical violence are themselves conventional. Cross-cultural generalization about conflict, honor, and violence therefore seems out of reach—again ironically, inasmuch as this conclusion seems to follow from a universal pattern.

The intent of this book is to press in the other direction—to derive some general understanding of violent human interaction from the welter of variation within and across social contexts. I aim to do so by combining systematic investigation of primary data concerning violence in a handful of disparate settings—feuding societies in some cases, urban areas in the contemporary United States in others—with a synthesis of historical and ethnographic research that encompasses the broadest possible range of secondary evidence. The crucial first step in pursuing such a project is to settle on a way of thinking and talk-

---

ignores the fact that A is a Catholic country, B is Hindu, and C is Muslim." Such objections are typically perfectly true but irrelevant, *unless* they show that the general claim is consequently either incoherent or empirically wrong. Imagine telling a physicist who has predicted the rate at which two different objects will fall in a vacuum that she has ignored the fact that one belongs to a hair stylist in Atlanta and the other belongs to the Berlin Philharmonic, or that one is blue and the other beige. Classical mechanics pointedly ignores the color or ownership of objects falling in a vacuum—and the empirical evidence justifies doing so when describing motion. Point out that one of the objects is on Jupiter and the other on Mars, on the other hand, and you have a valid objection. At present, the default assumption in many of the natural sciences is that until a potential factor has been shown to be important, it is assumed not to be. In the human sciences, the contrary holds, at least for some practitioners: one must demonstrate that a factor is *not* relevant before one is entitled to disregard it. Unfortunately, this policy makes it difficult to say anything positive about the world, because the list of potential factors is infinitely long.

ing about human uses of physical violence that can capture the range of its manifestations without either imposing an overly rigid framework or giving in to the temptation to revel in infinite variability. The remainder of this chapter will, accordingly, develop a set of claims about conflict and violence organized around the idea of social rank and its encoding in relations of dominance and submission. Broadly speaking, I propose that much of human conflict occurs when relations involving rank are ambiguous or under challenge. Such conditions arise in encounters between people whose relative rank has not been established, in existing ranked relations in which one party wants to alter the status quo, or in situations in which some exogenous event (including changes in adjacent social relations) alters the prospects for continued precedence of one person over another. Before explicating these claims, however, it is necessary to enter into more detail concerning their component concepts.

On the surface, there may not seem to be much of a connection between the honorific world of patrimonial rule, dueling, and deadly feuds and the contemporary, mundane world of careers in bureaucratic organizations. Indeed, we moderns tend to see bureaucracy and patrimonialism as incompatible systems, with one progressively replacing the other.[15] The latter is generally seen as archaic, particularistic, founded on ties of personal loyalty, and basically hierarchical, the former as modern, universalistic, impersonal, and essentially egalitarian. Two of my aims in this book, however, are to focus on a deeper level at which these two worlds resemble one another and to reveal the ways in which this resemblance makes itself felt in the bitterness, anger, resentment, and sometimes violence with which people respond to contests concerning social rank. If we can discern parallels across contexts in the way people compete for and respond to assign-

15. Almost all of the evolutionary social theorists of the nineteenth century, from Maine to Durkheim, contrasted traditional and modern society in ways that resembled this one. But it is Weber's emphasis on the centrality to modern social life of rationalized bureaucratic organizations (as opposed to the replacement of "status" by "contract," or "mechanical" by "organic" solidarity) that has had the greatest influence on the way twentieth-century writers view contemporary Western society. Norbert Elias extended this view by concentrating on the way this change at the level of institutions transformed the emotional and behavioral dispositions individuals were obliged to develop so as to successfully participate in them. Max Weber, *Economy and Society*, trans. H. H. Gerth and C. W. Mills (Berkeley: University of California Press, 1980); Norbert Elias, *The Civilizing Process* (Oxford: Blackwell, 1994), esp. "State Formation and Civilization," part 2.

ments of rank, then insights derived from behavior in one context can be applied—with due caution—in others. The remainder of this introductory chapter begins the work of drawing these parallels—not to prove my point but rather to spell it out in detail and if possible to make at least a prima facie case for its plausibility. My arguments and examples should thus be seen for the moment as illustrative, not probative. Subsequent chapters bear the burden of offering systematic evidence in support of the claims I lay out in this one and the next.

It appears to be common in contemporary industrial societies for people who are talented and accomplished to be rewarded with advancement of some kind, only to find themselves threatened and intimidated by their new peers. The reason this happens is intimately related to the way organizational life generates social hierarchies. In educational institutions and bureaucratic organizations, meritocratic practices sort individuals into higher and lower positions and roles of greater and lesser decision-making responsibility and, sometimes informally, tracks representing varying rates of mobility. Along the way, nearly every organization also assigns formal marks of distinction—positive ones, such as awards and medals, and negative ones, such as disciplinary actions, demotions, and periods of probation—that serve as cumulative indicators of success or failure. These markers are central both to the sorting of individuals within organizations and to their selection into new ones, as anyone knows who has passed through postsecondary education and into a professional, corporate, or civil service labor market. Elite colleges select their students on the basis of their distinction in secondary school. Graduate programs compete for those who have distinguished themselves in college, especially if the college itself is distinguished, and employers (law firms, courts, state agencies, hospitals, private enterprises, university faculties, and so on) repeat the process at the next level. Hence the Peter Principle: at each stage, the ambitious and (so far) successful are surrounded by increasingly tough competitors, while those who have done less well are grouped with other, similarly less tough competitors. Bureaucracies get the most out of people by pitting them against each other in perpetual tournaments—tournaments, moreover, in which it is hard to predict the winner because the contestants have been pre-sorted to resemble one another. That way, relatively few people fail to perform, either because they are certain of losing or because they are confident of winning.

Because the winners of these tournaments often reap spectacular economic rewards in comparison to those who have performed less well or to those who are just entering the system, it is tempting to think that it is the promise of financial benefit that drives people to compete as fiercely as they do for prestigious credentials, professional distinctions, and promotions. That view, firmly held by most economists, has a lot of commonsense validity: it is easy enough to predict what would happen in an organization that imposed a significant salary reduction with every merit-based promotion. It is surely reasonable to think that the prospect of multiplying one's income twofold or tenfold motivates many people to work extremely hard to impress their superiors. In addition, the idea that the primary reason people compete for promotions is monetary gain preserves the image of egalitarianism to which I alluded: the rewards and the basis on which they are distributed being impersonal, the inequality of outcomes is also impersonal. Unequal distribution of monetary compensation is more nearly detachable from the persons it affects than is, say, the labeling of some people as noble and others as common.

But even if economic rewards are a major consideration, that does not mean that they account for all or even most of the competitiveness so widely observed among employees of large bureaucracies. If it did, we should expect to observe the most intense rivalries in settings where the financial returns of success are the greatest and almost no rivalry where the financial returns are insignificant. I know of no rigorous investigations of the matter, but there is much anecdotal evidence to the effect that there is just about as much envy and competitiveness in settings where economic rewards are modest as in those where they are extravagant.[16] One reason for this, some economists have suggested, is that people care about what they receive *relative* to others, not what they earn in absolute terms. But that argument is still fundamentally about wealth—and thus has opened the door only halfway to the notion that rank *in itself,* not merely the material benefits that come with rank, is very important to those who toil in modern bu-

<hr>

16. Henry Kissinger is credited with the quip that academic competition is especially nasty "because the stakes are so low." It might be fairer to say that it is no more nasty than competition in the high-stakes world; it is just that the low stakes seem to make it less worthwhile. The point I am making is that the stakes look more similar when one recognizes the value people place on winning for its own sake.

reaucracies. Opening the door the rest of the way means recognizing
that wealth comparisons are but one means of establishing relations in
which one person gets to feel superior to another.[17] Dominant positions in social hierarchies of all kinds—not only hierarchies of wealth
or income—carry intrinsic value for their occupants. People compete
strenuously for such positions even when obtaining them brings no
tangible benefits whatever. It does not matter whether rank is symbol-
ized by earnings or epaulettes, by the size of one's office or the height
of one's hat, by the authority to determine the fate of others or by the
fear and deference this authority inspires. What matters is that bureaucracies sort people into positions, some of which are understood to be "above" and others "below," and that, although most people
would—all else equal—rather be above than below, they nonetheless
are willing to endure the latter.

Identifying this deep structure in organizational relations—
"deep" in the sense that it underlies a whole range of social relations
that differ greatly on the surface—is what makes it possible to see the
connection between the modern bureaucratic world and the traditional honorific one. Bureaucracies may have rationalized and formalized the practice of sorting and ranking, but they did not invent it. The
very vocabulary with which organizations enact and refer to distinctions of rank bears numerous traces of premodern origins. The link
is clearest in professional armies, but one can easily find examples
elsewhere. Colleges, universities, and professional associations give
"grades" and bestow "honors." Persons employed for many years possess "seniority," a word that invokes medieval lordship, and those with
substantial authority are "senior officers," combining lordship with
the idea of service. In all but the most progressive organizations, "su-

---

17. James Duesenberry, *Business Cycles and Economic Growth* (New York: Greenwood,
1958); Robert Frank, *Choosing the Right Pond* (Cambridge: Harvard University Press, 1985).
Frank argues that people in contemporary capitalist society compete for wealth not so much
because they want a lot of it but more because they want to have more than others. That helps
explain why rich people report greater happiness than poor people but no more happiness
than reported by rich people fifty years ago. I substantially agree with Frank's interpretation,
but it seems to me that he too readily reduces status competition to competition for relative
wealth. There are many other ways to compete for status, even within capitalist society—by
trying to be the best at something, for example, or by earning people's esteem. People also
regularly compete for status by showing how generous they are—a competition that, *pace*
Veblen and subsequent economists, is not only about showing how much extra money they
have.

periors" continue to give orders that their "subordinates" are expected to obey. Every one of these concepts makes distinctions between people or places them in asymmetric relations with one another, and each represents a borrowing from premodern social organizations in which social relations were steeped in authority and hierarchy. Administrators no doubt find it easy to explain such practices in terms of efficiency. They are not completely wrong. In work organizations, formal classifications aid in establishing who decides what, in keeping records, and in controlling labor costs. Awards and promotions, moreover, are useful incentives with which to promote productivity. In educational and professional institutions, the promise of distinction for a select few is a way to elicit the greatest effort from everyone, thereby enhancing the aggregate performance of students or association members. But this explanation operates at the level of organizations that impose distinctions of rank, not at the level of the individuals who compete for those distinctions. It therefore *presupposes* a generalized desire among these individuals to attain superior positions of some kind, as well as a general willingness to accept a certain amount of subordination. Entirely different incentive schemes could be imagined if human beings entered organizations without any prior expectation that they would occupy positions defined as above some of their colleagues and below others—and that they would be pleased with the first yet amenable to the second.

The efficiency argument also does not explain why the resulting distinctions themselves look so much like indices of status in times and places in which large bureaucracies and considerations of administrative efficiency were unknown. Of course, one might contend that the forms in which ranking is expressed are simply survivals—methods for inducing hierarchy that designers of bureaucracies picked up because they were available and familiar, rather than because they were particularly suited for the purpose of motivating civil servants, clerks, students, and professional soldiers. If that were the case, however, the pattern would not be as widespread as it is. Newer bodies, moreover, would exhibit it less sharply for the most part than older ones; in fact, younger organizations often seem more interested than older ones in honorific practices (witness American institutions of higher education as compared with many in Europe). It is more likely that complex organizations have good reason to impose seemingly archaic hierarchical imagery on role classifications that might otherwise be neutral with respect to rank. The reason, I suggest, is that hierarchy would emerge anyway—making it more practical to harness the process for organizational purposes than to suppress or disregard it.[18]

Rather than attribute the hierarchical nature of bureaucracy purely to administrative design or to mimicry of a vestigial form of social organization, let us consider the possibility that it is a formal elaboration of a principle that operates throughout social life. I am referring to a tendency for human beings to develop, over time and by means of face-to-face interaction, stable systems of relations in which some individuals systematically exert dominance of some kind over other individuals. (I avoid the phrase "pecking order," common though it is, because it denotes a fully transitive order—a pattern almost never observed in human interaction.) Formal hierarchies, whether in the guise of organization charts, caste ideologies, or Burke's Peerage, may make such systems explicit and even shape them—otherwise there would not be much point to formalization—but they are hardly required to bring them into being. A mountain of ethnographic and sociometric observation testifies to the fact. However attached one might be to the idea of equality as a moral commitment, as a description of how human beings actually relate to one another it does a dismal job.

I hope it is becoming clear why I began this section by asserting a parallel between social systems in which individuals maintain their honor by means of physical force and those in which achievement (and

18. Experiments in group decisionmaking are often cited in connection with the emergence of hierarchy, a point I revisit in chapter 2. The best evidence in the world outside the laboratory, however, is that groups organized explicitly with the intention of eliminating hierarchy experience great difficulty in preventing differences of rank from appearing. Student activists in Europe and the United States in the 1960s, for example, discovered repeatedly that despite a fervent commitment to open debate and consensus decisionmaking, some members consistently dominated discussions by means of verbal agility, mastery of theoretical arcana, or mere arrogance stemming from imported characteristics such as sex or race. See Francesca Polletta, *Freedom Is an Endless Meeting: Democracy in American Social Movements* (Chicago: University of Chicago Press, 2002); Sara Evans, *Personal Politics: The Roots of Women's Liberation in the Civil Rights Movement and the New Left* (New York: Random House, 1980); Clayborne Carson, *In Struggle: SNCC and the Black Awakening of the 1960s* (Cambridge: Harvard University Press, 1981); Doug McAdam, *Freedom Summer* (New York: Random House, 1993). Intentional communities have repeatedly been found to hide acute, even exploitative asymmetries of rank beneath a (well-meant) veneer of democratic participation. Rosabeth Moss Kanter, *Men and Women of the Corporation* (New York: Basic, 1993); Benjamin Zablocki, *The Joyful Community* (Chicago: University of Chicago Press, 1980).

hence social standing) is defined in terms of diligence or talent in the pursuit of a professional career. As I pointed out, it is customary to see the former as the antithesis of the latter. Honor systems encourage people (especially men) to react quickly, definitively, emotionally, and often physically to insults or other transgressions, whereas the modern bureaucratic world emphasizes dispassionate, rational deliberation and long-term planning, in both conflictual and cooperative situations. The character traits that made Edward Teach a highly successful pirate (known as Blackbeard) would not have stood him in good stead in a modern navy, let alone in hospital administration or at a consulting firm. The same could be said for Roy Bean, Wyatt Earp, and any number of other agents of so-called law enforcement on the American frontier. Sandra Day O'Connor, on the other hand, would not have found much use for her judicial skills either on board *Queen Anne's Revenge* in the late 1600s or in the American West in the 1800s. From this point of view, many aspects of daily life have utterly changed over the past three hundred years or so, at least in some parts of the world.

Seen from another angle, however, at least one aspect of life has not changed much at all. It remains a commonly observed pattern that people engaged in a collective endeavor or inhabiting the same community settle into arrangements of dominance and deference that reproduce themselves over time, are regarded as legitimate by group members, and distribute status (admiration, esteem, and so forth) unevenly among individuals. Male youth gangs in American cities have for the past century established social hierarchy on the basis of fighting ability, courage, and at times sheer intensity. Something similar can be said for errant knights in feudal society, whether in Japan or in western Europe. In religious orders, individuals earn respect and gain leadership positions by demonstrating deep faith and a capacity for self-renunciation. Parliamentarians strive for social rank by using their talents of persuasion, either in oratory or in informal caucusing. Scholars joust with public displays of erudition or wit (as did parliamentarians, once), often in ways that unfortunately have no relevance to the substantive question they are ostensibly debating.[19] But one can

---

19. Although it is unfortunate that arguments deviate from relevant matters (because the issue is therefore not resolved), it is at the same time quite revealing. My hunch is that when two people—academics or anyone else—get into an argument, the goal of each

readily recognize major differences in the content of the interactions by means of which relations of dominance emerge without forfeiting the right to see these relations as analogous in form. As I have noted, the temptation to concentrate on variation is strong. The conceptual maneuver of regarding all these settings as arenas for the emergence of networks of dominance therefore requires a leap of theoretical faith—an act of bravery (to borrow a notion from an arena where the contests are more concrete), because it has at present no justification other than intuition. It is pointless to engage in debate about whether the diverse forms of social organization I have chosen to regard as analogous are "really" the same or "really" distinct. Ontologically speaking, they are all absolutely distinct, just as you are from me. For that matter, so is the you reading this page from the you who (I trust) read the previous page a short while ago. But it is an uncontroversial matter to claim that there are significant ways, chemically and socially, in which last-page-you and this-page-you can be regarded as more similar than either you is to me at any time, and others in which all of us are more similar to each other than to my neighbor's beagle. It is uncontroversial not because these categorizations are truer or more right than some others but because they are heuristically useful. They call attention, for example, to the fact that you could be indicted at any moment, whatever page you happen to be on, because an earlier version of you neglected to pay taxes last year; to the fact that you could not be indicted at any point for not paying my taxes; and to the fact that no version of any beagle can be indicted for nonpayment of anyone's taxes.[20] (Surprising as it may seem, I will suggest in the concluding chapter why this very issue—the contingent link between a person at one time point and the "same" person at a later point—is central to dominance and to revenge.)

For now, it is surely a bit controversial to claim that there are significant—that is, heuristically useful—similarities among the many kinds of hierarchies I have cited, along with a whole range of others. To

---

changes very quickly from establishing a specific point to simply winning the argument. This common occurrence lends strong support to the view that arguments, like fistfights, are dominance contests. Occasionally, often incidentally, they clarify substantive issues as well.

20. These are all descriptions of social facts, of course, not descriptions of anything that could be taken as intrinsic to me, you, or beagles. This does not make them any less convincing as evidence for the heuristic value of concepts such as "person" or "beagle."

make the claim less controversial, I need to show that statements made about the way hierarchical relations form and articulate themselves in one setting also hold in other settings, with provisions made for mapping the elements of these statements (relations, persons, and so forth) onto one another. There are many kinds of statements one might make, but because this book is about conflict and violence I shall concentrate on the connection between the emergence and stability of dominance relations on the one hand and interpersonal and intergroup strife on the other. Accordingly, chapter 2 develops some general ideas about this connection and shows that they logically imply certain patterns in the sources of conflict and the way it unfolds. In the chapters to come, I present evidence concerning the existence of such patterns, notably in (1) the way disputes become serious and ultimately fatal, (2) the types of relations that are particularly likely to generate such disputes, and (3) the tendency for existing and stable relations to be disrupted by disturbances in *other* relations with which they interlock. The third of these patterns has the most far-reaching implications insofar as it explains why an event occurring at the level of a whole society, such as migration or regime change, can make itself felt on a very local scale in the form of anger, hatred, and violence—even in locations not affected directly by the event. But all three, and others besides, are important in establishing the explanatory utility of a perspective that ties violent disputes among individuals and groups, and by extension human conflict more generally, to relations of dominance and subordination.

CHAPTER 2

Dominance Relations

Domination in one form or another has been a preoccupation of social science at least since it adopted the indictment of inequality as a core mission. But there are various ways of talking about domination, and some are more fruitful for certain purposes than others. I want to suggest straightaway that the most common uses of the concept—uses that focus either on overt aggression or on group disparities in well-being and how they persist—will not turn out to be the most useful when it comes to making sense of conflict. After saying a bit about various ways the concept of domination is typically employed, I offer an alternative that I think bridges the differences while retaining some of the distinctive aspects of each. There is no "right" way to define domination—it is a concept, not a thing in the world—but some versions allow one to make more headway than others in the effort to understand conflict.

One way of talking about domination comes directly from ethology, in which the term "dominance" refers to overt acts of aggression by one animal against another. One organism is said to dominate another when the former attacks or threatens to attack the latter (for instance, by pecking, striking, chasing, snarling, or feigning a blow) more often than the reverse. On the other hand, one animal is said to be dominated by another when it typically responds to such acts of aggression by cringing, whimpering, running away, or prostrating itself.[1] (In the case of some primates, gestures of submission by a male who has just lost a dominance contest with another male include adopting a "female" sexual position while the latter feigns intercourse with him. The fact that such actions are coded by researchers in terms of dominance and deference shows either that ethologists have projected on nonhuman primates their vision of human gender domination or that the symbolic linkage of sexual difference with gender dominance is not a human invention. I do not feel qualified to decide, although I can guess which answer most social scientists would choose.)

Psychologists have broadened the concept somewhat in applying it to human behavior, notably by including verbal threats, insults, interruptions, and other distinctively human ways of being aggressive as examples of dominance behavior. Nevertheless, the psychological concept of dominance remains "thin" in comparison with the way sociologists, anthropologists, and historians use the term. When social psychologists refer to dominance, they mean observable interactions in which one person attempts to control the actions of another by means of sheer intimidation—as opposed to persuasion, appeals to norms, rules, or tradition, or the use of personal charm. Above all, the idea of dominance retains a behaviorist flavor inasmuch as it refers to observable, superficial actions. If a psychologist says that one person in a pair dominates another, he or she is talking about how the two visibly act toward one another in face-to-face situations, not about how their lives are arranged, how contented they are, or how they feel about one another. That is what makes it a thin conception: it is restricted to a small

1. In animal behavior, studies of dominance date to the nineteenth century. See Charles Darwin, *The Expression of the Emotions in Man and Animal* (New York: Oxford University Press, 1998); Konrad Lorenz, *On Aggression* (New York: Harvest, 1974); Nikolaas Tinbergen, *Social Behavior in Animals* (London: Chapman and Hall, 1953). Students of nonhuman primate behavior have increasingly argued for extension of their methods and ideas to human interaction; some social psychologists have taken the idea very seriously. See especially Donald R. Omark, F. F. Strayer, and Daniel G. Freedman, eds., *Dominance Relations: An Ethological View of Human Conflict and Social Interaction* (New York: Garland STPM, 1980); Frans de Waal, *Peacemaking among Primates* (Cambridge: Harvard University Press, 1990); Frans de Waal, *Chimpanzee Politics* (Baltimore: Johns Hopkins University Press, 2000); Allan Mazur, "A Biosocial Model of Status in Face-to-Face Primate Groups," *Social Forces* 64 (1985): 377–402; Cecilia Ridgeway and David Diekema, "Dominance and Collective Hierarchy Formation in Male and Female Task Groups," *American Sociological Review* 54 (1989): 79–93.

set of directly observable phenomena and accordingly contains little in the way of a theory about how or why people behave as they do. It is deliberately purged of theoretical assumptions. One virtue of keeping a concept thin is that it is easy to communicate to others, making it possible to replicate research findings. Another virtue is theoretical clarity: concepts with many dimensions (such as "culture," "capitalism," or "crime") often lead to inconsistent findings concerning the relation of their referents to other phenomena. Disaggregating thick concepts into sets of thin ones is valuable in experimental traditions because researchers can adjust the study environment, one dimension at a time, to match or modify previous work in a well-defined way. Similar considerations apply to the reliance on a strictly behavioral criterion: when a concept such as dominance is defined in terms of observable actions, coding is highly reliable. It is far easier, for example, for two observers to agree on whether subject A "struck" or even "threatened" subject B than it would be for them to agree that A was "disrespectful" to B. The drawback is that theories built on thin behavioral concepts are themselves thin and, usually, behavioral. Refusal to delve beneath the surface of human behavior and say things about subjective experiences shields a theory from accusations of vagueness or nonfalsifiability, but it also tends to preclude theorizing, however rigorously, about aspects of social life that are not directly observable.

There is a second limitation worth noting. The psychological approach to dominance relations has achieved an impressive level of scientific rigor—notably in the form of precise statements and replicable findings—but at the price of generality. In particular, the requirement that research take place in a controlled laboratory setting has made extrapolation to naturally occurring settings both questionable and rare. Experimental researchers are uncomfortable working with observations of real-world interactions, even if these look a lot like the dominance behavior they examine in the laboratory, because of the large number of confounding factors that might influence people interacting in everyday situations. Psychologists therefore rarely venture outside the laboratory to see how well their general findings hold up in natural settings. At the same time, nonexperimental researchers are mistrustful of laboratory findings because they come from a highly artificial environment and because the subjects are almost always college students (who may, moreover, have participated in other experiments and have specific ideas about what they are up to) rather than people from the general population. The link between laboratory behavior and real life tends therefore to be metaphorical and suggestive rather than direct and verifiable—as in the celebrated Milgram experiments, in which people administered what they thought were dangerous electric shocks to actors they believed to be fellow experimental subjects. Disturbing though the results were, they did not come with a license to generalize to human behavior more broadly. After all, the subjects understood that they were participating in a scientific experiment and were thus explicitly not acting as they would in everyday life. There is no agreed-on method for making inferences about human social behavior in general on the basis of experimental findings. Pending the development of such a method, laboratory experiments can tell us a lot about the way people behave in laboratory experiments but relatively little about the way people live.

Elsewhere in the human sciences, the concept of domination is comparatively thick. When sociologists, political scientists, historians, and anthropologists use the term, they typically intend to convey a lot of information at once, concerning not only observable behavior but also subjective experience, along with an implicit theory, and even a moral evaluation, of how the world works.[2] Where psychologists and animal behaviorists opt for a minimalist, microscopic, and consistent conception, ensuring reliable observational data, scholars in other disciplines have opted for a very rich, macroscopic, and variable one, aiding in evocative description but impeding reproducible research. One major advantage of working this way—perhaps the major advantage—is that it makes it possible to talk about domination in contexts where no obvious struggle is occurring. Indeed, probably the single most notable achievement of left-leaning social theory in the twentieth century is to have elaborated the idea that absence of conflict does not imply absence of oppression. From Marxist accounts of class hegemony to poststructuralist accounts of self-oppression, critics of mod-

2. I have pointedly excluded economists from this list. Economists do use the term "dominance" but use it in a highly technical sense referring to people's preference orderings. I am unaware of any research in economics, outside of Marxian economics, that specifically discusses domination of people by other people.

ern society have forged a formidable arsenal of weapons against the liberal idea that a just society is one in which everyone is content with his or her lot.[3] For scholars writing in these disparate traditions, domination can be observed anywhere, so long as one accepts in advance an elaborate account of how social life works. Whereas behavioral scientists talk about dominance in a way that sharply restricts its application, more humanistic approaches have greatly expanded the range and the scale of phenomena to which it can refer. There are reasons to believe that something in between might be worthwhile.

Four tendencies in the way social scientists outside of psychology write about domination underlie this assertion. First, the concept of domination as employed is typically not abstract but rather has a lot of content—each use is closely wedded to a particular form of domination such as wage inequality, slavery, cultural marginalization, or ethnic discrimination. Second, and as a result, domination is almost always seen first and foremost as a matter of subordination of one group by another. In the tales social scientists tell about domination, entire categories of people, defined in terms of sex, class, race, religion, caste, or some other criterion, collectively relegate other entire categories of people to an inferior position. Third, and despite the particularism implicit in the first tendency, domination is almost always understood as being a matter of differences in welfare. Regardless of the form (enslavement, manipulation, terror, legal disempowerment, and so on), domination is almost always ultimately a matter of one group benefiting while—and because—another suffers. Fourth, because they usually are directed at challenging it, if only rhetorically, discussions of domination tend to portray it as a system resistant to conflict and to change. The mechanisms sustaining domination therefore receive a great deal of attention, with relatively little thought given to the implications—or for that matter the possibility—of instability in dominance relations. Each of these tendencies makes understanding conflict difficult, for the following reasons.

The first tendency precludes generalization across concrete types:

3. Oddly, this idea is sometimes extended so far that generalized contentment is not only insufficient as evidence that society is just but is actually invoked as evidence that society is *unjust*. The most widely cited example of such work is Michel Foucault, *Discipline and Punish* (New York: Vintage, 1995), but the writings of the later Frankfurt School, notably Marcuse, also tend in this direction.

domination of workers by employers is one thing, slaves by slaveholders another, wives by husbands yet another. Just as the multiplication
of ethnographies and local histories breeds suspicion regarding general claims, the expanding number of studies of inequality provokes
the discovery of "new" and distinct forms of domination. Each study
works with its own definition, which is consequently rich in local color
and detail and correspondingly hard to transpose onto other social settings. Yet it is possible, and in my view desirable, to see these various
forms, and others (of which I will presently give some examples), as
special cases of a broader, more abstract category. Sad as it might
sound, a useful concept is one that has been drained of as much content as possible without becoming empty. Something must remain, of
course, or the concept can be applied to everything—but that something should not be much, for fear of attributing to one aspect of a phenomenon effects that belong to another. In the above discussion of the
formal aspects of hierarchy—its representation as a system of asymmetric relations that locates some elements in higher positions than
others—I was identifying what I believe should be retained.

The second tendency, that of seeing domination as taking place
between groups, offers a useful way to organize thinking about subordination in that it maps entire populations of relations into one relation, but at the same time it makes it easy to forget that the collective
relation is made of local interactions. Every time an employer fires a
worker, lengthens work hours, or cuts wages, what is "really" happening according to this way of thinking is that capital is asserting its
power over labor. Every time a white police officer uses a racial slur
while questioning a black suspect, what is "really" going on is that
whites as a race are asserting their superiority over blacks as a race.
And so on. It is easy to start believing that the abstract categories "capital" and "labor," "white" and "black," "male" and "female" are engaging in a battle of wills in which particular people are pawns.

To think this way, however, is to mistake abstract categories for
real things—to see them as agents rather than as heuristic devices for
classifying people and the things they do. The categories are built up
from the interactions of real people; they may inform but they do not
produce those interactions. "Capital" has never in its history either
hired or fired "labor," although employers frequently hire and fire
workers. They may even do so with the explicit thought that their ac-

tions could be subsumed under the broad rubric of power relations between capital and labor—but this does not change the fact that the actors in each instance are a particular worker and a particular employer.
If we remember this, then we will also remember that there are innumerable interactions between people that involve domination but have
nothing to do with such group categories as class, race, gender, nation,
caste, religion, or lineage. When the meanest, largest boy in a fifth-
grade classroom discovers that he can oblige a smaller child to give up
his or her lunch money (at least when the teacher isn't looking), he is
surely engaging in dominance over the latter. But he is just as surely
not doing so as an instantiation of the category "schoolyard bully" or
"boy," nor is the victim giving him money because he or she is an example of that category. The bully is not terrorizing his victim on behalf
or because of bullies in general but on his own account. The victim is
complying out of fear specifically of *him,* not because the culturally
available category "bully" has taught him or her to be afraid of bullies.
Thinking about dominance as a matter of social groups needlessly excludes interactions of this kind from consideration, although they may
be just as numerous and just as painful for their victims as group subordination. Moreover, such interactions may turn out to be the raw in-
gredients from which group-level dominance is assembled.[4] If so, then
it is a major theoretical error to leave them out simply because they are
not already integrated into relations of subordination between social
groups. On the contrary, group dominance can be seen as a special
case of interpersonal dominance: one in which many separate interactions are seen by the people implicated in them to be analogous to one
another.

   The third tendency leads to a different kind of blind spot—
namely, an inability to think about domination without thinking about

   4. In an earlier work I argued that collective identities are conceptual devices by means
of which people acknowledge and act on parallels between patterns in their own social relations and those in others' relations. Collective identities ("Irish-American," "landowner,"
"man," or "prisoner") then influence behavior because they coordinate the actions of multiple people, but they only do so if the people in question mutually recognize the parallels.
Local relational patterns are thus the building blocks of abstract collective identifications. The
point I am making here is very nearly the same. Dominance relations can easily exist in the
absence of collective identities that map such relations onto intergroup relations, but relations of dominance between social groups only exist because of patterns of interaction
among individuals. See Roger V. Gould, *Insurgent Identities: Class, Community, and Protest
in Paris from 1848 to the Commune* (Chicago: University of Chicago Press, 1995).

harm. When social scientists talk about domination, they very often have in mind some kind of material exploitation: the overriding concern of scholars who write about social inequality (in Europe and North America, anyway) is economic inequality. This is most explicit in Marxist scholarship, of course, inasmuch as the idea of class position is fundamentally tied to location in the system of production. Apart from the more philosophical versions of Marxism, which concentrate on such abstractions as alienation, the central feature of class domination in the Marxist tradition is therefore that it makes some people rich at others' expense. Other aspects of social inequality, such as the representation of poorer people as inferior, less civilized, or less deserving, serve as instruments of domination: they are useful ideological tools for the maintenance of material domination but are not constitutive of domination. Liberal analyses of economic inequality are if anything more materialist: they attend almost exclusively to disparities in measurable financial outcomes such as earnings, returns to schooling, and chances for promotion. Conservative explanations of inequality as the result of innate variation in ability, intelligence, or diligence are seen as errors or outmoded attitudes rather than as integral parts of a system of domination.

Things are not quite the same with other dimensions of inequality, notably those involving race and sex, but they are not far off, either. Although earlier formulations—in particular those that accompanied feminist and civil rights activism in the 1960s—concentrated on unequal distribution of material resources and unequal political access, attention rapidly turned to the interpretation of race and sex differences as cultural or ideological products. Critiques of this kind are numerous, so there are many varieties of constructivist analysis in the area of race and gender (and ethnicity, and disability, and beyond). Nonetheless, there is a common thread running through these discussions, in that ideologies legitimating inequality are portrayed not only as a factor contributing to its persistence but an intrinsically important component of it. In this view, disparities in material well-being are among the consequences of ideologically produced perceptions of difference, but the perception of difference is itself a form of harm, particularly when internalized by those the ideology defines as inferior. Scholarship in this area has thus usefully broadened the idea of domination to include nonmaterial forms but retains the understanding of domination as exploitation.

Debates about these matters are frequently more about making moral judgments—about whether this kind of inequality is as bad as, or not so bad as, some other—than they are about achieving analytical understanding. That is not such a terrible thing in itself—social criticism is inevitably a part of social science—but it is unfortunate in at least one way that relates closely to my claim that existing conceptions of domination are not general enough. Because domination is seen as necessarily a matter of engendering inequities in well-being, dominance relations that are *not* exploitative cannot be incorporated within existing definitions. It ought to be possible to say that parents dominate their children without committing oneself to the idea that parents necessarily *exploit* their children—even if some do. State authorities, especially those exercising coercive functions, systematically dominate civilians and often enough do so in harmful ways. But again, that does not mean that domination of civilians by state actors is in itself a harmful thing. In fact, contractarian defenders of the state, who should be expected to be quite suspicious of centralized authority, argue that citizens need states to oblige them to behave properly in certain areas. They are therefore better off if they permit themselves to be controlled by a central authority, provided that there are limits to this control. In short, domination of citizens by state actors or of children by adults can be harmful and exploitative, but it is not intrinsically so. Given extant uses of the concept of domination, however, it is impossible to apply the term to these sorts of relations and condone them at the same time. In this book I propose to view harm as a contingent rather than essential characteristic of dominance relations. Domination of one person by another undoubtedly makes exploitation possible, even likely, but it is important to make the analytical distinction between a relation of dominance as such and *abuse* of that relation. Otherwise, for instance, there would be no way to explain why somebody might willingly submit to another person's authority without claiming that the former is a dupe.[5]

5. Such claims, of course, are open to the charge of elitism. I see no way to make arguments about "false consciousness" without implying that one's own understanding is supe-

The fourth tendency stems from the fact that most discussions of domination seek to describe a system—a complex set of arrangements that, sometimes with and sometimes without anyone's intention, conspire to reproduce patterns of inequality between categories of persons. Class analysis seeks to explain why, generation after generation, children of wage-earners are more likely to become wage-earners (and thus more likely to be poor and powerless) than children of professionals, property owners, or managers. Analyses of racial inequality offer explanations for persistent differences in life chances, residential location, and relations to official authorities among groups distinguished by race or ethnic origin. Discussions of "male domination" search for the mechanisms that sort people into two socially distinct categories called "men" and "women" and make it possible for the former to exert authority over the latter, usually to the benefit of the former.

All of these traditions, then, concentrate on relations among whole groups and on the sources of stability in these relations. They are about social categories, real or ideological, and about the maintenance of patterns. What distinguishes them from functionalist social science—that is, from accounts that see institutions as fulfilling general social needs—is that the latter are fairly sanguine about the patterns they describe, whereas the former are critical. To put it crudely, the main innovation in social science since functionalism came under attack in the 1960s is that it has shifted from portraying society in a generally positive light to portraying it negatively. Naturally, one result of this shift is greater sympathy with socially disruptive behavior, above all but not exclusively when it is organized and directed at specific social change. But such disruptions are then not part of the social order; rather, they are its antithesis, or in the language of one of the orthodox traditions in the study of conflict, expressions of its internal "contradictions." As far as the mechanisms invoked to explain social *continuity* are concerned, many look quite a lot like the ones a more conservative Talcott Parsons described in explaining "system integration"—with perhaps a greater emphasis on the power of symbols and language relative to that of institutions and material resources.

---

rior to that of the unwitting victims. The implication may be justified, but it is dishonest not to acknowledge it. Pity is, after all, a way to place oneself above another. So is correcting someone else's mistake.

An important consequence of this emphasis on stability—both in systems of domination and in the groups these systems place in relation to one another—is that it encourages the portrayal of conflict as a residual phenomenon, as what happens when domination doesn't. In this way of thinking, if systems of domination operate in general to sustain themselves, then they should suppress conflict when everything is working smoothly. It follows that conflict—especially violent conflict—is a sign that the system is somehow failing to do its job. Strife is the appearance of cracks in the system rather than an aspect of it.[6] And this is indeed how, for example, the strife-ridden 1960s and 1970s are usually described: as a period in which, on a global scale, established arrangements for the domination of some by others were thrown into crisis and in some cases overturned. Sociologists and political scientists generally see the upsurge in conflict in these two decades—much of it quite violent, particularly in colonial settings—as the achievement of militant activists who had no other means to press their claims. These movements included groups in places such as South Africa, the United States, and various British Commonwealth countries demanding civil rights for blacks, ethnic migrant workers, and indigenous peoples; feminist, gay rights, and immigrant movements in Europe and North America; resurgent labor movements in a variety of industrialized countries; democracy movements in Soviet-bloc nations; and anticolonial insurgencies throughout Asia, Africa, and Oceania. Conflict, ranging from disruptive but peaceful protest tactics to guerilla warfare, was an instrument in the effort to overthrow oppressive elites or oblige them to create more egalitarian social and

---

6. Proponents of "conflict approaches" in the social sciences, including Marxism, might take issue with this statement, arguing that they indeed view conflict as endemic to social life. But they would be talking about underlying conflicts *of interest* thought to account for behavior, whereas I am talking about the behavior itself—about observed conflict, not conflict as an unobserved theoretical construct. Writers in the conflict tradition see observable conflicts such as protest movements as challenges to domination explained by a deep structure of contending interests. In contrast, I contend that observable conflict is an aspect of domination, an interaction that helps set its terms: it is a way contending individuals or groups establish or reestablish their dominance relations. In the conflict tradition, then, violence used by elites is qualitatively different from violence by subordinates: one supports, the other undermines the status quo. In the perspective I am advocating, they are two sides of the same coin: in each case, violent conflict is a way ego signals to alter what ego will and will not accept. Among other things, this interpretation helps explain why protest might be worth the trouble even if it is sure to "fail," that is, even if it has no chance of securing concrete concessions.

political institutions. It was, in short, a coercive tactic made necessary by the de facto or de jure exclusion of subordinate groups from the mainstream political process. In other words, conflict was a weapon wielded against the existing system by people who had managed to step temporarily outside it.

An alternative view is that violent struggles are intrinsic to systems of dominance, not because such systems necessarily give some people grievances against other people but because struggle is the primary means by which people individually or collectively set the terms of their relations with others. According to this way of viewing matters, conflict is an intrinsic part of many social relations, even if it is not always a visible part, because people in these relations continually jockey for greater discretion over what goes on in them. People implicated in relations with others—on the microscopic level of families and friendships and on the macroscopic level of national institutions—remake those relations on a daily basis using what has repeatedly happened in the past as a guide. But only as a guide: if one party decides to change things, for instance by demanding the right to vote, going on strike, or insisting that the other party do the laundry, that does not mean that the existing relation has been destroyed. It means that one party has challenged the terms of the relation as constituted by past interactions and obliged the other to accept the new terms, offer an intermediate arrangement, or resist the challenge.

That, I suggest, is where conflict comes from: not from the collapse or destruction of stable arrangements but from recurrent negotiation, explicit and implicit, verbal or violent, about the terms of those arrangements. If this view has merit, then it is a mistake to think of stability as a basic component of dominance relations, and it is likewise a mistake to think that conflict is a matter of overthrowing domination. Stability may or may not characterize systems of dominance, depending on whether one party or the other believes that an adjustment of terms is possible and desirable; but even when stability does obtain, it is a good idea to remember that conflict is still present as a threat enforcing the current arrangement.

It may be useful to summarize what I have been arguing before moving to a positive statement about what domination is and how it relates to conflict and violence. Although it would be unreasonable to describe the literature concerning domination as a coherent body of thought, there are nonetheless several threads tying it together, so to speak, under the surface. I have claimed that research in the behavioral tradition limits the kinds of theoretical generalizations one can make because, for the sake of rigor, it concentrates narrowly on observed acts of aggression. More subtle kinds of domination go undetected, and their effects on conflict are disregarded. Outside the behavioral tradition, current thinking exhibits four related tendencies in the opposite direction that also hamper a full understanding of the connection between domination and conflict: (1) the current thinking is highly contextual, that is, tied to specific domains, and therefore fragmentary; (2) it concentrates heavily on relations among groups, thereby excluding relations of dominance among individuals; (3) it represents domination as fundamentally a matter of disparities in well-being; and (4) it casts domination as a feature of self-sustaining systems and conflict (therefore) as the antithesis of such systems. I wish to make the case for a view of dominance relations that escapes the limitations described in the preceding pages yet encompasses the range of examples I have mentioned—and, most important, yields testable implications along with insights into a variety of kinds of social conflict.

It is not an accident that people find it so easy to equate the idea of domination with that of exploitation. There is, after all, a strong empirical correlation. Dictators commonly amass great wealth at the expense of dutiful, uninformed, or terrorized subjects. Directors of large corporations pay themselves handsome bonuses even as they announce massive layoffs in response to the need to cut costs—indeed, the bonuses are themselves explained as rewards for success in the cost-cutting effort. Schoolyard bullies tax their classmates much as racketeers extort protection money from small businesses, and parents, though in many instances capable of great kindness toward their children, in others oblige them to work yet deprive them of minimal living standards or a nurturing environment in which to develop. When one person exerts dominance over another, the results can often be ugly.

What is ugly in these examples is not domination itself, however, but its result. Exploitation is what happens when one party to a relation exercises more control than the other over how its benefits will be allocated *and* does so in a self-serving way. But domination, I shall insist, is the fact of exercising that control, not the specific way it is exercised.

If a mother deprives herself of breakfast so that her children will eat enough to stay awake in class that day, it is she who determines how the resources at her family's disposal will be distributed (particularly if she must cajole the children to get *them* to eat), but no one would suggest that she is taking advantage of anyone else. She is, nonetheless, the dominant person in her household. The connection between domination and exploitation, however common, is therefore contingent on the way dominant people choose to act, not intrinsic to the fact that they are dominant.

The way to tell whether one party to a relation exerts dominance over the other, then, is to look at who decides what goes on in the relation. This is a highly general criterion, inasmuch as the question can be asked and answered with regard to an enormous variety of relations. At the same time, it is not very hard to decide in most cases what the answer is, as I shall demonstrate with a set of real and hypothetical examples. To be sure, there are some relations in which one person believes he or she is the source of decisions that the other has in fact maneuvered him or her into making (hence the popularity of books about how to manage one's boss), and it is possible for the maneuvering to involve multiple levels—for example, I can allow you to think that you have subtly persuaded me to make the decision you prefer, when in fact you prefer it only because I have subtly persuaded you to. Still, most relations are not that complex, because most people are not that good at being tricky. Consequently, the issue of who dominates and how much can be decided with fairly high reliability across a broad range of contexts—the hallmark of a usable, workable concept.[7] (I refrain from saying "useful" because consistency, clarity, and reliability ensure only that a concept *can* be used, not that it ought to be. What determines whether a concept is *worth* using is whether it helps clarify or make sense of something. There are plenty of concepts that are easy to

---

7. People often ask for precise and formal definitions of concepts, believing that they will thereby learn what the concept means. The real test of whether one knows what a concept means, however, is whether one can use it reliably—hence the difference between being able to recite the definition of a word and actively employing it in one's vocabulary. I am far more concerned with showing how I mean to *use* the concept of domination than with defining it; hence I will demonstrate what I mean by it with repeated examples. See Hilary Putnam, *Reason, Truth and History* (Cambridge: Cambridge University Press, 1981); John Searle, *Intentionality: An Essay in the Philosophy of Mind* (Cambridge: Cambridge University Press, 1983).

apply, such as Nelson Goodman's color grue, but not very useful in making sense of things.)[8]

Take what is surely the archetypal example of a human dominance relation: that between master and slave. Although the temptation is to see slavery as the most extreme form of exploitation, this is again to mistake one of its results for the thing itself. What makes someone a slave is not forced labor—in many slave societies, slaves were a costly form of conspicuous consumption, not a source of productive labor. Nor is it ill treatment, since the most pampered slave is still a slave. Rather, what makes someone a slave is the mere fact that every detail of his or her existence is, formally or in practice, under the absolute discretion of another. It is this thoroughgoing asymmetry that led Hegel to use the relation of "lord and bondsman" as the ultimate expression of "divided consciousness," which is to say the condition in which a subject becomes an object, in this case, the object of another's consciousness. In some cases by law, in others by virtue of force or circumstance, the master completely determines not only the content but also the very existence of the relation. The latter is actually more significant than the explicit allocation to the master of authority over the terms of the relation: slaves by definition are deprived of the capacity to unilaterally terminate the relation and are thereby stripped of a major source of implicit bargaining power. Hence the overwhelming importance of fugitive slave laws in the nineteenth-century United States, home of the most fully developed slave society in recorded human history.[9] Hence, also, the determined efforts by slaveholders to crush communities of escaped slaves, known as Maroon societies, in the Caribbean and in Brazil from the seventeenth to the nineteenth

---

8. At any given moment, an object is "grue" if it has been examined at some prior moment and found to be green *or* if it has not yet been examined and it is blue. The grueness of objects is as easy to establish as their greenness: all known emeralds, for instance, are grue as well as green. "Grue" is an entirely reliable and usable concept; it simply isn't very useful, in our world at any rate. See Nelson Goodman, *Ways of Worldmaking* (Indianapolis: Hackett, 1977).

9. Kenneth Stampp, *The Peculiar Institution: Slavery in the Antebellum South* (New York: Vintage, 1989); Eugene D. Genovese, *Roll, Jordan, Roll: The World the Slaves Made* (New York: Vintage, 1972); Marc Bloch, *Slavery and Serfdom in the Middle Ages* (Berkeley: University of California Press, 1975); Orlando Patterson, *The Sociology of Slavery: An Analysis of the Origins, Development, and Structure of Negro Slave Society in Jamaica* (London: MacGibbon and Kee, 1967); Orlando Patterson, *Slavery and Social Death: A Comparative Study* (Cambridge: Harvard University Press, 1982).

centuries.[10] The capacity of a master to dictate terms is guaranteed above all by the ability to prevent exit. Because of this ability, relations between masters and slaves are, in effect, absolutely hierarchical: they represent domination in its purest form.

In contrast, employment relations are typically portrayed by free-market advocates as nonhierarchical, because both parties are formally free to enter into and to terminate the arrangement. Legally speaking, this characterization is entirely accurate: labor laws in liberal democracies forbid the use of outright coercion, either by employers or by workers, to maintain an employment relation that one of the parties wishes to terminate. As far as the law is concerned, wage earners and employers are equal parties to a contract each enters freely. And, indeed, workers often quit jobs for others that they find more rewarding or remunerative, just as employers terminate workers they find unproductive or nonessential. It might seem, therefore, that employment relations do not involve domination. However, common sense and a variety of theories agree in observing that real employment relations are often far from this picture of symmetry. It is easier for managers to discipline or fire workers than the other way around, easier for senior managers to fire mid-level managers than the reverse, and so on. Managers issue orders to workers, whereas workers can only make suggestions to their managers. Workers can register complaints about their superiors—but whether the complaints change anything depends on their superiors' superiors. As I observed in chapter 1, no matter how symmetric the formal arrangement might seem, the actual experience of work is anything but egalitarian.

The reason hierarchy can persist in formally free labor markets is not terribly complex. Employment relations are hierarchical because individual workers need jobs more than the people offering jobs need workers. If you own a factory or have a lot of savings from your ample executive salary, then you have enough wealth to live on while your employee tries to hold out for a higher wage. Workers—at any rate, those with skills that are not scarce—will starve or be evicted from their homes before their actual or potential employers will be. Unions, collective bargaining agreements, and strike funds equalize this imbal-

10. See Richard Price, ed., *Maroon Societies: Rebel Slave Communities in the Americas* (Baltimore: Johns Hopkins University Press, 1979).

ance to some degree but not completely. So long as there are people without savings, that is, people who need work right away, wage earners are in a weaker bargaining position than wage payers. As a result, the contracts they sign give the latter more discretion than the former, within limits defined by labor laws—discretion, notably, over hours, basic working conditions, productivity goals, disciplinary measures, promotions, evaluations, and so forth. Managers dictate how workers experience work, how much they will be rewarded for it, and whether they will be permitted to keep doing so, in part because organizations operate more efficiently that way, but more important, because they can. No matter how organizationally useful it might be for the employment relation to involve domination of workers by employers, it would be far more difficult to achieve were it not for asymmetry in bargaining power. Another way of putting this is to say that the employer-employee relation, which is intrinsically one of dominance, would not exist in the absence of such asymmetry. Instead, the exchange of work for payment would resemble the kinds of contracts executed between, for instance, small enterprises in buyer-supplier relations, between professionals and their clients, and so forth. The existence of hierarchically organized firms built of interlocking employment relations is contingent on the prior existence of unequal bargaining positions.[11] We can thus infer that the amount of domination in an employment relation varies with the circumstances that affect each party's exit options—and thus varies considerably more than in the relation of slaves to masters.

The world of production is not the only place where domination of some people by others goes on. I have already had occasion to mention the role of hierarchical relations within families, for example. In most societies, children are largely subject to the authority of their biologi-

11. In economic theory, the existence of firms was regarded as an anomaly for precisely these reasons—that is, because firms seemed to be an inefficient way to execute labor contracts that could be made in a spot market. In a pathbreaking article, Ronald Coase offered an explanation in terms of transaction costs, later elaborated by Oliver Williamson and others into the "markets and hierarchies" perspective. The basic idea is that long-term relations offer solutions to monitoring and knowledge-accumulation problems that cannot be addressed in pure markets. Oddly, however, this argument is seen as having explained *hierarchy* along with the existence of firms. But long-term relations need not be hierarchical, and even if they are there is no transaction-costs explanation for the fact that workers consistently occupy the subordinate position in them. The fact that firms are almost invariably hierarchical in this way needs to be distinguished from the mere fact that firms exist.

cal parents (with substitutes in anomalous cases such as orphans and abandoned children), whereas in other settings they may fall under the authority of whole collections of related adults, of uncles or aunts, or of older siblings. Industrial societies have progressively wrested a portion of this authority from families, particularly with regard to older children, and placed it in the hands of schools, juvenile courts, social service agencies, health organizations, and other institutions. But the fact remains that social life is everywhere based on the essential domination of particular children by particular adults. For the most part, it appears that children and adults alike view this domination as legitimate, even if they might take issue with specific versions. Children, even when protesting what they see as painful privations, for the most part accept the background fact that ultimately their parents decide where they will live and attend school, what they will eat and wear, and the like. Parents, even when they see their authority as a duty rather than a privilege, nonetheless believe that it is sometimes legitimate to justify a decision with the phrase "because I said so"—a most succinct expression of dominance—rather than rational debate. Families and schools alike are coercive to children not simply for the fun of it but to oblige them to develop in certain directions. It is important to note this instance of domination as a reminder that to dominate is not necessarily to harm or oppress—sometimes it really is for a child's own good that adults make choices the child dislikes. Conversely, it is entirely possible to harm without dominating—indeed by failing to do so, as when parents allow their offspring to run into traffic.

It is relatively easy to decide who is dominant in the foregoing examples because the people in them occupy roles for which there is an explicit terminology. Children and parents, workers and employers, slaves and masters typically have a vocabulary for the way they relate to each other—a vocabulary to which they can appeal in deciding whether some action or other is inside or outside the bounds of the relation. Children, for instance, often pressure parents by pointing to what other parents do for or with *their* children, and parents use the behavior of their own parents as a model (if occasionally a negative one). This use of analogies to what happens in other families, facilitated by parallel kinship terms, makes parent-child relations more rigid, more predictable, and more uniform across family groups than would otherwise be the case. The existence of an accepted terminology is thus important both because it explicitly describes the pattern of who decides what and because it helps enforce that pattern. A large body of cross-cultural evidence shows that kin terminologies, for example, serve as powerful guides to action in such domains as gift-giving, economic assistance, and regulation of sexual behavior.[12]

But there are many relations that are less easily described in terms of a conventional and precise role vocabulary. Such relations are correspondingly difficult to inspect for signs of inequalities in control: there is no ready-made language for representing and highlighting the asymmetries they involve. But the absence of formal and explicit languages of dominance like those found in work organizations, slave institutions, or families does not mean that the people in other relations cannot be sorted into dominant and subordinate positions—even if it does mean that dominance in such cases is less stable, a point to which I shall return below. For example, everyday experience reveals that social groups are often sharply differentiated with regard to the amount of deference paid to various members' stated views and the amount of respect accorded to their actions. One person's remarks may be greeted with nods of assent while another's—even if they are substantively identical—are immediately subjected to sharp criticism or summarily dismissed. Conversely, criticisms leveled by a respected group member are given greater weight than those coming from a member with low status.

Systematic research on small-group interaction confirms this impression and, fortunately, adds to it. For one thing, experiments reveal that people in small and medium-sized task groups sort themselves quite quickly—sometimes in minutes—into leader and follower roles, with one or two people doing the most talking and receiving a disproportionate amount of credit for group achievements. For another, characteristics that are associated more broadly with status, such as age, race, education, or sex, influence the way members are allocated to roles, independent of their actual behavior. Unlike cases of for-

---

12. See Maurice Bloch, "The Long Term and the Short Term: The Economic and Political Significance of the Morality of Kinship," pp. 75–87 in Jack Goody, ed., *The Character of Kinship* (Cambridge: Cambridge University Press); W. H. R. Rivers, *Kinship and Social Organization* (London: Athlone, 1968); Bronislaw Malinowski, *Argonauts of the Western Pacific* (New York: Waveland, 1994); Theodore Caplow, "Rule Enforcement without Visible Means: Christmas Gift Giving in Middletown," *American Journal of Sociology* 89 (1984): 1306–23.

mal assignment of people to roles, informal "group structure" of this kind is principally observed sociometrically, that is, by observation of repeated interaction or occasionally by questionnaires. Yet despite the more diffuse character of small-group social differentiation, it unmistakably shares features with the foregoing examples. Most important, the fact of unequal attributions of esteem in social groups means that some people largely dictate what others will do. A majority of members find themselves following the suggestions of a minority, silencing themselves or being silenced when their opinions diverge from those of the group's leaders. This pattern of deference, moreover, persists even if leaders refrain from using explicit threats or promises of rewards. Indeed, in certain situations, for example, when artificially chosen leaders (that is, people assigned the leader role by experimenters) have an ascribed trait usually associated with subordination, the use of threats reduces compliance by followers.[13] Hierarchy based on interpersonal influence, although more subtle than in formal hierarchies, is thus another example of domination according to the criterion I have described.

The small-group research tradition has concentrated since the beginning on groups performing tasks. But purely social relations, that is, relations with little or no instrumental component, can also be hierarchical, in ways that can be even more painful, because more deeply personal, than is the case in task groups. Ethnographies of youth groups and sociometric studies of schools repeatedly find what anyone who has spent time in such settings already knows (but might have trouble expressing in a general way): a small number of individuals re-

13. Many of these results come from experiments by Robert F. Bales, A. Paul Hare, Muzafer Sherif, and their colleagues. See Robert F. Bales, Fred Strodtbeck, T. M. Mills, and Mary E. Roseborough, "Channels of Communication in Small Groups," *American Sociological Review* 16 (1951): 461–68; A. Paul Hare, *Handbook of Small Group Research* (New York: Free, 1962); A. Paul Hare, Edgar F. Borgatta, and Robert F. Bales, eds., *Small Groups: Studies in Social Interaction* (New York: Knopf, 1966); Muzafer Sherif, *Social Interaction: Process and Products* (Chicago: Aldine, 1967). See also George C. Homans, *Social Behavior: Its Elementary Forms* (New York: Harcourt, Brace, and World, 1961), for a lucid synthesis and reinterpretation through a behaviorist prism. More recent developments have focused on the role of ascriptive status characteristics and responses to the use of sanctions. See Joseph Berger, M. Hamit Fisek, Robert Z. Norman, and Morris Zelditch Jr., *Status Characteristics and Social Interaction: An Expectation States Approach* (New York: Elsevier, 1977); Cecilia Ridgeway, "Nonverbal Behavior Dominance and the Distribution of Status in Task Groups," *American Sociological Review* 52 (1987): 683–94; Linda Molm, *Coercive Power in Social Exchange* (New York: Cambridge University Press, 1997).

ceive a great deal of publicly displayed esteem and approval from others, whereas most receive little or no esteem and a few (usually a very few) are targets of nearly unanimous ridicule and shame.[14] Remarkably, these settings are even closer than work organizations to the fiercely competitive world of honor societies, albeit in a form that is somewhat less extreme because it is more closely regulated by institutional authorities. Although the dimensions on which people compete for status can vary (athletic ability and physical attractiveness being the most common, intellectual and artistic ability far less so), the typical pattern is that elite membership is common knowledge: widely shared and recognized as widely shared. In fact, schools and informal youth groups alike employ stylized attire—called "colors" in both cases—to mark both distinctions of rank and group membership.

It is clearer in the case of informal groups why status distinctions might be connected to relations of dominance. After all, members of groups by definition interact frequently, and it is unsurprising to observe that the high-status members of youth groups direct the actions of others much as superiors direct subordinates in formal organizations. Schools, however, can be quite large, making interaction between any arbitrary pair of students rare—and especially rare between students who differ in status. Moreover, students are for the most part tightly regulated while in or near school, leaving relatively little room for any student to tell another how to behave. In such cases, one might conclude that status rankings have little to do with dominance as I have been defining it, that is, as a relation in which one party has greater say than the other over what both will do.

Yet even in this case there are clear examples of asymmetry in social relations, and these asymmetries do have implications for the way students behave. Within the limits imposed by official dress codes, high-status students' clothing choices exert enormous influence on the choices of other students, both implicitly and as a result of verbal pressure (this latter sanction being applied as much by other non-

<hr />

14. There are many studies documenting the existence of status hierarchies in informal groups, but I will cite only a handful of prominent examples: James S. Coleman, *The Adolescent Society* (New York: Free, 1961); Theodore Newcomb, *The Acquaintance Process* (New York: Holt, Rinehart, and Winston, 1961); Muzafer Sherif, *Group Conflict and Cooperation* (New York: St. Martin's, 1966); Jacob L. Moreno, *Who Shall Survive? Foundations of Sociometry, Group Psychotherapy, and Sociodrama* (Beacon, N.Y.: Beacon House, 1953).

elite students as by social superiors). Similar processes permit high-ranking students to determine hair styles and other aspects of bodily presentation, musical tastes, linguistic behavior, and evaluations of other students. This last detail is the most significant in the present context: to the degree that social approval is important to adolescents, and to the degree that high-status students influence the distribution of approval by their own actions, the average student is far more dependent on the approval of a high-ranking student than the latter is on the former. With smiles, gestures of respect, attention, and invitations to sit at the same table, elite students can elevate others to near-elite rank. At the other end of the scale, they can relegate those of whom they disapprove to pariah status or at least to social invisibility. Other students can reject these elite-led classifications; some openly do so by constituting counter-groups (nerds, delinquents, Goths, and so forth). But many profess to admire and like the varsity athletes, cheerleaders, and their hangers-on and cherish the occasional moments of recognition they receive in return. In this respect, popular students do in fact dominate the non-elites who do not defy the mainstream status ranking. When social relations form, it is at the discretion of the former and on terms they dictate—whereas the latter count themselves lucky to be included at all.

Friendships in general often follow a similar logic. Even if adults have outgrown the insecurities of adolescence, differences in social appeal persist. Take any two people at random, and it is unlikely that they will match exactly in the degree to which they appeal to one another as friends. The mismatch might result from differences in social attractiveness on which everyone might agree, or it might be the result of purely idiosyncratic factors leading Alice to like Beth more than Beth likes Alice; the implication is nearly the same. Even if they do form a friendship, the asymmetry will manifest itself in a wide range of patterns that will consistently make one party to the relation feel neglected and cause the other to feel crowded if the former demands more attention. Alice may call more often than Beth, having discovered that the two-week interval Beth prefers is too long; Beth will regularly show up late for, cancel, or simply forget engagements, whereas Alice is eager to get together, consistently punctual, and loath to postpone. Beth might make carelessly hurtful remarks and think nothing of it, whereas Alice may worry for days about whether a minor misunderstanding has irritated Beth. (Beth, meanwhile, is most likely worrying about what she might have said to *her* favorite friend, who hasn't called in a while.) Any of the transgressions Alice routinely suffers at Beth's hands would, if committed by Alice, be sufficient for Beth to drop her as a friend. Beth consequently dictates the terms of the friendship, although the category "friend" connotes no such asymmetry. Here again, then, is an example of a relation involving dominance: for fear of losing Beth as a friend, Alice submits to her will concerning what they do together and when.

The example of Alice and Beth is a caricature, naturally, but I suspect most readers will recognize a muted version of such patterns in their own social relations and in others of which they are aware. Many romantic relationships and marriages, even those in which the parties adhere to the equal partnership model, endure similar asymmetries—often in the form of unequal effort and occasionally to the point of emotional abuse. At either end of the scale, then—from the most openly hierarchical types of relations to those that in principle are fully egalitarian—it is possible to envision and observe domination as I have defined it, namely, asymmetry in discretion regarding what parties to the relation will do. By this definition, there are many ways for people to achieve dominance over others, some of which my examples have cited: threats of force, personal charm, superior debating skills, bargaining power, and even claims of arcane knowledge or divine inspiration are all viable means of exerting control over what other people do. Domination, the way I am using the term, is an abstract concept that encompasses all sorts of mechanisms for social influence: authority, coercion, unequal exchange, manipulation, deception, persuasion, demonstration of superior competence, and so on.

Although abstract, this is nonetheless a quite primitive conception of dominance insofar as it only concerns relations between pairs of individuals. There is no immediate extension to relations among multiple individuals, which we might describe as networks of dominance. Nor is there a simple analogy from the relation between two individuals to the relation between two social groups, which is the most common kind of domination discussed in the social sciences. I will extend my arguments to these higher-order forms of domination in subsequent chapters, but I wish to emphasize here that the extension is not straightforward. The reason is that it is problematic—however frequently social scientists do it—to speak of collections of people "do-ing" or "deciding" things, either alone or in relation to other groups. To say that a group, say, "employers" or "landowners," dominates another group, such as "workers" or "peasants," is to attribute a degree of unity of purpose and action to these collectivities that they may not in fact possess. The assertion that landowners as a group dominate peasants as a group is quite different from the assertion that each specific peas-ant is controlled by a specific landlord. However, it is a virtue of the conception of dominance I have offered, not a vice, that it resists ready transposition from individual-level relations to group-level relations. It calls attention to the possibility—to which I have already alluded—that group-level domination is derivative of, not identical to, domi-nance relations among individuals. In fact, I shall offer evidence in chapter 4 that conflict between social collectivities such as families or ethnic groups occurs precisely because the cohesion of these groups is crucial to the domination of one by another and because cohesion is often in doubt. Beginning with a primitive, or thin, notion of domi-nance is what makes the second-order nature of group domination visible.

I am jumping ahead, however. The goal of this section has not been to make theoretical claims about the connection between domi-nance and conflict but to set out a definition of dominance and to show that it can be meaningfully and reliably applied to a range of instances. The definition I have offered is not as thin as that employed by psychol-ogists and ethologists, but it is a good deal thinner than others avail-able in the social sciences more generally. What is useful about thin definitions, as I have just suggested, is that they permit one to start simply and only gradually build toward more elaborate propositions. Starting with a thicker, more complex notion only leads to confusion by making it hard to separate definitions (for example, "when I say X, I am referring to . . .") from empirically falsifiable claims ("the occur-rence of X is usually accompanied by . . ."). The remainder of this chapter will propose a set of such claims.

I have taken pains to separate the issue of who dominates whom in a social relation from the issue of who is better off—in other words, to distinguish asymmetry in control from asymmetry in well-being. The point of underlining this distinction is to make sense of the fact with which I introduced this book: that a lot of very violent behavior in a lot of places appears to be attributable to disputes about small matters. My argument is that, once we recognize the intrinsic importance of struggles for dominance, independent of the material benefits at stake in a given dispute, we will find it much easier to understand the intensity of conflicts about materially insignificant concerns. The following hypothetical example illustrates my reasoning.

Suppose you have a friend whom you meet for coffee on a regular basis, although the location and time vary. If you and your friend are like most people, you probably discuss where and when to meet, taking into account schedules, weather, traffic, and so on. Most significant, you probably see the discussion as mutual in the sense that each person's preferences bear equal weight most of the time and in the sense that occasions on which one person essentially chooses the location are about as numerous as those on which the other decides.

Of course, your friend may consistently have a busier schedule and will thus more frequently express a strong preference for a convenient meeting place. Or you may be more sensitive to noise levels and therefore more likely to veto certain choices depending on your mood. According to the definition I have sketched, if one of you routinely decides where you are going to meet, then your supposedly symmetric friendship involves a certain amount of dominance. This is particularly true if the person who decides does so without much consideration for the other—for instance, by simply announcing the rendezvous rather than suggesting it, by neglecting to ask whether the arrangement is suitable, and so forth. Frequently, showing consideration consists precisely of these sorts of verbal gestures because they signify the speaker's recognition that both parties are entitled to a say. Asking "Is that all right with you?" is a way of signaling one's readiness to change plans if the answer is no. If your friend offers a reason for preferring a specific place or apologizes for having expressed a strong preference, she is renouncing the right to make a unilateral decision: the first tactic invites you to agree or object rather than assuming your acceptance, the second acknowledges that the current asymmetry in decisionmaking is a little outside the normal bounds of your friendship. If, on the other hand, your friend *tells* you where you will meet, with no accompanying markers (such as "Shall we," "How about," or "What do you think?"), she has implicitly asserted the right to decide unilaterally.

Assuming that your friend is the one announcing a peremptory decision, it may turn out that the location in itself is fine with you, or it may turn out that it is unacceptable. You will, however, be irritated either way, possibly to the point of starting an unpleasant argument. That, at least, is the implication of my main thesis concerning disagreements in general—that the *substantive* issue of where you will meet is less important in producing conflict than the *procedural* issue of who makes the decision. People occasionally justify their anger over materially insignificant matters like this one by insisting that it is the "principle" that concerns them; I contend that what they mean, in the terms I have been using, is that the other party has arrogated to himself or herself a level of discretion, a dominant role, that has not previously characterized the relation.

My reference to the relation is not incidental but critical. If the coffee-shop rendezvous were a one-time event, it ought to matter little that one of you has asserted a dominant position in making a decision that would otherwise have been shared evenly. But in the case of a friendship, there will be more decisions like this one. Consider, then, what might happen if you were to go along wordlessly with your friend's unilateral choice. If she is someone who generally likes to be in charge, she might be pleased to discover that she had got her way without discussion and be inclined to try again the next time. After a few more such episodes, she might feel entitled to decide for the two of you. You might likewise begin to see it as her privilege or at any rate be reluctant to challenge her after having said nothing for so many weeks, recognizing that *she* might take it amiss. In short, a unilateral decision, left unchallenged, might become a regular feature of your ongoing relation. Foreseeing this (consciously or not), you ought to be considerably more bothered by the initial display of dominance than if the person you are meeting were someone you did not anticipate meeting again.

To push things a bit further, your concern about your friend's behavior will become more intense to the degree that dominance concerning the narrow question of where to meet might generalize to other domains—how often to meet or for how long, for instance, what to talk about, who will pay, or entirely separate aspects of the friendship. The broader the potential implications of a specific assertion of dominance for future encounters, the more disturbed the other party will be, independent of the inherent significance of the present decision.

The idea behind this proposition is that current interactions concerning small matters are more important than they might appear because they have effects on future interactions that potentially involve big matters. If my brother has always decided what games we play, who sits in the front seat, and other issues of minor import, he will also expect to dominate later on, when the decisions concern such things as whether to sell the family home. If I have been accustomed to deferring throughout our childhood, it will take much more courage for me to challenge him later. To the degree that I recognize this fact about our relationship and its major implications for the future, I will be more reluctant to defer with respect to minor issues. Indeed, the effect of current interactions on the outcomes of future interactions makes the present one more important than it seems even if later decisions will *not* involve significantly bigger issues. Deferring now makes it harder to raise objections about tomorrow's similar decision, which makes it even harder to object the next day, and so on. Integrating the stream of future decisions, even if they will not increase in intrinsic importance, makes today's decision much more significant than it would be in isolation.

In short, the pattern of past interactions sets the tone for current ones. Current interactions either conform to expectation, thereby reinforcing it, or deviate from it, altering expectations if the deviation goes unchecked. In existing relations, people come into conflict when one party acts in a way that departs from the pattern, but not simply because such departures are disturbing in their own right. They bother people for the same reason that they had expectations in the first place, namely, that current actions serve as guides for future ones. If you are accustomed to an equal say in decisions, a unilateral action by a friend will offend you not only because you want an equal say now but because you want to preserve your equal status for the future. Objecting to your friend's behavior is a way of countering the shift in the friendship that acceptance of the behavior would entail. If your friend insists, then he or she is implicitly saying that the new terms are the only acceptable terms. What started off as a small matter can become a serious conflict because the way it is resolved will influence the outcome of subsequent decisions. Even if the current discussion ends with a joint decision, things will still not be the same unless you receive an apology as well: otherwise, your friend will have arrogated at least the right to make further *attempts* at shifting the terms of your relationship. My argument, then, is that interpersonal conflict stems mostly from disagreements about the amount of dominance exerted in social relations. When two people get into a fight about a debt or about ownership of a mule, about whether the ball was in or out or whether it was all right to divulge a secret to a mutual friend, it is conventional to say that the fight was "about" the debt, the mule, the ball, or the secret. The disputants themselves seem to say so: asked why they are angry with someone, people in most societies will tell a story about something the person did, or said, or failed to do, or refused to do. I am suggesting that this view can easily get things just about backwards: rather than say that Kim and Kelly got into a fight because Kelly revealed Kim's secret, it might be more accurate to say that Kelly revealed Kim's secret because that was a good way to start a fight or that Kim made an issue of the secret because Kelly's decision to divulge it was a sign of indifference to Kim's desire for discretion. The mule, the debt, the ball, and the betrayal of confidence are not so much causes of conflict as occasions for it—the superficial expressions of attempts to renegotiate the terms of the disputants' relationships. When people get into serious conflicts about material things such as money, land, and merchandise, it is not because these are the important things in life but because they are a very concrete, visible way in which people show each other who is in charge: they are, to distort a famous phrase, good to compete with.

All of this bears directly on the puzzle of violence I raised at the beginning of chapter 1—namely, the fact that a lot of serious violence occurs because of seemingly minor matters. This is indeed a puzzle if one expects conflict to be more severe when the dispute is "about" something important than when it concerns something minor. But the puzzle goes away if we draw back from the immediate dispute—the incident precipitating violent conflict—and concentrate instead on the social relation the disputants have with one another. To the extent that today's interaction is linked to tomorrow's, and the next, and the next interaction after that, the difference between "minor" and "major" disputes is diminished. So long as the parties to a relationship base their expectations about future interactions on the dominance pattern established in the present one, arguments about a two-dollar bet can become nearly as serious as arguments about a two-thousand-dollar loan. In a sense, the disputes are not about what they seem—they are disputes about social relations.

I mentioned another noteworthy fact about violence in chapter 1: the regular occurrence, all over the world, of tragic violence due to (to put it provocatively) mere words. On the face of it, a two-dollar bet is much more like a loan of two thousand dollars than it is like a verbal jibe—whether in the form of ritualized insults like those I cited above or in the form of offhand remarks about a host's cooking (too much salt), the true reason a friend had gone to war for the duke of Burgundy (the prospect of plunder), or a fellow barber's haircutting ability (not as good as the speaker's).[15] In the former instances, tangible resources are at stake, regardless of their amount; in the latter, what is at stake is, literally, sound waves. Utter this stream of syllables, and someone might smile and say "thank you"; utter that one, and you may end up dead. Even the tone of the delivery might make the difference between a remark that provokes a chuckle and one that sends someone into a murderous rage.

I am describing the difference provocatively so as to make something explicit. Obviously, it is not the sounds that make people angry, it is what they mean. Moreover, it is what they mean in a particular time and place, and with reference to specific people: not being someone who cuts hair for a living, for instance, I cannot imagine being terribly angry if someone were to tell me I was no good at it. Nor can I imagine a friend trying to goad me by accusing me of incompetence in spear-fishing, since I do not inhabit a society in which adult males are expected to have that skill. I *can* imagine being angry if someone were to say I was a bad writer, or a bad thinker, especially if I thought the person would be believed by others. (Even in this case, I have trouble imagining that such a remark could make me turn violent. Keep in mind, however, that it is common for people to be surprised by their own extreme reactions to certain situations. Those of us who have no

15. These are genuine examples of insults leading to homicide, to which I will return in the next chapter. The first occurred in Madhya Pradesh in the 1960s, the second in the Low Countries in the 1500s, and the third in Corsica in the 1850s. I have selected these cases arbitrarily, but they are similar to hundreds of other incidents in the contexts I have examined in which insults led to murder.

experience of reacting violently to insult should be cautious about inferring that such reactions belong to other cultures. Recognizing that insults make people angry because of what they mean does not require us to believe that insults make people angry or violent only in certain cultural settings.)

In short, the meaningfulness of insinuations, accusations, and gestures of disrespect results from the social setting in which they are made. This fact makes them symbolic forms of harm; thefts, beatings, unpaid debts, and demotions, on the other hand, are immediate, intrinsic, material forms of harm.

Even purely symbolic harm, however, has real consequences. In the context of social relations, verbal insults can cause as much trouble as stealing a cow or slapping someone in the face. Doing damage to someone's reputation by deriding his or her abilities (or physical appearance, or parentage, or taste) has material consequences by virtue of its impact on future interactions; conversely, doing damage to someone's material well-being also diminishes his or her reputation. Just as it is possible to recognize the larger implications of an unpaid two-dollar debt, it is possible to see the real damage inherent in a verbal slight: someone willing to insult you in public is likely to challenge you in other, more concrete ways as well, unless you respond decisively. The very fact of the insult reveals the speaker's belief that he or she has little to fear from you, a belief that will only be reinforced if you do nothing. Those who witness it will feel similarly emboldened if you fail to counter the symbolic challenge. They will likewise be emboldened by your failure to counter a concrete offense, for example, if an acquaintance takes one of your possessions, makes a decision that affects you without regard for your opinion, or forces you to do something you do not want to do. As far as your reputation as someone whose will must be respected is concerned, there is little difference between a disparaging remark and an action whose material consequences imply disregard for your wishes. Because both the person challenging you and those present can presume that you do not wish to be insulted, a symbolic gesture of disrespect conveys the same message as a concretely harmful action. Both types of action assert, and in so doing effect, dominance over you. Verbal exchanges, like material resources, are good to compete with—better, in fact, inasmuch as they are always available.

This reasoning seems to suggest a self-fulfilling, conventional quality to verbal insults. All it takes is a conventional understanding that a gesture is disrespectful for it to be so. Likewise, it is sufficient that a gesture be a conventional expression of respect (shaking hands, tipping one's hat, saying good-bye) for its omission to be construed as insulting. It is this conventionality that motivates the widespread commitment—which I noted in chapter 1—to studying "honor" as a cultural complex. From the commonplace observation that a phrase or hand movement that expresses deference in one place can express the opposite somewhere else, it is a small step to concluding that the best position from which to make sense of the link between insults and violent conflict is within the relevant cultural system. After all, if biting one's thumb prompts a bloody brawl in Elizabethan England but invites a comment about nervous habits in late twentieth-century New York, then the cultural context—it is often claimed—must be a mediating factor in any explanation of the bloody brawl that mentions thumb-biting behavior as a cause.

In introducing this issue in the previous chapter, I pointed out that the focus on specific behaviors and their meanings might lead us to miss the larger fact that every society offers its members symbolic tools with which to elevate or demean others. Standing back from the specifics of hat-tipping, hand-shaking, nose-thumbing, and thumb-biting, that is, from the visible markers of respect and disrespect, it is possible to see a broader picture in which people everywhere employ both symbolic and material means to express dominance and deference toward one another. In this, human beings have a lot in common with other social animals, although the range and perhaps the subtlety of the symbolic resources they employ exceeds that of macaques, sea lions, and highland ponies. In complex organizations in the West, dominance is most often displayed by issuing spoken or written commands, deference by compliance with those commands, occasionally accompanied by salutes or phrases like "Yes, sir" and followed if necessary by abject apology for failure to comply. In athletic endeavors in many societies, dominance is achieved by "winning" and expressed by physical gestures such as vigorous dancing, jumping, baring teeth, and thrusting arms into the air (followed, in some instances, by gracious expressions of admiration or affection for the defeated opponent—a sort of reimbursement of some of the status wrested from the humiliated rival). In Hindu society, dominance is frequently expressed by means of asymmetric contact prohibitions that correspond (more or less) to caste categories and both enacted and expressed in the *jajmani* system of food distribution.[16]

True, the hierarchies so expressed vary in the breadth and content of their implications. In Hinduism, a caste superior does not have the presumptive right to give orders to a caste inferior, whereas, for instance, whites in the postbellum American South regularly asserted the right to give commands to blacks they did not know. In athletic competition in the West, winners do not usually have a recognized right to oblige their opponents to do anything besides acknowledge defeat (and perhaps give up an item of clothing, as in rowing events). Yet whatever else each version of hierarchy may involve, all involve at least a socially enforced allocation of greater discretion to one party than to the other.[17] Managers, tournament winners, high-caste persons, and members of dominant racial groups have various means to relinquish or at least not insist on their rank (means that, admittedly, they rarely exercise), whereas their inferiors are not free to disregard theirs. Beneath the surface of rich variation in the mechanisms, signs, and consequences of dominance relations, it is possible to discern a generic asymmetry in control that corresponds to the (moderately) thin conception of dominance I have set out.

Even in societies that initial observation and wishful thinking per-

16. Murray Milner, *Status and Sacredness* (Oxford: Oxford University Press, 1994); Louis Dumont, *Homo Hierarchicus: The Caste System and Its Implications* (Chicago: University of Chicago Press, 1967); McKim Marriott, *Caste Ranking and Community Structure in Five Regions of India and Pakistan* (Poona, India: Deccan College Building Centenary and Silver Jubilee Institute, 1965); Adrian C. Mayer, *Caste and Kinship in Central India: A Village and Its Region* (Berkeley: University of California Press, 1970).

17. By calling these forms of dominance "socially enforced" I am implicitly referring to a more complex kind of domination than that shown in many of the dyadic examples I have been using in this chapter. Although it may be the case that a particular manager can expect compliance with commands because of her personal authority over subordinates, that authority is backed up by an elaborate system of rules to which she can appeal in difficult situations. The rules have force because they guide other people's actions, which are subject to the commands of yet other authoritative people, and so forth. Similar considerations apply to the fact of winning a game with conventional rules and to the operation of caste distinctions: relations of dominance in these examples are necessarily linked to a broader social arrangement, whereas dominance in dyadic examples like that of Alice and Beth, or you and the friend you meet for coffee, can be self-contained. It is this distinction that makes it difficult, as I noted above, to apply statements about dyadic dominance relations directly to group-level dominance.

mitted some anthropologists to describe as egalitarian, it turns out that many social relations are hierarchical and marked as such with verbal signs, physical acts (including but not restricted to aggression), or maneuvers of other kinds that either directly or in their effects show that one person's fate is subject at least in part to the will of another.[18] The absence from small hunter-gatherer communities of stratification by class or of formal institutions of kingship is no obstacle to relations in which adults dominate children, men dominate women, or assertive people dominate passive people, individually or collectively. So, although the way domination is achieved, maintained, or expressed can be conventional, the *fact* of its achievement, maintenance, or expression is not conventional in the least. Nor, as I show in chapter 3, is the role of verbal exchanges in the trajectory of violent conflict. Across a wide range of social settings, a substantial proportion of deadly conflicts begin with a casual remark.

What this implies is that, if the form verbal insults take is subject to cultural variation, their relevance to the enactment and expression of dominance may not be. Abstracting from the specific forms of dominance, on one hand, and from the specific forms of insult, on the other, makes it possible to see their connection as a general matter. So long as we do not make the mistake of *equating* insult with dominance by definition (for instance, by defining conversations in which one person calls another a coward as dominance contests), observing an empirical association between verbal jousting and dominance would

18. See, e.g., Elizabeth Marshall Thomas, *The Harmless People* (New York: Vintage, 1959), on the !Kung San; Robert K. Dentan, *The Semai: A Nonviolent People of Malaya* (New York: Holt, Rinehart and Winston, 1979). Although these and other "nonviolent" peoples live much less hierarchically than, for instance, "warrior" peoples such as the Masai and the Yanomami, they nonetheless maintain some asymmetric relations of deference and respect. A common reason for the original attribution of social equality—although this does not apply to the !Kung—was restriction of attention to the lives of adult men, a move some authors have argued was facilitated by the fact that the ethnographers themselves were predominantly men. See Michelle Z. Rosaldo and Louise Lamphere, eds., *Woman, Culture, and Society* (Stanford: Stanford University Press, 1974), especially Michelle Z. Rosaldo, "Woman, Culture, and Society: A Theoretical Overview," and Sherry Ortner, "Is Female to Male as Nature Is to Culture?"; see also James G. Flanagan, "Hierarchy in Simple 'Egalitarian' Societies," *Annual Review of Anthropology* 18 (1989): 245–66; Marilyn Strathern, *The Gender of the Gift* (Berkeley: University of California Press, 1990); Eleanor Leacock, "Women's Status in Egalitarian Society: Implications for Social Evolution," *Current Anthropology* 19 (1982): 247–76; Jane F. Collier, *Marriage and Inequality in Classless Societies* (Stanford: Stanford University Press, 1988).

carry major implications for understanding conflict. If it really is the case that social relations—and the amount of asymmetry they involve—are sensitive to what the people in them say to each other, then we have one of the keys to understanding why interpersonal violence among human beings seems to be such a common occurrence.[19] Situations in which the criteria for establishing dominance are clear and leave little room for debate—as is ordinarily the case in formal hierarchies, monarchical succession, and organized tournaments—discourage conflict. In these settings, only one person can plausibly lay claim to preeminent status, at least if the rules are followed. (Hence the frequency with which monarchs' illegitimate children have been the occasion for wars of succession.) On the other hand, the more evenly or ambiguously distributed the tools for achieving dominant positions are, the harder it is for people to agree on who ought to prevail. That makes it more likely that both parties will persevere in a dispute, which in turn increases the likelihood of violent resolution. Because talk is difficult to concentrate in the hands of one person or a few, dominance contests based on talk are prime candidates for conflict.

The insight that almost anyone can engage in disparaging talk, making conflict possible in any relation, underlies a more general proposition about the conditions in which conflict is most likely to occur and to become serious. I have already observed that some relations are governed by a more explicit set of terms than others, making hierarchy easier to observe, say, in family relations or in formal organizations than in informal friendships. The proposition is that, if conflict occurs when people cannot agree on who dominates whom, it should occur principally in relations for which the social cues for deciding the

---

19. Calling interpersonal violence "common" presupposes a baseline. Most often, people seem to use a normative reference point, namely, the rate of interpersonal violence they would like to observe in human communities—which is usually zero. Because my purpose in this book is explanatory rather than evaluative, I have in mind an empirical baseline. It is the amount of intraspecific violence in communities of nonhuman vertebrates, above all, primates. Although it turns out that intraspecific killing is more common among nonhuman primates than was once thought, it nonetheless appears to occur less frequently than among humans. One reason for the difference may be technological, as Hobbes pointed out long ago. Another reason is social: with verbal resources at their disposal along with material ones, people are more reluctant to accept defeat in dominance interactions. The central argument, though, is that human social structure is more complex than primate social structure; consequently, ambiguity over relations is more intense, and the lashing of relations, as discussed subsequently, more commonplace.

issue are unavailable or inconsistent. The more clearly specified a relation is, from past experience, from explicit role terminology, or from
preexisting status characteristics such as age, the easier it ought to be
for people to agree on how to distribute control. Disputes should end
more quickly, and more definitively, when one person can legitimately
say "I'm the boss," or "you never objected before," or "I know more
about this than you."[20] They should be more difficult to resolve, and
should therefore be more likely to escalate, when there are no such appeals to be made or when they are available but contradictory—for example, when a formal superior is younger than his or her subordinate.
As with the equal availability of verbal insult, the equal distribution of
claims to superior rank (or the general absence of such claims) intensifies the likelihood of conflict.

Further inferences follow from this one. The existence of formally
organized authority—dominance backed up officially by other relations, themselves conditional on yet others, all described in official
rules and procedures—suggests another way in which conflict can
be more likely in some circumstances than others. Some contests for
rank can be decided in isolation, that is, on the sole basis of the differences in strength, resolve, or skill at argument between the two persons directly involved. But in complex societies, and especially in adult
life, such gladiatorial competition is the exception. It is much more
common for dominance contests to depend on third parties, whether
these are superiors with decisionmaking authority, followers with the
freedom to choose allegiances, peers forming coalitions, or simply
people in comparable social positions. (The interweaving of ranked social relations is one of the things to which social scientists are referring
when they use the term "social structure"—although, as with my use
of the term "domination," it is one of the thinner conceptions.) Most
of the time, this embedding of relations in other relations ought to be

20. My use of the word "legitimately" might mislead. In saying that some claims are legitimate I do not mean to imply any moral evaluation of the reasons people give in their attempts to dominate others. Rather, I mean that there is general recognition and acceptance
by the relevant parties. When everyone in W. F. Whyte's "Corner Boys" gang agreed that Doc
was their leader, then he could legitimately claim to have the authority to give orders. This
was the case despite the complete absence of any formal criteria giving Doc higher rank. Incidentally, Whyte's study is, in my judgment, one of the most lucid and insightful accounts of
informal hierarchy ever to have appeared. See William F. Whyte, *Street Corner Society* (Chicago: University of Chicago Press, 1993).

pretty stable, as people discover what kinds of support they can and cannot expect from third parties. If you find yourself in a disagreement with a colleague, for instance, you can probably count on the moral support of people who are closer to you than to your colleague, and you can probably expect those who are closer to your colleague to take his side. If your organization is hierarchical, you can also expect your superior (or if you and your rival do not share a boss, then someone higher up) to take a position somewhere in between, thereby adjudicating the dispute—and in so doing reinforce *her* authoritative position.[21] If the relation belongs to a commonly recognized category such as "employer-employee," "parent-child" or "roommate," you can expect that disputes will include comparisons with what other people tied by the same relation do—as when children justify their demands with references to their siblings or to schoolmates' arrangements with *their* parents. These various ways in which what goes on in one relation is shaped or constrained by what goes on in neighboring ones contribute to the stability of such relations by, so to speak, roping them together—just as fishing boat crews lash their vessels to one another to prevent capsizing in a sudden storm.

Conversely, then, a social relation that is *not* lashed to others, whether these are parallel to it (as in "Becky's parents let *her* stay out past nine o'clock!") or adjacent ("But you let *Chris* use the circular saw!"), ought to be less stable. A relative lack of reference points or arbitrators has the same effect as equally distributed resources with which to compete for the dominant position: it is harder to say in advance who ought to prevail.[22] And if it is harder to decide in advance, it

21. Morris Friedell has offered a succinct formal analysis of organizational structure concentrating on precisely this functional requirement of authority relations—namely, the necessity that every disagreement between two members of an organization be adjudicable by some unique third party. Although highly static and relatively detached from real-world examples, the argument nonetheless captures an important aspect of the embedding of interpersonal disputes in their structural context. Morris Friedell, "Organizations as Semilattices," *American Sociological Review* (1967) 32: 46–54.

22. "Ought" in this context should be read in both its normative and its predictive senses. This is not simply a matter of equivocation: my claim all along has been that legitimate domination—domination acknowledged by both parties as right or at least acceptable—results from repeated instances of domination, leading to the mutual expectation that future interactions will resemble past ones. To the extent that expectations based on past interactions are the basis for legitimate domination (as opposed, say, to elaborate ideological justifications that are often thought to be essential preconditions for legitimacy), then the normative "ought" is actually the product of the predictive "ought."

is more likely that the decision will be made by means of overt conflict, because both parties will persist in their claims in hopes of winning the contest, or at least not losing too badly. Relations with fewer external checks in the form of adjacent or reference relations should therefore experience more conflict, and by extension more violent conflict, than relations with relatively many such checks.

On the most macroscopic level, this pattern is already widely recognized. When national regimes collapse or autocratic leaders suddenly die without having designated a successor, violent conflict may ensue. In fact, everyone anticipates that it may ensue, occasionally with self-fulfilling results. The reason is that the death or imminent fall of a paramount leader creates a vacancy that subordinates will compete to fill. Because doing so requires the allegiance of other influential actors and of their followers, and so forth, and because there are often multiple pretenders, there is no predetermined outcome. There is, above all, neither an agreed-on procedure for selecting a new leader or (by hypothesis) an existing dominant actor with the recognized authority to choose one. Such situations thus precisely match the one I have just described, and the civil wars to which they frequently lead offer provisional empirical support for my argument.

On a less grand scale, however, the pattern is not so widely recognized. It is nonetheless plausible that it can be observed locally as well as nationally. This is so, I would like to suggest, in two distinct ways. The first and more obvious way is that disruption of small-scale networks of dominance relations, for example, at the level of towns, organizations, or social groups, can have consequences similar to those that accompany disruption on a national level. The mechanism I am describing—in which, for instance, the removal of a single person or the eruption of conflict between two individuals sets off a chain of conflicts in which those remaining sort themselves into new positions—can in principle occur at any scale of social organization. Although state collapse directly affects more people than any one small-scale event, the aggregate impact of all such events on people's lives may rival regime changes in importance. Our attention is drawn to the latter type of event not so much because its effects are more profound as because it is easier to see these effects as stemming from a single cause. Airplane accidents attract more attention than automobile accidents despite accounting for far fewer deaths because the deaths are concentrated in time and space; yet it is a commonplace that automobile fatalities should be viewed as a more significant issue than airplane fatalities for policymakers and for people in general. The same may be said of the truly small-scale conflicts that take hundreds of thousands of lives every year across the globe. They receive less press than revolutions and civil wars, but taken together they are no less disastrous.

The second sense in which the pattern might hold more locally involves the potential impact of national disruptions on local social relations. To the extent that social hierarchies at the national level are indirectly connected, often through long chains of patronage, mobility, or loyalty, to local hierarchies, shifts at the center can be expected to induce collateral shifts elsewhere. This possibility suggests that national political transformation—even in the form of democratic elections or legislative initiatives directed at redressing inequality—exerts conflict-generating effects far from the domain of political competition. Political players whose party has recently been ousted can find themselves suddenly commanding less respect and attention in ordinary social interaction, which may intensify their thirst for dominance in relations (for instance, close friends or family) over which they still have substantial control. In addition, newly influential people will shift attention away from some of their less consequential relations and toward their new ones, leaving the former arena open for competition among pretenders—just as managerial promotions provoke strife among junior managers vying for the newly vacated spot. The central insight these scenarios offer is that disruption at the center of any large hierarchy will indirectly set off conflicts in the periphery that may appear to have nothing to do with what happens at the center. The connection is hard to spot because the events are linked by an underlying network of hierarchical relations, not by the overt substance of the conflicts. A brawl started by a poker hand in Duluth might seem entirely unrelated to the resignation of a CEO in Atlanta—until we realize that the new CEO initiated a reorganization that included the dismissal of a regional manager, triggering the promotion of a line manager to the vacated slot, which intensified the resentment of the latter's rival, who the same day humiliated a subordinate, who as a result responded poorly to the derisive remarks of his good friend at the weekly poker game. It is this aspect of violent conflict that we are most likely to miss if our explanations concentrate too heavily either on the violent propensities of individuals or the details of the disputes that most immediately provoke violent behavior.

In closing this chapter I want to both reiterate what I have been arguing and make explicit the theoretical procedure I have been following. Too often, writers and readers of social science conflate theories and hypotheses—as if a theory of, say, political behavior amounted merely to a pile of testable hypotheses about political behavior, and as if a good theory of political behavior would be a pile consisting of a lot of confirmed hypotheses with some relevance to politics. I prefer to think of a theory as an integrated set of propositions, some of which might be intrinsically untestable, from which specific and testable hypotheses can be derived logically and nontrivially. If your hypotheses are simply restatements of (that is, propositions derived trivially from) your core assumptions, you do not have a good theory—no matter how strongly confirmed they might all turn out to be. The simple reason is that, if your hypotheses essentially restate what you already knew when you started building your theory, then confirming them is not much of an achievement. You know you have a good theory when it generates a statement you had *not* already thought about and when further empirical investigation confirms the new statement.[23]

In this and the previous chapter I have been laying out a theory of conflict whose core assumptions involve the achievement of stable dominance in social relations and the dense interlocking of such relations. By construction, the core assumptions cannot easily be verified, but I have tried to derive some implications of them that can be. A few of the implications—for instance, that struggles about dominance can be expressed in conflicts about symbolic matters at least as easily as in those about material conflicts—are in an important sense trivial, because the core assumptions were designed to lead to them. The theory will be seriously undermined if these implications turn out to be

23. Actually, it would be sufficient if the statement were already known to be true but not known to have been connected substantively to the subject of the theory. People knew, for instance, that the sun was larger and redder at the horizon than at the zenith long before the theory of optics was shown to imply that this would be so. Nonetheless, the fact that the theory of optics made sense of a familiar phenomenon added to its value as a theory, because the theory's ability to do so was not known in advance. On the other hand, if the concept of refraction had been invented precisely to explain why the sun is redder at the horizon, observing that it is would not have scored any points for the theory.

falsified by systematically collected evidence, but on the other hand it will be no great victory if they are verified, inasmuch as my theory-building exercise began with the conjecture that they would be. The real test of the theory is to be undertaken with reference to the implications that were not obvious at the outset and for which there is so far no evidence. They are the following:

1. Conflict, including violent conflict, is particularly likely to occur in relations that are explicitly symmetrical, such as "friend" or "sibling."
2. Violent conflict is particularly likely in relations that are inconsistent with respect to rank—as when the formally subordinate party to the relation is older than the formally superior party.
3. Conflict is more likely to occur in relations that are adjacent to *other* relations undergoing instability. Consequently, violent conflict of any sort, including interpersonal disputes, is more widespread during moments of political transformation than during moments of political stability.

In short, the key "inferences" I have laid out should not be taken (yet) as empirically warranted assertions about how and when conflict occurs. Rather, they are hypotheses: propositions that follow logically from the core assumptions with which I began. The chapters to follow offer evidence bearing on these propositions that ought to enhance our confidence in the theory.

[CHAPTER 3]

Strife out of Symmetry

Let us return to one of the well-known patterns in interpersonal violence to which I alluded in chapter 1: most violent conflict takes place between people who have prior social relations. By "well-known" I do not mean known by most people but rather known by most people who study the topic. Common sense has not entirely caught up with a century of systematic research, largely because incidents of what people like to call "random violence," including but not limited to grisly mass attacks, are overrepresented in news reports, remembered by more people for longer periods, and viewed by more people as events that (by definition) are as likely to strike their lives as anyone else's. Except in unusual circumstances, people who walk down dark streets fearing an attack are not imagining that the attacker will be someone they know.

Yet the odds are that, if someone *is* the target of violence, it will not be on the part of a stranger but on the part of an acquaintance, relative, or friend. (Nor, for that matter, is it particularly likely to happen on a dark street.) Taking the kind of violent incident for which the evidence is most reliable, namely homicide, roughly four out of five victims in the contemporary United States are socially tied to their attackers. That figure, moreover, is at the low end of the scale compared with other societies: the proportion in other urbanized industrial societies is closer to nine out of ten, and is even higher in small-scale rural communities along with tribal groups and hunter-gatherer societies. Stranger violence, in the form of robbery-murders, predatory attacks of other sorts, or traffic altercations, may seem more threatening to urbanites, but that is a function of their unpredictability, not of their relative frequency.

If there is a received explanation for the fact that violence occurs primarily among intimates and acquaintances, it is analogous to the explanation of the fact that most motor vehicle accidents occur close to home. Driving near home is not necessarily more dangerous than driving elsewhere; it might in fact be less so. It is simply that (apart from tractor-trailer drivers) people do most of their driving near where they live. It is not the likelihood of an accident at any given moment that is higher close to home but rather the total number of moments spent there. Similarly, people spend most of their time with family, friends, and acquaintances and fairly little time with strangers. In any event, except in a society overrun with vicious hermits, strangers could not be more dangerous, on average, than one's associates: one person's stranger is nearly always someone else's associate. Naturally, then, if a conversation or transaction turns nasty or homicidal, it is most likely between two people who know each other—just as any other interaction (other than an introduction) is likely to occur between people who know each other.

It surely helps to recognize the role of relative exposure in accounting for the fact that homicide victims usually know their attackers. All else equal, I will stub my toe more often in my own house than in other people's houses, although I know my house better than any other. My toes are at home, and therefore at risk of stubbing at home, more often than they are at other homes.

Nevertheless, straightforward though it is, this explanation is not sufficient to account for many robust and noteworthy patterns in homicide. Indeed, it is at odds with a good many. For instance, if relative exposure were the main issue in determining who ends up attacking whom, immediate kin, who spend more time with each other than with anyone else, should kill one another more often than anyone else. That is decidedly not the case: homicides between acquaintances and friends are considerably more common than family homicides, even

in small-scale communities in which people typically have as many relatives as acquaintances. Likewise, if exposure were the main factor,
homicides within nuclear families would also be fairly evenly distributed across relationships, with brothers killing sisters, mothers killing
sons, sons killing fathers, and so forth in numbers proportional to
their occurrence in the average family unit.[1] That pattern also does not
hold, even after taking account of the obvious fact that men are more
likely to kill and to be killed than women, both inside and outside the
family. Brothers are more likely to attack brothers than sisters, whereas
sisters are—relatively speaking—more likely to kill their sisters. When
a son kills a parent, the victim is usually the father, whereas when a
daughter kills, the victim is typically the mother. Spouses are far more
likely to kill each other than anyone else in the nuclear family. It is also
well known that children are more likely to be killed by an adoptive parent or stepparent than by a biological parent.[2] Whatever explanation
one chooses for these patterns (some writers suggest kin selection to
explain the stepparent phenomenon, for instance, but there are many
other explanations), they make clear that the relative prevalence of certain relations in violent incidents is not simply a function of relative
exposure.

The argument I sketched in chapter 2 offers a more satisfactory account for the fact that violence typically occurs between people who are
connected to one another, and moreover for the kinds of connections
most likely to lead to this sort of trouble. My thesis is that violence happens when people get caught in contests for social rank and when for
various reasons the contest is difficult to resolve using external social
cues concerning the proper outcome. If this notion is right, then some
kinds of relations are more vulnerable to serious conflict than others, regardless of the kinds of people in those relations. The more ambiguous the relation is with respect to who should be expected to out-
rank whom, the more likely violence is.

To see how the argument works, take the following archetypal example of a social tie in which there *are* readily available cues on which

---

1. If, for instance, families average three offspring, and everyone spends about the
same amount of time interacting and arguing with everyone else, there ought to be three sibling homicides for every spousal homicide and two parent-child homicides for every sibling
homicide.

2. See Martin Daly and Margo Wilson, *Homicide* (Chicago: Aldine de Gruyter, 1988).

to call: the relation between a boss and an employee. The reason we know how disagreements between a boss and a worker will typically be worked out is that it is *part of the definition* of the boss-worker relation that the former gets to decide what happens when differences of opinion arise. A good heuristic in deciding whether a relation carries an implicit ranking is whether one person can legitimately close off discussion by saying something like "We will do it this way because I said so" or "You will do what I say because I am the boss." The fact that one person, by virtue of the name of the relation, has the right to say something of this kind does not imply that the other person will cooperate, but it does imply that refusing to comply necessarily occurs in the absence of an agreed-on right to refuse (whence the recurrent organizational drama in which a subordinate resigns rather than comply with an intolerable command). To deny the boss's right to make peremptory decisions is to deny that she is the boss. Conversely, to insist on having one's way without elaboration—for instance, an explanation of why it would be in everyone's interest to comply (not counting threats) or an offer to reciprocate by making a concession on some other front—is to imply that one is the boss. The first action entails exit from, or at a minimum reconstitution of, the relation; the second entails reaffirmation of the existing terms.

I contend that conflict is harder to resolve, and violent conflict thus more likely to occur, when cues concerning which person outranks the other are absent or mixed. The cues can come from a variety of sources, but in many situations they are derived from mutually recognized and explicit names for relations and roles. On one end of the scale are organizations with highly formalized codes of conduct specifying not only who gives orders to whom but furthermore what the content of such orders can and cannot be, what recourse individuals have when the code is violated, and so forth. Military organizations, with an explicit allocation of rank expressed in formal titles and in costume, bearing, and physical gestures, are the obvious example, but bureaucracies, paramilitary groups, certain church organizations and religious orders, and in some instances hospitals and schools approximate armies in the extent to which they explicitly allocate social rank to persons or to roles. In these contexts, it is usually very easy to decide, when selecting any pair of individuals, who the superior is and who the subordinate is. This fact further implies that it is (relatively) easy for

both observers and participants to predict how differences will be resolved, which in itself contributes to their resolution. Naturally, subordinates in such organizations do not always heed their orders; what is
important is that the decision *not* to follow an order is understood by
all as insubordination—even when most people would agree that the
order is unjust or out of bounds. The essence of hierarchy is that it is
not up to the subordinate to decide that question. A subordinate who
attempts to do so without, for instance, appealing to the next level of
authority is rejecting the role of subordinate.

At the other end of the scale are groups, relations, or organizations
with no explicit or implicit ranking. Examples include freely forming
crowds in public places, most friendship groups, radically democratic
social movement organizations, some religious sects (usually small
ones), neighborhoods, and, most important for present purposes, any
relation in which ego's term for alter is the same as alter's term for ego.
In relations approximating this type, it is not easy to say how differences will most likely be resolved. Because each party to a dispute has
an equivalent basis on which to claim the right to have a say, neither
has an agreed-on right to override the views of the other. It makes no
sense to say, "You must stand aside as I walk by because, as your neighbor, I demand that you do so."[3] Absent some other criterion such as
seniority or status, people who are neighbors cannot demand unilateral deference from each other. Consequently, ill-defined or symmetric relations such as "friend" are at least in principle democratic.

The reason is not hard to find. The symmetry in relation terms
such as "neighbor" or "friend" implies that if I am your neighbor, then
by definition you are also mine. Consequently, I cannot legitimately
use the fact of the relation to claim any sort of gesture from you, such
as getting out of my way, that you could not also and simultaneously
demand of me.[4] I could demand that you stand aside when we meet in

---

3. I am not suggesting that people never make such demands, but rather that they cannot do so with the reasonable expectation that the other person will assent to them. Obviously, people do make demands in the absence of a shared understanding that such demands
are reasonable. Indeed, it is one of the hallmarks of unreasonable people that they expect others to do more, rhetorically and materially, than they are willing to do in return—even when
there is no basis, either in experience or in available terms for describing the relation, for
counting on or justifying such asymmetries.

4. Another caveat is required here. When I speak of some behavior as "legitimate" or
"illegitimate," I am using these terms descriptively, not normatively. An action is legitimate,

front of my house, but only if I grant that I will stand aside for you in front of your house. I can insist that you say "excuse me" if you bump into me, but only if I grant that I should excuse myself if I bump into you. Any departure from symmetry in expectations or demands must be justified, if it is justified at all, with reference to some asymmetry, in the terminology of the relation itself or at least in some relevant aspect of the relation. For example, in the basic Anglo-American kinship terminology brothers are not differentiated with respect to age; nevertheless, older brothers can legitimately invoke their seniority in demanding deference from their younger counterparts. The tactic works structurally, as well as rhetorically, because only one sibling can claim to be older than the other. It is very difficult to imagine a stable arrangement in which asymmetric expectations and asymmetric behavior could coincide with complete symmetry in the rhetorical resources parties to a relation can call on to justify their actions or their requests.

Or to make the same argument another way, a situation in which one person tries to establish precedence *without* some criterion—formal, verbal, or experiential—on which to base the demand for it is a situation in which conflict is very likely to occur: in the absence of any external criterion for deciding who should prevail, disputants will persist in pushing, hoping that doing so will persuade the other to give in. Disputes heat up accordingly, because neither party sees a reason to back down.[5]

It may be helpful to make this argument concrete with a collection of actual cases, taken, moreover, from a wide range of social settings. I make no claim regarding the representativeness of these stories—that issue will be addressed below with systematically collected data—but rather intend them as illustrations of the way struggles for superior rank in relations turn into serious conflicts. The cases are accordingly selected for the relative salience of symbolic, as opposed to substantive,

in the present usage, if people in the relevant setting treat it as such—no matter what you or I might say about it. When nineteenth-century schoolmasters rapped their pupils' knuckles for speaking out of turn, it was legitimate for them to do so in this descriptive sense, whether or not people of the twenty-first century might see such a sanction as legitimate in the normative sense (i.e., as worthy of their approval).

5. Alternatively, they can exit the relation, forestalling escalation. But the exit option is available in many ranked relations as well. Barring a demonstration that exit is easier in symmetric than in ordered relations, there is no reason to expect the exit option to alter the pattern my argument implies.

motives: they are examples of the kind of homicides that would normally be classified as disputes of "relatively trivial origin." Throughout, what is most striking is how explicit actors can be about the fact that disputes take on lives of their own, whatever the substantive matter, if any, that occasioned the dispute. What makes people angry enough to kill in these stories has as much to do with the little things adversaries say and do while struggling as with the things they are ostensibly struggling about. It is this sensitivity to process—to tone, demeanor, gestures or turns of phrase—that suggests that winning the fight matters at least as much to disputants as walking away with the material stakes. This is not to say that material or substantive stakes, when they exist, do not matter, but rather that, when they do play a role, this role diminishes in relative importance as the dispute continues, allowing symbolic grievances to pile up. One might infer, as I indicated above, that substantive stakes are in a sense pretexts for conflict rather than reasons for it. Following my discussion of largely symbolic (though no less deadly) disputes, I offer examples of more substantive conflicts suggesting that these too can be seen as contests for superior rank.

The first story is also one of the oldest: it comes from Lille (then part of the duchy of Flanders) in 1459, a time and place in which a lot of men shifted back and forth between everyday village life and participation in the wars waged against (or with) the dukes of Burgundy. One evening Jehan, "bastard of Carvin," along with Pierot Malet, Bernardin Delecroix, Jehan Dupont, Gilles Duhem, Gossel d'Escamaing, Jean Wastiel, and a few others went to the Au Beau Regard tavern following an afternoon of tennis. As dinner was being cleared away, one of the above (possibly Wastiel) tossed a piece of bread at Jehan, striking him on the lapel of his jacket. The latter countered this by throwing a half-full glass of wine into Wastiel's face. Wastiel good-naturedly cried, "Now I can see better," poured wine into his own glass, and declaring, "Eye for an eye!" (actually, in the parlance of the time, "cabbage for cabbage!"), threw the contents at Jehan. Jehan, the bastard, was no longer amused: furious, he overturned the table, drew his dagger, and dealt a thrust at Wastiel, which the latter parried with his arm. Wastiel drew his own dagger and made several thrusts at Jehan, although he was unable to say afterward whether the instrument had struck its target. At that moment, Gossel d'Escamaing rose, drew his own dagger, and stabbed Jehan fatally in the back.

This brawl combines culturally unfamiliar elements (bastards, daggers, and talk of cabbages) with a remarkably though sadly familiar script: playful taunts in a social setting are taken one step too far, enraging one of the parties to the point of violent attack. It does not matter that the first person to draw a weapon in this story was the one who was killed; our interpretation of how escalation occurred is independent of the outcome. What appears to have happened was that Jehan, perhaps already mildly annoyed, threw his glass of wine at Wastiel as a riposte to the latter's initial crumb toss. More than likely, Wastiel viewed being doused with wine as rather more than he deserved—that is, as a more serious affront than being hit by a morsel of food—so he responded in kind, while continuing to treat the exchange as all in good fun. For his part, Jehan saw this act as a *second* aggression and hence no longer a joking matter. As a man with no avowed family, he may have been a frequent target of ridicule and thus more sensitive than the average young man in Lille.

The misunderstanding, then, resulted from the lack of fit between Wastiel's and Jehan's views of how far "good-natured" taunts could be taken without turning into something uglier. Wastiel thought he was still on the safe side with his second gesture; most likely he did not anticipate that it would provoke a knife fight (although this alternative cannot be entirely ruled out). In contrast, Jehan may have viewed the first gesture as already close to the limit, which would account for his initial escalation from a crumb to wine in the face. If each man had perceived more clearly exactly how much impertinence the other was willing to tolerate, the exchange might have ended peacefully.

The second episode occurred a few centuries later, on the Mediterranean island of Corsica, whose feuds will form the empirical centerpiece of chapter 5. This one took place early one February morning in 1852, near Sartène, as a result of what we might now call a traffic altercation. Pietro Giovanni Balesi, a young wagon driver, was traveling up the narrow road into the Falcanaja forest when he encountered a convoy of wagons hauling lumber to town. The supervisor of the wagon team, Luigi Galanti, observed that Balesi's wagon was taking up the middle of the road and that if he could pull over to the left, the convoy could pass. Rather than comply, Balesi hurled insults at Galanti, calling him a starveling and a "Lucchese." (The term was a slur Corsicans used in referring to Italian immigrants from the area around

Lucca, many of whom found employment in the construction trades in Corsica. Galanti was indeed an immigrant from the duchy of Modena, but it is unclear from the records whether Balesi was already acquainted with Galanti or whether he was reacting to the latter's accent.) He then picked up a stone and prepared to throw it at his adversary, who, being considerably larger than Balesi, walked up to him and knocked it out of his hand. Balesi then drew a knife, which Galanti also managed to seize.

By this time quite exasperated, Galanti slapped Balesi several times, finally pushing him away. The latter, visibly humiliated, ran back down the road leaving his wagon behind and, running into an acquaintance in a settlement a short distance away, announced that he had just been treated in an unacceptable manner and would soon avenge his wounded pride. Borrowing a rifle from someone in the settlement, he made his way back up the road until he once again found himself face to face with Galanti. The latter, evidently seeing Balesi's brandishing of a rifle as just another idle threat, walked up to Balesi, said, "If you're going to kill me, here I am." To this challenge Balesi responded by firing his weapon. Struck in the head and chest, Galanti died four days later.

Balesi was convicted of murder later that year and sentenced to five years in prison. Remarkably, at least from the standpoint of the reporting magistrate, the Corsican jury declined to classify the murder as premeditated and went so far as to accept the defense attorney's claim that the homicide was "provoked," in this case by the rough treatment Balesi had received half an hour earlier. They were responding sympathetically, as inhabitants of "honor societies" usually do, to the public humiliation Balesi had obviously experienced in being rendered helpless, twice, by a larger and more confident yet unarmed adversary. It did not matter that, as the prosecutors pointed out, it was Balesi who had clearly been the aggressor. The magistrate attributed this anomaly in the jury's attitude to the fact that the defendant was Corsican whereas the murder victim belonged to a low-status immigrant group.

It is possible to see in this incident another process of escalation stemming from incompatible expectations about deference. Galanti saw his team of wagons as entitled to the right-of-way because they were many, whereas Balesi was alone; Balesi saw Galanti's request for right-of-way as impertinent, at least in part because of the latter's low-status ethnicity. Having staked a claim to right-of-way on this basis, Balesi found it intolerable that his bid for superior rank over Galanti, backed by a threat of physical force, had been so thoroughly rebuffed. The symbolic defeat surely swamped in importance the delay that waiting for the caravan would have entailed: in the first place, the lumber market in nineteenth-century Corsica hardly depended on just-in-time production, and in the second place, Balesi was obviously willing to spend more time disputing with his adversary than it would have cost him to wait. The only substantive matter at stake in this dispute, waiting time, was self-evidently not the reason the dispute occurred; yet, given the obvious importance to Balesi of the deference denied him, it would be a mistake to describe the altercation as having "trivial origin."

Consider, finally, a contemporary incident from urban America, more precisely St. Louis in 1994. In the prelude to this homicide, two brothers were talking to their sister at the latter's house. According to the woman's subsequent account, they were inquiring about why her partner had attacked her violently earlier that afternoon; according to them, she was complaining to them about it and they were not terribly concerned, in part because it was a common occurrence. The man in question then arrived at the house but she refused to admit him, at which point her two brothers asked him to give them a ride in his van. When he angrily refused, one of the brothers said, "Don't talk to me that way. I'm not a punk." The boyfriend responded by saying that he didn't have to do anything he didn't want to do. The offended brother repeated his demand. When the boyfriend retorted, from behind the wheel of the van, that it was not a serious matter, his interlocutor leaned into the van and shot him. Afterward, the other brother told police that he didn't think his brother would shoot the man—"not over something like that."[6]

By the time the episode became deadly it evidently did not, either for the witnesses or for the disputants, have much to do with the victim's aggression earlier that afternoon against the killer's sister—although this earlier assault indirectly led to the homicide by giving the woman a reason to turn her boyfriend away at the door. Rather, the conflict centered on the boyfriend's dismissive behavior concerning the matter of a ride in his van, along with his refusal to apologize or

6. Richard Rosenfeld, St. Louis Homicide Project, Case No. 94-112318 (1994).

even to acknowledge that there was something to apologize for. We may conjecture that the victim's irritable response and subsequent stubbornness were related to his frustration and perhaps humiliation at being refused entrance to his own house, but the available evidence indicates that the victim's fight with his girlfriend was largely irrelevant to the offender. What was important to him was the fact that his sister's boyfriend had treated him as if he were a "punk."

The basis for escalation in this incident, then, was the victim's refusal to disown a verbal slight—a refusal that seems to have been prompted at least in part by the aggressive way in which the retraction was demanded. Convinced that accepting the slight, or even asking politely for its retraction, would make him look weak, the offender *insisted* that the victim talk differently to him; by the same token, the victim seems to have believed that he could not comply without implicitly acknowledging that his girlfriend's brother had the right to give him orders. What had apparently been a relation among peers (note that, if the union between the cohabiting couple had been a formal one, the killer and his victim would have been brothers-in-law) was destabilized when one party adopted an imperious tone with the other.

I hasten to reiterate that these episodes are not representative of homicides occurring in the settings from which they are drawn; I chose them precisely because they illustrate so vividly the potential for largely symbolic concerns—a tossed drink, a disagreement over who moves out of the way, the tone with which someone refuses a favor— to become matters of life and death. But I do not, on the other hand, mean to suggest that these incidents are somehow qualitatively different from conflicts about substantive matters—debts, thefts, sexual rivalries, terminated relationships, property damage, inheritances, and the like.[7] On the contrary, as I will show in a moment, many disputes about matters that we would not be inclined to call trivial turn violent

---

7. I use the term "substantive" rather than "material" to reflect my judgment that there are many disputes not involving money or property that nonetheless seem to have intrinsic importance for the participants. Consider infidelity, abandonment by a significant other, testimony that leads to an arrest or criminal conviction, or serious physical injury. These are not "material" concerns, at least not in the narrow economic sense, yet most people, in most societies, would likely see them as inducing as much or even more unhappiness. Perhaps the clearest criterion distinguishing these sorts of dispute from purely symbolic disputes is that in symbolic matters a verbal apology might be sufficient to mollify the aggrieved person, whereas it would not be enough to make amends for a substantive offense.

in ways that strikingly resemble the episodes just described. My purpose in recounting disputes about almost entirely symbolic matters is not to suggest that there is something special about these conflicts but rather to avoid being distracted by the substantive concerns—sizable debts, property damage, personal betrayals, and so forth—that so often dominate interpretations of interpersonal conflict. Once sensitized to the processes that can lead to violence when substantive concerns are almost entirely absent, we are in a better position to appreciate the relevance of such processes in disputes in which such concerns are undeniably present.

Consider, then, the following incidents, in which matters of genuine substantive importance indisputably played a role. Beginning once again with the most temporally distant setting, fifteenth-century Flanders, we have the sad story of Yeulvain Voet, whose best friend, known as Maître Jean, betrayed him by seducing his wife (or at least that is how Voet characterized the matter). Voet's wife and Maître Jean moved away, compounding the double betrayal by making off with a number of Voet's possessions. Three years later, accompanied by two friends, Voet chanced upon Maître Jean in a neighboring town and, filled with rekindled rage at the wrong he felt he had suffered, set upon his enemy with the aid of his two companions. Severely beaten, Maître Jean died within a few days of the attack.

It is easy enough to see this murder as stemming from a serious conflict when compared with the essentially verbal and thus, in my terminology, symbolic altercations I described above. Maître Jean earned Voet's anger and hatred by violating his trust, breaking up his marriage (again, this was how Voet saw it; we do not know what other reasons his wife may have had for leaving him), and stealing from him. In almost any society, these actions would qualify as genuine harm, and rage (though not necessarily murderous rage) would be seen as an eminently justified response. Police, criminologists, and lay observers would readily classify this homicide under the rubrics "jealousy," "theft," or "sexual rivalry." The term "retaliation" might also be used, inasmuch as the homicide occurred well after the original offense. But it is virtually certain that, regardless of time or place, Voet's motive in this killing would *not* be characterized as trivial.

Yet it would be a major error to conclude that concern for social rank, however it might be achieved, did not contribute to Voet's rage or play a significant role in determining his actions. It is fair to say that he killed Maître Jean because the latter had run off with his wife, but it would be going too far to claim that in doing so he hoped to bring about a material improvement in his own situation—which a narrowly instrumental interpretation of the murder would imply. There is no evidence that Voet either won back his wife or recovered his purloined items, and considering that he was banished shortly thereafter, it seems unlikely that he did. Nor does it seem particularly likely that this was his intention, let alone that of his two accomplices in the homicide. This murder was a fairly pure example of revenge, in the sense that it destroyed Voet's enemy but did nothing to reconstitute the state of affairs that had obtained prior to the original offense.

Nothing, that is, unless "state of affairs" includes the relative standing of Voet and Maître Jean. As best friends, the two had been peers until the moment Voet, and presumably the larger community, became aware that Mme Voet (her own name is not given) had chosen Maître Jean instead of her husband. It is no great cultural stretch for us to see Voet as having been at that moment humiliated by—and thus reduced in stature in relation to—both his rival and his wife. If Voet could not restore equilibrium by doing to his former friend precisely what the latter had done to him, he could nevertheless humble Maître Jean in a different way—by beating him into submission, in this case with lethal consequences. It would be going too far to say that the physical attack was restitutive in the sense of putting matters right because, even if it had not been fatal, it almost certainly would not have restored the friendship. But it would *not* be going too far to say that, in his own estimation and that of his community, Voet had restored his dignity— his rank relative to Maître Jean—by showing that, in the end, the latter had not gotten the better of him. In this respect, it is hard not to see this homicide as being every bit as "about" social rank as those that did not involve anything so intrinsically significant as the breakup of a marriage.

Returning to Corsica, we find another conflict that, although obviously growing out of a material dispute of consequence, cannot fairly be said to have become violent *because of* the material dispute. In late November 1851, Francesco Marchi was tending his property outside the village of Antisanti when he noticed that Martino Tristani, plowing the adjacent field, had allowed his oxen to trample the hedge separating the two properties. A heated exchange ensued, and the two were apparently about to come to blows when several neighbors, who had been drawn to the scene on hearing loud voices, broke up the argument.[8]

One week later, at nightfall, Marchi was heading down the path to his cabin in Antisanti, accompanied by his younger brother and thirteen-year-old cousin, when he spotted a man whom the group soon recognized as Tristani crossing a field in their direction. When Tristani reached the path, he loaded his rifle and said to Marchi, "So, you said you were going to kill me?" Marchi responded by saying that he meant Tristani no harm and asked that he and his companions be allowed to pass. At that moment Tristani discharged his weapon. Struck in the arm and chest, Marchi tried to run but collapsed a few seconds later. Tristani walked over to his victim and, in full view of the two witnesses, shot Marchi a second time. Although the defense argued that the accused had acted in self-defense, noting the open knife with which Marchi had been whittling a myrtle branch moments earlier, the jury convicted Tristani of murder with extenuating circumstances. Tristani was sentenced to twenty years of forced labor. The reporting magistrate found the granting of extenuating circumstances to be overly indulgent, observing that Marchi was well-liked in the community whereas Tristani had been characterized by witnesses as an irascible troublemaker and even as "the scourge of Antisanti."

It is no surprise that the city of St. Louis in the 1990s had its share of violent conflict about money, property, and other matters of substantive importance to disputants. Consider this example, which began as a dispute over money the killer claimed that the victim's friend owed him. According to witnesses, the offender, an unemployed man in his early forties, allowed young dealers to spend time and use drugs in his apartment on Enright Avenue, in return for which they made their merchandise available to him. On one such occasion, in March

8. It is probably not part of the commonsense image of Mediterranean honor societies that bystanders intervene in scuffles, but this was in fact a very regular occurrence even for disputes that ultimately became violent. It is all the more remarkable when one takes into account the frequency with which interveners were themselves injured or killed. Of course, these reports are selected on the dependent variable—scuffles that become homicidal—and we do not know what proportion of all interactions, scuffles or not, had bystanders present. Still, the association is intriguing.

1996, the older man got into an argument with one of his regular visitors, a twenty-one-year-old dealer, claiming that the latter's best friend (an eighteen-year-old man who was also present) owed him money. The argument subsided, and after spending most of the afternoon at the apartment the two younger men left. The eighteen-year-old wanted to visit a female friend, so the dealer dropped him off at the woman's apartment, saying that he was going back to meet the older fellow in back of the apartment building on Enright and would swing by later that evening. He never did.

What happened, according to an eyewitness, was that when the dealer arrived at the lot behind the building, the older man and an unidentified companion approached him and an argument ensued. The offender and his friend suddenly began stabbing the younger man, who collapsed. After going through his pockets, which according to the victim's friend contained several hundred dollars, they carried his body to the garage and left. Later that night, the older man also confronted the victim's friend and stabbed him, though not fatally. Neither the murder nor the assault went to trial because, on returning to his apartment the next day, the offender was shot to death in his front yard, evidently by friends of the two young stabbing victims.[9]

Convention dictates that the motive in this homicide was "argument over drugs and money," and indeed this was the police classification. Moreover, although we do not know exactly what was said in the two arguments, we do know—assuming that the victim's friend accurately reported how much money he had been carrying—that the offenders made off with between four and five hundred dollars after the attack. There can be little doubt that material interests informed the offenders' actions.

Yet it would be as incorrect to stop there as it would be to ignore the role of money in setting off the dispute. In the first place, it was not the victim who owed money to the killer but rather his associate. The argument occurred because the victim had stood up for his friend, not because he himself had committed some material trespass. Mutual acquaintances reported, moreover, that the older man had been telling them that the young dealer was "getting too big for his britches." This colloquialism transparently tells us that he saw himself as struggling

9. Richard Rosenfeld, St. Louis Homicide Project, Case No. 96-88283 (1996).

to maintain, or achieve, superior rank in relation to the dealer. (I specifically exclude the possibility that he saw the dealer as a peer trying to achieve superiority because his choice of expression indicates his belief that the younger man owed him deference.) The argument about money may even have been a pretext—an opportunity for a verbal disagreement to express on the level of interaction the underlying problem of uncertainty about who was superior in the relationship.

These stories, and the interpretations I have offered for them, have been intended as illustrations of, not evidence for, my argument. Even if I had selected the cases randomly, rather than with the specific goal of illustrating a process I believe underlies many conflicts, their small number would stand in the way of concluding anything about conflict generally. The most I can legitimately say, if my interpretation of these specific cases is accepted, is that homicide *can sometimes* occur because each disputant expects the other to back down. To make the further assertion that homicide *frequently and in many contexts* occurs because each party persists in demanding deference from the other, I need to present systematic evidence drawn from a large number of disputes.

To make the evidence systematic rather than suggestive, and analytical rather than interpretive, requires a set of methodological constraints that make it hard to manipulate the data into confirming the argument. In the first place, it is no longer acceptable to take each event as it comes and weave a tale about it *ex post facto*. Even with a large and representative set of incidents, the risk of finding confirming evidence is too great if we allow ourselves to peek at the data before deciding how to classify it. If I apply enough imagination and allow myself to use sufficiently flexible criteria, I can successfully interpret *any* incident in such a way as to show that a contest for dominance was at stake and that escalation resulted from mutual (hence erroneous) expectations of submission by the other person. But if confirmation is guaranteed in this way, then finding that the argument is confirmed cannot enhance anyone's confidence in the theory. Consequently, it is necessary to classify cases naively, that is, without knowing how the theory says things ought to turn out. In the analyses I report below, the data were either coded by third parties, as in the case of the large-scale Chicago Homicide Project, or, in the case of the smaller data sets, by research assistants to whom I did not reveal the hypotheses I planned to test.

In the second place, it is important to derive specific implications of the argument that empirical data *might or might not confirm,* no matter how dearly one might hope for confirmation. This is what empiricists mean when they say they want the data to "speak for themselves." The phrase is not meant to imply, as is often suggested by critics of empiricism, that the researcher has brought nothing to the data in the way of classification, selection of some phenomena to record and others to ignore, and so forth. It implies only that the data are given the opportunity to falsify the researcher's argument. If the argument is that people behave more strangely when the moon is full, then the argument can only be tested if *in principle* it is possible to show with empirical data that people behave no more strangely, on average, when the moon is full than when it is not. Almost all unfair tests of arguments begin with violations of this principle, as when the researcher only records strange behavior during a full moon or only classifies behavior as strange if it entails howling at the full moon. So a careful and systematic test of the dominance argument is called for.

Empirical Patterns in Homicide

Probably the best way to test my claim that symmetric relations are prone to struggles about dominance would be to assess the relative rates of conflict in symmetric and asymmetric relations. Starting with a sample of actual relations, we could ask whether the rates of conflict in symmetric and asymmetric ties differed in the predicted direction, net of other factors and of the competing risk of tie dissolution. In the absence of data of this sort, a more indirect strategy is necessary. Here I take advantage of two facts about data on homicide that make an indirect yet systematic approach possible. First, in contrast with many social phenomena, homicide is a very well defined event. Even after one acknowledges cultural variation in definitions of death, murder, intent, and guilt, most homicides look like homicides from almost any standpoint.[10] Moreover, most of the homicides that occur are known

10. Obvious exceptions include homicide by neglect, euthanasia, physician-assisted suicides, and infanticide. Another exception, in many non-Western societies, is the imputation of sorcery as the cause of deaths that Westerners would attribute to illness. Aside from the last example, most of these are easily enough excluded from consideration on the ground that they are quite different from the sort of homicide that grows out of overt disputes. In

and thus likely to be recorded in some way, even in societies with predominantly oral traditions, in contrast to arguments, fistfights, or incidents of domestic conflict, of which only a tiny fraction generate a durable record.

The second fact is that, when a homicide is recorded, we usually know something about how and (more problematically) why it happened. Although the growth of urban centers has meant that homicides go unsolved more frequently than was the case a century ago, the proportion of all homicides that are classified as mysteries is still small relative to the comparable figures for more low-level acts of aggression. Most of the time, investigators establish and record the relation (if any) between the attacker and the target along with a description of the circumstances motivating the attack. These two types of information, moreover, can be drawn both from official sources (in bureaucratized societies) and from informal sources such as oral accounts (in societies where police do not always compile data on homicides). In other words, whenever we know something about a homicide, we almost always know about the circumstances leading up to it.

With the right information, then, it is possible to inquire whether there is an association between the kinds of relations homicide victims have to their killers and the kinds of disagreements that lead to homicides. For instance, we can ask whether homicides between friends or acquaintances—two kinds of relation in which there is no presumptive rank and relatively little structure—disproportionately involve disputes of a symbolic nature, that is, disputes about verbal or gestural insults, disrespectful behavior, and so forth. If it is true that unranked or unstructured relations—those in which expectations about what interaction consists of are vague—are more prone to conflict and escalation than are relations in which rank and expectations are clear or decidable, then the following pattern should hold: a greater proportion of homicides between friends should stem from symbolic disputes than homicides in other relations. If one-third of all homicides are based on arguments, then more than one-third of homicides between friends or

---

other words, the harder it is to decide whether something is a homicide, the less relevant it is to a study of the origins of interpersonal conflict. Inasmuch as accusations of sorcery, which in some contexts are not simply interpretations of past fatalities but also justifications for violence, are easily seen as elements of social conflict, they cannot be so easily dismissed. I take up this difficult example of culturally mediated homicide below.

acquaintances should grow out of arguments, and less than one-third of those occurring in other relations should stem from arguments. Stated in the most general terms, killings due to symbolic matters should be more typical of symmetric relations, whereas killings due to substantive matters should be, relatively speaking, more typical of asymmetric relations.

The reasoning behind this prediction is as follows. Remember, there is no way to follow a large-scale sample of relations (some symmetric, some asymmetric) to see which ones erupt into violent conflict and which ones do not. But we *can* look backward, given a set of violent incidents that have already taken place, and see which kinds of relations seem to have been particularly vulnerable to violent escalation of symbolic conflicts. If a homicide resulted from an argument and little else, then we can infer that that pair of individuals moved relatively easily from verbal conflict to violence, or to put it another way were unable to resolve the dispute at the verbal stage: even in the absence of a substantive reason such as a borrowed car or a stolen television set, the pair in question managed to find themselves in a lethal struggle. So, if a given kind of relation turns out to exhibit a higher rate of "argument" homicides than other relations, we can conclude that that kind of relation is particularly prone to conflict escalation. Such a conclusion would lend support to my contention that conflict and violence owe at least as much to struggles about the character of social relations—notably who outranks whom—as they owe to struggles about resources, material things, or sexual exclusivity.

Table 1 reports the argument-nonargument comparison for homicides occurring in Chicago from 1965 to 1994—about eighteen thousand homicides in all. There were four thousand for which relations could not be established because the offender was not identified. Most of these appeared to have resulted from armed robberies and are thus not particularly relevant to the question at hand. The two columns compare the proportion of homicides between friends or acquaintances that stemmed from verbal argument to the proportion for all other relations (husband-wife, parent-child, employer-employee, landlord-tenant, bar patron–bartender, and so on). As I have suggested, the relation "friend" is notable for the lack of hierarchy it implies; although it is undoubtedly the case that friendships involve varying degrees of dominance, nothing in the concept "friend" justifies or expresses hi-

Table 1 Proportion of Chicago Homicides Involving Argument, by Relation Type

	Character of Homicide		
Relation	Nonargument % (N)	Argument % (N)	Total % (N)
Friend or acquaintance	60.8 (3,768)	39.2 (2,430)	100.0 (6,198)
Other relation	86.0 (9,783)	14.0 (1,596)	100.0 (11,379)
Total	77.1 (13,551)	22.9 (4,026)	100.0 (17,577)

Pearson χ^2 (d.f. = 1) = 1440.72; $p < .001$

erarchy. This is evident in the way the term is used: if you are my friend, then unless something peculiar is happening between us, I am also your friend. As far as the relation *concept* is concerned, then, anything I can expect from you is also something you can expect from me. The same goes for "acquaintance," except that this is a social tie which carries even fewer implicit prescriptions for how people ought to treat each other. (Friends are presumed to feel affection for one another, something that cannot in general be said of acquaintances.) Both are therefore good examples of the kind of relation that, according to my thesis, ought to be conflict-prone.

Comparing the proportions in table 1 shows that homicides between friends or acquaintances are particularly likely, compared with other kinds of social ties, to occur because of verbal disagreements as opposed to substantive disputes. Indeed, the figures are starkly different for friends or acquaintances. Looking at all other relations together, 14 percent of homicides—about one in seven—resulted from verbal arguments; the rest, by implication, began as disagreements about something substantive or material (jealousy, money, drugs, and so forth). But nearly 40 percent of homicides involving friends and acquaintances began as verbal disagreements. In other words, given that a homicide occurred, it was about three times more likely to be based on a verbal altercation if the killer and victim were friends than if they were connected in some other way. (Recall that, because there is no information about arguments that *didn't* lead to homicides, we cannot conclude that friends are more likely to kill one another than people tied in other ways—only that, if they *do* end up killing each other, the dispute is more likely to have been symbolic rather than substantive.)

These data come from Chicago alone. Although there is no reason to think that the city of Chicago between 1965 and 1994 was unusual in this regard, it is nonetheless worth knowing whether the same association holds in other times and places—that, after all, is the kind of cross-context regularity I suggested was a useful thing to search for in studying conflict. In addition, a more general classification than "friend or acquaintance" versus "other relation" is desirable: my thesis is not about friendship or acquaintanceship but about *symmetry*. Friends and acquaintances are simply good examples, in urban America around the turn of the twenty-first century, of people who are tied in a diffuse and specifically symmetric way. The further we stray from urban North America, the more important it is to adopt the abstract classification "symmetric or asymmetric" in place of possibly symmetrical but nonetheless highly concrete and context-bound relation terms (such as "tennis partner," "employer," "matrilateral cross-cousin," "co-wife," "classificatory sister," "godson," or "teacher").

This maneuver is not just a matter of devising a flexible coding scheme. Abstractions of this sort, that is, analytical distinctions that call attention to commonalities across disparate objects without presupposing that the objects are identical, are indispensable to the quest for cross-cultural regularities in social processes. I can only find a regularity, or for that matter demonstrate the absence of the regularity, if I willfully disregard most of the properties of a concrete object and concentrate on *one or a very few of its aspects*—in this case the symmetry in a social tie—with respect to which it can be compared to another object somewhere else. The tie between a young man and his mother's brother in the Trobriand Islands is, naturally, many things that the tie between doctor and patient in San Francisco is not. But one thing both relations *are* is asymmetrical, and it is that aspect that the present argument makes salient.

Consider first the pattern for Chicago. Table 2 cross-classifies the variable "argument-nonargument," as before, with "symmetric tie or asymmetric tie." In addition to friends and acquaintances, the "symmetric" category includes roommates, business partners, co-workers, rival gang members, fellow gang members, brothers, sisters, neighbors, brothers-in-law, and so forth. The "asymmetric" category includes such as relations as landlord-tenant, employer-employee, parent-child, uncle-nephew, drug buyer–drug seller, and lawyer-client. Strangers, although socially related in the abstract sense described by Georg Simmel, are not included. The reason is not theoretical but practical: most of Chicago's homicides involving the tie "stranger" were street robberies or store hold-ups gone wrong. These were confrontations that, as I suggested above, have little relevance for the issue of how relation form is tied to dispute type: it would be a stretch to consider the killing of a robbery victim the result of a dispute.

Another coding principle that deserves mention involves homicides between spouses, ex-spouses, or people of opposite sex tied by (or formerly tied by) sexual relationships. About four thousand of the seventeen thousand Chicago homicides involved such relationships. In all the analyses reported here, I coded these relationships as asymmetric, despite the existence of the symmetric concept "spouse" alongside the asymmetric concept "wife or husband," and more important, despite the prevalence in the United States of the idea that marriage and its extralegal equivalents ought to be equal partnerships. The continued salience in practice of gender as an organizing principle for relationships, and more specifically for the distribution of authority in intimate relationships, makes it unrealistic to view husband-wife, ex-husband–ex-wife, boyfriend-girlfriend, and other such relationships as genuinely symmetric.[11] In any event, examining only nonfamily relationships reveals the same association that appears in the full sample.

As table 2 indicates, the abstract classification of ties as symmetric or asymmetric again yields the predicted pattern. Whereas 6.4 percent of homicides involving asymmetric relations stemmed from arguments, the figure for symmetric relations is 29.2 percent. In other words, homicides occurring between people tied symmetrically were nearly five times as likely as homicides in asymmetric relations to result from verbal altercations. There is a strong association between symmetry in a homicide dyad and the likelihood that the dispute lead-

11. Same-sex couples, on the other hand, are coded as symmetric relationships; although this is surely a controversial choice, the number of such homicides is so small that it cannot affect the overall pattern

Table 2 Proportion of Chicago Homicides Involving Argument, by Relation Form

	Character of Homicide		
Relation	Nonargument % (N)	Argument % (N)	Total % (N)
Asymmetric	93.6 (4,564)	6.4 (312)	100.0 (4,876)
Symmetric	70.8 (8,987)	29.2 (3,714)	100.0 (12,701)
Total	77.1 (13,551)	22.9 (4,026)	100.0 (17,577)

Pearson χ^2 (d.f. = 1) = 1041.15; $p < .001$

ing to the homicide occurred principally because of symbolic concerns.

Using the same scheme for classifying relations and homicides, tables 3 and 4 repeat the analysis for two other American cities, Miami and St. Louis, respectively.[12] Although the data in these cases cover a shorter period (1994–96 in St. Louis, 1980 in Miami), the number of homicides in each instance is, sadly, high enough to permit reliable estimates of the association between relation type and homicide motive. Once more, the same pattern holds: for Miami in 1980, homicides within symmetric relations are four times more likely than in the case of asymmetric ties to result from argument. The comparable figure for St. Louis homicides committed between 1994 and 1996 is similar if somewhat smaller: whereas only about 6 percent of homicides between nonpeers stemmed from an argument, 19.5 percent of homicides between relational equals did. This represents a ratio of about 3.3 to 1, showing once again that symmetry in relations makes it easier for verbal altercations to become deadly.

Although the consistency with which the association holds across contexts is impressive, the contexts in question are nonetheless all

12. The data from St. Louis were derived from homicide narratives compiled from police records by the St. Louis Homicide Project, Richard Rosenfeld, Principal Investigator, Washington University of St. Louis. Miami data were coded from similar narratives drawn from William Wilbanks, *Murder in Miami* (New York: University Press of America, 1984).

Table 3 Proportion of Miami Homicides Involving Argument, by Relation Form

	Character of Homicide		
Relation	Nonargument % (N)	Argument % (N)	Total % (N)
Asymmetric	96.4 (133)	3.6 (5)	100.0 (138)
Symmetric	86.7 (262)	13.3 (40)	100.0 (302)
Total	89.8 (395)	10.2 (45)	100.0 (440)

Pearson χ^2 (d.f. = 1) = 9.55; $p < .01$

urban settings in the United States in the late twentieth century. They therefore share a number of characteristics that influence the patterns in violent conflict. These characteristics include substantial economic inequality, a racially divided population, the existence of illegal drug markets, and the presence of youth gangs (of varying sizes and levels of organization) committed to policing territorial boundaries with sometimes lethal force. The connection between relational symmetry and violence caused by symbolic matters could be limited to settings of this kind. Although it is not immediately obvious why this should be so, it is worth investigating whether a similar pattern can be observed in very dissimilar settings.[13]

Two distinct indigenous groups in central India provide an opportunity to find out. One group is known as Bhils, the other, which in fact comprises two tribes who inhabit the same villages, as Munda and Oraon. Both groups, part of the roughly five hundred Scheduled Tribes of India, live in mountainous areas and practice a combination of pastoralism and small-scale cultivation. Although the population of each group is more than one million, they live primarily in small villages lo-

13. As I observed in chapter 1, there is an undeclared war in the social sciences between people for whom different contexts ought to be assumed to operate according to different principles unless the contrary is shown and people who think that contexts should be assumed to operate similarly unless the contrary is shown. My commitment to the latter position derives from the pragmatic consideration that propositions holding across contexts, if discovered, will be far more important than propositions true, say, only of early modern Europe—or, for that matter, only of bourgeois circles in Vienna between the wars.

Table 4 Proportion of St. Louis Homicides Involving Argument, by Relation Form

	Character of Homicide		
Relation	Nonargument % (N)	Argument % (N)	Total % (N)
Asymmetric	94.1 (64)	5.9 (4)	100.0 (68)
Symmetric	80.5 (214)	19.5 (52)	100.0 (266)
Total	83.2 (278)	16.8 (56)	100.0 (334)

Pearson χ^2 (d.f. = 1) = 7.25; $p < .01$

cated in India's central and south central states of Madhya Pradesh, Bihar, and Orissa. Indeed, more than one-quarter of the population of Madhya Pradesh, where the Bhil homicides examined here took place, belong to these and other Scheduled Tribes. In the Ranchi district of Bihar, the location of the Munda and Oraon homicides, 60 percent of the population is composed of tribals, with most of those classified as Munda or Oraon. Neither the Bhils nor the Munda and Oraon explicitly practice Hinduism, although some urbanized tribals have converted to Hinduism or to Christianity; in the village communities, both groups recognize some of the caste distinctions that Hindus observe. Both, finally, are viewed as "aboriginals" by the state and by people in urban settings; the latter are also likely to characterize the aboriginals as criminals, savages, or both. In part this image is the result of the high homicide rate in both groups—a feature of indigenous social life that, along with such other matters as alcoholism and illiteracy, motivated the studies from which the data I employ here are drawn. Among the Munda and Oraon of the Ranchi district, police records together with the accounts of native informants generated detailed information about 103 homicides during the study period, 1955 to 1959; for the Bhils, 101 homicides were recorded between 1965 and 1972. The narrative accounts of these homicides established relations and motives for 87 of the Bhil homicides and for 81 of the Munda and Oraon homicides.

    The limited number of cases obliges us to treat the likelihood ratios as rough rather than precise estimates. For instance, if argument

Table 5 Proportion of Bhil Homicides Involving Argument, by Relation Form

	Character of Homicide		
	Nonargument % (N)	Argument % (N)	Total % (N)
Relation			
Asymmetric	96.7 (29)	3.3 (1)	100.0 (30)
Symmetric	79.0 (45)	21.0 (12)	100.0 (57)
Total	85.1 (74)	14.9 (13)	100.0 (87)

Pearson χ^2 (d.f. = 1) = 4.86; $p < .05$

homicides appear to be four times more likely in symmetric dyads than in asymmetric dyads, the actual ratio might be anywhere between three and five. The data nonetheless yield statistically significant results that resemble those observed for U.S. cities; in other words, the ratio is almost certainly larger than one. The implication is that, given the observed pattern, sampling error might exaggerate or understate the *size* of the association, but it is very unlikely to mislead us as to the *fact* or the *direction* of the association. Among the Bhil, according to table 5, homicides are about six times more likely to have begun as arguments for dyads tied symmetrically than for those tied asymmetrically. In the Munda and Oraon data, reported in table 6, the association appears yet again—although the corresponding likelihood ratio for these homicides cannot be estimated because *none* of the twenty-two homicides occurring between people tied asymmetrically resulted from arguments, compared with twenty-one argument homicides in the fifty-nine symmetric dyads. (A conservative estimate of the ratio that one would observe with a larger sample is 6:1, the figure that would have resulted if one case from the "argument" category had been classified in the "other" category. Again, given the small number of observations, the numerical estimates themselves are less informative than the overall direction of the associations.)

The association, then, holds for some sharply different contexts—three urban centers in the United States and two fairly isolated indigenous groups in South Asia whose everyday life differs enormously from that of city dwellers in America. In all of these locations, the avail-

Table 6 Proportion of Munda and Oraon Homicides Involving Argument, by Relation Form

| | Character of Homicide | | |
Relation	Nonargument % (N)	Argument % (N)	Total % (N)
Asymmetric	100.0 (22)	0.0 (0)	100.0 (22)
Symmetric	64.4 (38)	35.6 (21)	100.0 (59)
Total	74.1 (60)	26.0 (21)	100.0 (81)

Pearson χ^2 (d.f. = 1) = 10.57; $p < .001$

able data indicate that lethal violence occurring within symmetric relations is more likely to start symbolically, in the form of verbal altercation, than is violence occurring between people tied asymmetrically. Reasoning back from this pattern, we have evidence that symmetric ties are more conflict-ridden and violence-prone than other kinds of ties. To state the point somewhat starkly (the comparison is, after all, a matter of degree), people connected in ways that allow rhetorically for the recognition of asymmetry, and hence make structurally possible the assertion of rank, are on average more likely to resolve their disputes before they become lethal. People whose connection offers no rhetorical basis for the achievement of dominance are more likely to find themselves locked in lethal battles before their disputes end. Hence the relative prevalence of arguments in homicides within symmetric dyads: with fewer brakes on conflict relative to asymmetric dyads, the proportion of violent incidents that start "small" is higher for the former than for the latter.

Another source of evidence relevant to the symmetry thesis, as it might be termed, derives from the fact that some disputes end violently although there is, so to speak, a break in the action. As with both Corsican incidents recounted above—the Balesi-Galanti and the Marchi-Tristani homicides—it often happens that one party to a dispute exits the scene, only to return later with a deadly weapon and put a violent end to a conflict others thought had already ended peacefully. In such incidents, the symbolic character of conflict seems to be particularly visible: the assailant is not as angry about whatever set off the conflict as about the humiliation of having lost. Recall, for example, that Balesi specifically announced to an acquaintance that he planned to seek revenge against Galanti for the way he had been treated—calling attention not to the inconvenience of having been denied the right-of-way but rather to the fact that he had just lost a fight.

Or consider the following homicide in St. Louis in 1994, in which once again someone who demanded deference was instead publicly humbled. The offender in this incident was a twenty-four-year-old un-employed man (as before, names are protected) who, according to witnesses, made a habit of bullying other young people in his neighbor-hood but was also known as a drug seller. On one Saturday evening in late November, he encountered an acquaintance, a nineteen-year-old neighbor, and ordered him to make a trip to a local store. On this occasion, the young man refused. Surprised by this act of defiance, the older man began to call his adversary names, including, once again, the term "punk." Emboldened, perhaps, or irritated by being harassed in this way, the younger man punched the neighborhood bully in the mouth, knocking him to the ground, and then said, "You're going to have to get your nine [nine-millimeter handgun]. You're the punk—you need a gun to be tough!" Victorious, he headed home, about a block away. The offender asked friends to bring him a washcloth and his gun, saying he needed to "take care of business." About half an hour later, as the younger man sat in a car with friends, the drug dealer walked up to the car, fired a single shot at his antagonist, and fled. His friends later told police that they knew he was going to shoot the man because he was "not a fighter"—as the victim himself had declared.[14]

Such incidents can be found in interpersonal violence almost everywhere, including contexts in which the set of motives for violence includes such unusual considerations—unusual from the Western point of view—as witchcraft. I shall comment presently on the challenge the existence of culturally specific motives raises to cross-cultural generalization, but the current point is that even when these appear, the overall ensemble of motives and dispute trajectories looks familiar—and there are *always* cases in which the loser in a confrontation returns to exact vengeance a few hours or days later. In a

---

14. Richard Rosenfeld, St. Louis Homicide Project, Case No. 94-178059 (1994).

study of a conglomeration of Bantu tribes in Kenya, for example, the anthropologist Paul Bohannan documented slightly more than one hundred homicides that occurred between 1949 and 1954. Along with homicides caused by sexual and domestic matters, disputes about land or livestock, and killings resulting from suspicion of witchcraft, there was the usual collection of disputes (about thirty in all) about such matters as payment for a drink, jostling, disparaging remarks, or disrespectful behavior. And in a subset of these are found the incidents in which one party retreats from a heated conflict only to return a short time later with homicidal intent.

One of these occurred at a customary gathering following the burial of a young girl. The deceased girl's father, Shiamala, had brewed beer for a gathering in honor of a regional official, or olugongo—a local custom for dignitaries visiting "in times of sadness." The olugongo arrived in the middle of the afternoon along with his retinue and a phonograph. After many hours of drinking beer from a common pot, the guests were invited to pay for the music. Each guest (all were men) was permitted to preface his contribution with a short speech in praise of his own importance, stature, and wealth. Licheberere, nephew of the host, delivered his self-congratulation and paid ten cents, which a policeman accompanying the olugongo rejected as insufficient. Licheberere retorted that the amount was reasonable in light of the fact that he could not collect bribes as an olugongo's policeman could. The official unsuccessfully tried to calm Licheberere, who continued to express his anger. Shiamala, roused from sleep in the adjoining room, ordered his nephew from the house and, after throwing Licheberere's drinking reed to the floor, pushed him out the door. Some time later, Licheberere returned to the house and, entering the room in which Shiamala was sleeping, stabbed him fatally with an arrow.

The theme that most clearly runs through these incidents is that, for at least one disputant, the conflict continued after the parties involved had parted company. These homicides were not committed preemptively or in self-defense, inasmuch as the victim in each case had demonstrated no interest in pursuing the matter further—not surprisingly, since the matter had ended in his favor. The homicide accomplishes nothing apart from the annihilation of a rival. The killings are therefore most plausibly seen as responses to perceived humiliation, that is, clear and typically public defeat in a dominance interaction. In this interpretation, by destroying the person responsible for humiliation, the offender has tried to seize the dominant position in the relation. In reality, of course, both the relation and the victim have ceased to exist, so that the offender's presumed goal of extracting deference from his rival cannot be achieved. It is fair to suppose, nevertheless, that the killer in such a case sees himself for a fleeting moment as having won the contest and that he believes his achievement of priority, however short-lived with respect to the actual relation, will extend into the future in the minds of third parties. This is a decidedly second-best outcome from the viewpoint of the offender, who would have preferred to relegate the living victim to a subordinate role in relation to himself.[15] Even so, it is consistent with the dominance-contest interpretation insofar as the most desired outcome in these stories seems to be out of the offender's reach.

If retaliatory violence of this sort is indeed an expression of the desire to establish priority over a rival, then it should be possible to find in retaliatory homicides a pattern akin to that observed in the previous section. That is, retaliatory violence should be more typical of symmetric relations than asymmetric ones. To be sure, people might want revenge for a public put-down regardless of whether the antagonist was a peer, a superior, or a subordinate, but, following the lines of my earlier argument, disagreements between individuals tied symmetrically should be more likely to reach the point at which the put-down in question is intolerable. Asymmetry in relations ought to be associated with relatively early resolution of disputes, diminishing the possibility that insults or physical affronts will be serious enough to provoke retaliatory violence.

For all five contexts examined above, table 7 cross-classifies symmetry or asymmetry of relation with an indicator of whether a given homicide was retaliatory—that is, whether the assailant was seeking revenge for a prior offense against himself or herself. (Note that this criterion excludes vendettas, to be examined in part II, in which the attacker specifically avenges a prior killing. It also excludes preemptive homicides—those in which the assailant believed that the victim intended future physical harm). As in the case of argument homi-

---

15. Konrad Lorenz makes an illuminating comment to this effect in his celebrated book *On Aggression* (New York: Harvest, 1974).

Table 7 Relative Frequency of Retaliatory Homicide in Symmetric and Asymmetric Relations, Across Five Social Contexts

Context	Retaliation	Number of Cases
Chicago, 1965–94	3.7**	17,577
Miami, 1980	3.9*	440
St. Louis, 1994–96	8.0**	334
Bhil, 1965–72	4.2*	87
Munda and Oraon, 1955–59	5.3*	81

Note: The numbers in the column labeled "Retaliation" compare the proportion of retaliatory murders in symmetric dyads to the proportion of retaliatory murders in asymmetric dyads. For example, the Miami row shows that retaliation was 3.9 times more likely to be the basis for murder in symmetric relations than in asymmetric ones.

*p < .05   **p < .001

cides, retaliatory homicides occur disproportionately within symmetric dyads. In four of the contexts examined, retaliation is about four to five times more likely to feature in symmetric than in asymmetric relations. The ratio in St. Louis is 8:1, possibly reflecting a tendency for youth gang killings to be described in police reports as retaliation if there is a history of conflict between the relevant groups. Overall, the proposition is strongly borne out by the evidence: when someone kills a peer, the attack is much more likely to be a retaliation for a perceived wrong than when the assailant and the victim are tied asymmetrically.

Cross-Cultural Consistency in Patterns of Violence

A simple but not very precise way to summarize the results of this chapter is to say that, when people come into conflict, the kind of relation they have to each other makes a difference for the outcome. It seems, in particular, that small or symbolic disputes are more likely to figure in violence between peers than between nonpeers—suggesting that conflict between peers is more likely to escalate to violence. It would be useful to be able to say in addition that conflict of any sort, not only violent conflict, is more prevalent in certain types of relations than in others—that is certainly an implication of my argument—but the data required to explore that claim are not yet available.

It is nevertheless a striking result that the data that are available consistently reveal a link between relational symmetry and violent conflict across a range of settings that differ significantly in the character of everyday life and by implication in the *content* of interpersonal conflicts. It is worth pausing for a bit to consider the significance of finding an abstract regularity in a domain so rife with cultural variation. There is, of course, much overlap in the content of symbolic disputes, and even more coherence in the kinds of substantive conflict that lead to violence—sexual rivalries, land boundaries, theft of property, political control of communities, and perhaps a few others. Still, the ensemble of things people argue about—the content of disputes— varies impressively across social settings. In urban North America, people can wound each other's pride with remarks about athletic ability, sexual behavior (or the sexual behavior of relatives, especially female relatives), trustworthiness, courage, and any number of other matters, but they are not likely to offend with comments about how much facial hair a man has. Elsewhere, notably in rural Latin America and many Mediterranean societies, noting that a young man has no moustache can carry quite a sting.[16] So can the physical gesture suggesting that a man has horns, implying that (like a billy-goat) he is unable to control the sexual activities of his mate.[17] This metaphor carries little significance for people to whom goat herding is unfamiliar, even if it is common in many settings for insults to cast doubt on a male rival's sexual prowess or control over his wife's behavior.

In Muslim societies, particularly in the Middle East, comments about the sexual behavior of wives or daughters have not been observed to provoke violence against the speaker, but extramarital sex itself often does lead to violence, at least when it is a matter of public knowledge.[18] In these contexts, it is the woman in question who most often pays the price. Elsewhere in the Mediterranean region, it is more often the male partner in a clandestine relationship who becomes the target.

16. See Pierre Bourdieu, "The Sentiment of Honor in Kabyle Society," pp. 191–242 in Jean G. Peristiany, ed., *Honor and Shame: The Values of Mediterranean Society* (Chicago: University of Chicago Press, 1966); James B. Greenberg, *Blood Ties: Life and Violence in Rural Mexico* (Tucson: University of Arizona Press, 1989).

17. Anton Blok, "Rams and Billy-Goats: A Key to the Mediterranean Code of Honor," *Man* 16 (1980): 427–40; David D. Gilmore, *Manhood in the Making: Cultural Concepts of Masculinity* (New Haven: Yale University Press, 1990).

18. Gideon M. Kressel, "Sororicide/Filiacide: Homicide for Family Honour," *Current Anthropology* 22 (1981): 141–58; Jane Schneider, "Of Vigilance and Virgins," *Ethnology* 10 (1971): 1–24.

Finally, of the eighty-seven Bhil homicides examined in table 5, three resulted from arguments about a drum in which one person wished to play and others protested.[19] It is hard to avoid the inference that the desire to play a drum, or not to listen to it, could arouse especially strong emotions in this community. On the other hand, it is unlikely that disputes about drum-playing will turn out to be a common, cross-cultural feature of interpersonal conflict.

In short, the visible fact of variability at the level of explicit content might easily lead one to expect corresponding variation in the way relation form is associated with the likelihood of violent conflict. The coherence across settings found here is, from this point of view, quite surprising. It is all the more surprising when we recognize that the kinds of enmity people harbor toward one another are sensitive even to differences in fundamental metaphysical beliefs. As I noted above, accusations of sorcery or witchcraft figure prominently in annals of violence in many non-Western societies, notably in Africa but also in many parts of Asia and Oceania. In such settings, it is quite common for disputes to erupt when one person accuses another of casting spells—or, to describe the same thing in a more experience-distant way, for one party to an interpersonal enmity to express that enmity in the form either of a witchcraft accusation or of a threat to use magical means against the other party.

For example, in a study of homicides drawing on a larger ethnography of the Gisu of Uganda, La Fontaine describes an incident in which two young men severely beat an elderly man they suspected of practicing sorcery. They killed him by hammering a nail into his head, believing that this technique would be effective against his magical powers.[20] Three of the 99 homicides examined in La Fontaine's study involved suspicions of witchcraft or sorcery—certainly a far higher proportion than in Western societies, where the category "witchcraft" does not even appear in official records. More remarkably, a sample of 114 homicides among the Nyoro of western Uganda from the same time period includes 15 in which the killer believed that the (typically female)

---

19. Sushil C. Varma, *The Bhil Kills* (Delhi: Kunji, 1978). As with the analyses in tables 5 and 7, this figure results from my own tabulation of the homicide narratives.

20. Jean La Fontaine, "Homicide and Suicide among the Gisu," pp. 94–129 in Paul Bohannan, ed., *African Homicide and Suicide* (Princeton: Princeton University Press, 1960).

victim had bewitched him or his children; in some of these incidents the accusation of witchcraft was based on mere suspicion, whereas in others, one or more children had actually died.[21] Verrier Elwin's classic examination of homicide among the Bison-Horn Maria (like the Bhil and the Munda and Oraon, an aboriginal group of central India) reports 5 witchcraft-related murders in a sample of 100 incidents.

In one Maria homicide from 1941, Vedta Sukra suspected his uncle, Kola, the village headman, of having magically induced the death of his young daughter. When Sukra's month-old son died three years later, he consulted a Siraha—a medicine man with mystical powers of diagnosis—who confirmed his suspicion that Kola had brought about both deaths. In a further test, a chicken was presented with five piles of rice, one designated with Kola's name and four with names of various deities. The chicken pecked at two piles of rice: the one representing Kola and the one named for Mirchuk Deo, killer of children. Concluding that Kola had invoked the deity Mirchuk to cause the two children to fall ill, Sukra murdered his uncle the next day and immediately confessed to the homicide.[22]

Perhaps the most unusual instance of the link between homicide and witchcraft beliefs occurs in a rainforest region of lowland New Guinea, where, according to Bruce Knauft, the Gebusi attribute *all* sickness deaths to sorcery or witchcraft. Because deaths caused by magic are understood to demand the death of the perpetrator, Gebusi communities identify a guilty party by means of divination and proceed to a ritualized execution either immediately or soon after. Although in practice only about 25 percent of deaths from illness are so avenged, the attribution of illness to sorcery leads fairly directly to a population-threatening rate of homicide. Most surprising of all, this astonishing level of "violence" in the purely behavioral sense occurs in a society that pointedly lacks the usual traits of the honor complex: men do not engage in the status contests typical of honor societies, and the Gebusi in general place a great deal of value on harmony and peaceful resolution of differences. Indeed, they justify the swift de-

21. J. H. M. Beattie, "Homicide and Suicide in Bunyoro," pp. 130–53 in Bohannan, *African Homicide*.

22. Verrier Elwin, *Maria Murder and Suicide* (Bombay: Geoffrey Cumberlege/Oxford University Press, 1943).

struction of individuals identified as sorcerers or witches with reference to the need to eliminate malice and hostility in the community.[23]

From the Western (or, more precisely, Western rationalist) standpoint, it would be difficult to imagine more compelling evidence for the claim that the roots of conflict, even lethal conflict, are fundamentally arbitrary. It is one thing to recognize that patterns in social conflict can vary with respect to the set of things people may view as symbolic affronts; it seems quite another to discover that societies vary with respect to basic beliefs about the physical means available to people who wish to inflict physical harm. With the recognition that fundamental ontological principles concerning possible types of aggression are socially flexible, the goal of establishing cross-culturally valid propositions about conflict begins to seem impossibly remote.

Yet the association between relational symmetry and conflict is robust across all the settings I have examined—including two in which witchcraft accusation often crops up as a conflict motive—suggesting a deep structure to human conflict that is masked by observable cultural variation. Excessive reliance on the categories and relations social actors invoke in explaining their own behavior (sociologists like to call reliance on native categories "grounded theory," whereas anthropologists refer to it as offering an "emic" account) would render such patterns invisible; hence the value of conceptual frameworks constructed autonomously from the subjective experience of those actors.[24]

One might stop there and conclude that the subjectively available content of disputes is mere noise: uninformative surface appearance or local color interesting to tourists but not to serious scientists. In fact, though, there is reason to believe that witchcraft and sorcery accusations are in many settings specifically driven by the very same kinds of conflict I have been discussing—but within relations whose character renders explicit reference to contests for rank embarrassing or un-

23. Bruce M. Knauft, "Reconsidering Violence in Simple Human Societies: Homicide among the Gebusi of New Guinea," *Current Anthropology* 28 (1987): 457–500.

24. Many critics of theory-driven research see this imposition of categories onto experience as a Procrustean enterprise in which the world is forced to fit the analyst's theory. This criticism is, frankly, misguided and unfair. If theoretically derived categories imposed on the data were mere inventions with no relevance to how the world works, then the data would say so: the variables examined would exhibit few or no statistically significant associations. Imposing a theoretically generated framework on data cannot by itself produce statistically significant results.

acceptable. In Tiv homicides involving agnatic relatives, for example, Paul Bohannan observed an association between witchcraft accusations and generational difference: suspicion of witchcraft occurred in eight of thirteen homicides in which killer and victim came from different generations and in only one of the eight homicides between members of the same generation. (Although Bohannan did not perform a statistical test on the cross-classification, the association is indeed significant at $p > .05$.) Even the single case of a same-generation witchcraft killing turns out to conform to the overall pattern: the victim was an elder half-brother who exerted parental authority over the killer. According to Bohannan, Tiv cosmology represents tribal elders as possessing magical powers that are usually used to protect tribe members but can also be turned to evil purposes.[25] It is not a long stretch to see witchcraft accusation in such cases as a culturally sanctioned expression of a structural fact, namely, that younger community members cannot be confident that their elders exert authority benevolently.[26]

Despite the strength of the association for Tiv homicides, it is by no means the case that witchcraft suspicions in general coincide with authority relations. But they need not do so to sustain the claim that accusations of malevolent use of occult powers are systematically connected to inadmissible contests for rank. The case of the Gebusi reveals why: if interpersonal conflict is unacceptable generally, then witchcraft suspicion can fall anywhere. Principles governing who can legitimately compete with whom for social rank vary cross-culturally; so, accordingly, does the set of social relations for which witchcraft accusations provide an acceptable rhetoric for such contests.

Conclusion

My focus in this and the previous two chapters has been interpersonal conflict. The aim of this study, however, is to say something about

---

25. Paul Bohannan, "Homicide among the Tiv of Central Nigeria," pp. 30–64 in Bohannan, *African Homicide*.
26. There is a striking and informative parallel, at least in my judgment, between these sorts of suspicions and the paranoid fears of anti-elitist social groups in democratic societies. Rumors concerning the supposedly conspiratorial activities of economic and political elites, in the United States in particular but elsewhere as well, routinely refer to occult practices and secret gatherings that bear an impressive resemblance to images concerning sorcery.

the connection between conflict and hierarchy in general, not simply within isolated pairs of individuals. The two concepts themselves demand a more general approach: although people inflict a remarkable amount of harm on one another in dyadic conflicts, comparable and sometimes greater harm occurs when conflict pits collectivities, rather than individuals, against each other. And, although it might be reasonable to talk of hierarchy between two isolated people,[27] it is an undeniable feature of social organization that dyadic relations are nearly always attached to other relations with which they form higher-order structures. Many of these structures are hierarchical, and many of the forms of dominance in them are, as in complex organizations, sustainable only because of connection to other relations. In fact, the more formal features of hierarchy, such as transitivity, are only meaningful for higher-order systems of relations.

In subsequent chapters, therefore, I turn to conflict on a different scale: that of social groups. The burden of chapter 4 is to establish the extent to which the idea of contests for rank can be detached from the interpersonal context and shown to have relevance for conflict among collectivities. To address this question, I shall concentrate substantially on a phenomenon that has emerged so often and in so many different parts of the world that it is impossible not to see it as a generic type of group conflict. I refer to the phenomenon of feuding.

27. As indeed one must in the case of Crusoe, who despite the existence of his forgotten subordinate Friday has become the iconic reference for the isolated, pre-social individual. The fiction in the story is the detachment of the dyad, not the individual, from social structure.

CHAPTER 4

Solidarity and Group Conflict

Most of what has been said up to now has pertained to conflict, violence, and dominance between individual persons. I have suggested that a focus on the matter of dominance helps account for a range of patterns in interpersonal conflict. These patterns include, above all, the large role symbolic disputes play in violence, the concentration of such disputes among pairs of individuals whose social connection does not establish rank, and the related concentration in such dyads of retaliatory violence, that is, attacks meant to restore the pride of the assailant without achieving much else.

In looking to the concept of dominance for an explanation of such patterns, I have, as I acknowledged in chapter 2, departed from the usage conventional to most social science disciplines other than psychology and the small subset of anthropology devoted to studies of primate behavior. In the first place, I have employed an abstract (and thin) conception of what interpersonal dominance is—one that picks out merely the fact of one person's occupying a superior rank relative to another, with minimal reference to the content of their interaction. One might call this a "structural" version of the idea of dominance, in that it abstracts from the concrete details of a relationship so as to highlight its form. The abstraction allows me to say that Frank exerts dominance over Joe if any of the following conditions (for instance) holds: Joe tends to do what Frank says, Frank belittles Joe's abilities while extracting approval or admiration from Joe, or Frank sees no need to offer an explanation for arriving twenty minutes late for their rendezvous while expecting (correctly) that Joe will apologize for keeping him waiting for only five minutes. It should not be hard for the reader to find such asymmetries in her or his own dealings with others. That should make it easier to achieve an intuitive grasp of the concept in the absence of a formal definition.

Naturally, if one views these relatively benign patterns of interaction as indicators of a dominance relation, then one is also committed to recognize dominance in any number of more serious patterns: Joe does not form an opinion on most topics without asking Frank what he thinks, Joe is afraid of Frank, Frank regularly causes Joe physical or emotional harm without repercussion, and so forth. In a "thick" conception, each of these concrete patterns in interaction might be part of the *definition*, which would also include a series of statements tying the patterns to each other. To avoid the resulting confusion between definitions of a concept and theories about its referent, I have treated such statements as concrete realizations of the abstract phenomenon of interpersonal dominance.

The second departure from convention lies in the fact that I have so far avoided discussion of dominance of one social group by another, although most sociologists, anthropologists, political theorists, and historians typically begin and end discussions of domination at the group level. The chief advantage of thinking about dominance as a matter of groups—whether these are defined in ethnic, racial, confessional, economic, or sexual terms—is that it permits discussion of broad and macroscopic (and hence, to most social scientists, important) phenomena without having to worry too much about the millions of microscopic interactions among individuals that are presupposed and summarized by such discussion. Concentrating on collective forms of dominance therefore offers a convenient shorthand, but it also makes it possible to forget that dominance relations between social groups actually comprise large numbers of interpersonal relations among members of such groups.

In defining and thinking first about dominance and conflict

among persons, and only then moving to groups, I aim to make explicit, and make progress in answering, the question of how these billions of interactions add up to relations among groups that are stable enough to permit macroscopic statements about the domination of children by adults, workers by employers, women by men, people of color by white people, Tamils by Sinhalese, and so forth. Unless small-scale interactions are nothing but reflections of general and abstract categories, formed by those categories but having no influence on their existence, it is unlikely that any social-scientific theory of group dominance will successfully account for observed patterns without addressing this question. Now, it is true that from Plato to Hegel and on to Althusser there have always been theorists willing to see abstract categories as prior and constitutive and concrete realizations as secondary and therefore dependent or illusory. That will surely continue to be true. Nonetheless, a goal of this and succeeding chapters is to highlight what is gained by rejecting that sort of idealism—that is, by taking group categories not as source but as result of patterns in interpersonal interaction.

What Intergroup Relations Are Made Of

It will already have occurred to the astute reader that interpersonal relations might be so messy that it is impossible to say whether Frank dominates Joe or Joe dominates Frank. Frank might be able to get Joe to defer to him about whether we can really know anything with certainty, whereas Joe might be much more knowledgeable about professional football; Frank might consistently decide what is for dinner but defer to Joe concerning the proper way to play the Caro-Kann opening in chess. Complete domination of one person by another, across the full range of domains of interaction, might be a relatively rare pure case—although it is likely that most people know at least one pair of people who relate to each other this way. Still, it bears pointing out that, although this possibility complicates what it means to talk about a dominance relation, it does not obstruct the core argument of part I: One should expect, all else equal, that social ties in which rank is inconsistent across domains should resemble symmetric ties in their capacity to engender conflict. On entering a new domain, pairs of people who lack a *consistent* principle telling them who outranks whom are in a similar position to the position of people who lack such a principle entirely.

Consider, however, the implications of this observation for talking about relations between social groups. Except, perhaps, in the most extreme forms of group hierarchy, such as slave systems, the statement that group X dominates group Y (or group X controls, exploits, persecutes, or receives deference from group Y) will never perfectly describe all the relations between each member of X and each member of Y. Indeed, even in slave systems, it is surely the case that some master-slave relations are less asymmetrical than others. Saying that social group X dominates group Y, even when the issue of who belongs to which group is easy to settle, amounts at best to the claim that on average, or most of the time, members of X expect and receive deference from members of Y.

This must be true even when group relations are formally regulated by law, explicit custom, or religious doctrine: Even in the most formally patriarchal of social systems, for instance, there are numerous examples of women who have exerted influence, achieved respect, given orders to men with the reasonable expectation of compliance, and in general exerted dominance over some members of the presumptively dominant group. Most people would not seriously contest the proposition that "men dominated women" in France between 1300 and 1600, in Venice during the Renaissance, or in Argentina, Israel, the Philippines, the United States, and the United Kingdom from before the nineteenth century roughly to the present. Yet each of these social contexts has contained a significant number of women who exerted clear dominance over a range of adult men—and the list goes well beyond Jeanne d'Arc, Diane de Poitiers, Veronica Franco, Golda Meir, Corazón Aquino, Carrie Nation, Florence Nightingale, and Margaret Thatcher. Many common households also harbored strong female characters, fear and resentment of whom has frequently been expressed in peasant folk tales.[1] The heavy price many of these women paid for inverting prevalent hierarchies, and the nonstandard methods

---

1. Some excellent examples of the way folk tales portrayed the menace of dominant wives can be found in chapter 3, "Peasants Tell Tales," in Robert Darnton, *The Great Cat Massacre and Other Episodes in French Cultural History* (New York: Random House, 1985).

many employed in doing so, make clear the force of the currents against which they swam; yet the fact that many nevertheless got as far as they did reinforces the point that dominance relations at the group level express tendencies, not invariant rules, at the level of individuals.

The realization that dominance relations among groups is nearly always a statistical matter—a matter of what happens on average between group members rather than all of the time—leads immediately to the question of how the statistical pattern is reproduced over time, leading to relatively stable, but not permanent, group hierarchies. The pattern surely derives some of its stability from cultural reference points—myths, analogies, stereotypes, and so forth—that subtly and overtly affirm the superiority of Xs and the inferiority of Ys. But to stop there is to ignore the fact that cultural reference points have to come from somewhere. If rebellious slaves led by the Thracian Spartacus had seized power in 73 B.C. and subjugated Roman slaveholders—and we know that prevailing cultural schemata did not stop them from trying—the cultural images that had once legitimated Roman dominance over Greeks and "barbarians" would soon have given way to a myth according to which the slave peoples had demonstrated their natural superiority by means of their heroic victory over the corrupt and unjust Romans. (This is not to say that Romans, to the extent there would still have been a group identified by that name, would not have told themselves the reverse story, presumably one ending with the future restoration of Romans to their rightful place.) Such myths surely play a role in coordinating and reinforcing dominance arrangements, but in the long term they too must receive support in the form of concrete social interactions that appear to conform to culturally prevalent notions. Stable though hierarchies might be, they are not permanent—and neither are the collective representations that give them cultural expression.

For group hierarchies to persist, then, there must be something in observable social interaction that lends solidity to the idea that one social group outranks another. Cultural legitimation of a particular group ranking is not sufficient, because it is vulnerable to behavioral falsification. The statistical pattern in behavior is not sufficient, because with regular deviations—every subordinate group has some strong-willed people, and every dominant group some who are weak—there would be little on which to base the idea that *groups* are involved at all.[2] Another factor must be at work, one that specifically makes it possible for one collectivity, *as* a collectivity, to exert dominance over another. And this factor must be observable in behavior, even if the behavior is itself subject to culturally influenced interpretation.

In this chapter I shall make the case that observed group solidarity is a crucial ingredient in establishing intergroup rank—more crucial, in some contexts, than the properties most often invoked in accounting for the strength of social groups, such as numbers or material resources. I say "more crucial" rather than "more important" because in many group encounters it is obviously of tremendous importance whether one party outnumbers another or is better equipped— whether with horses or checking accounts. What makes solidarity more crucial is that, unlike resources or numbers, it is only observable in action. If the Sharks wish to intimidate the Jets, they can display their numbers, their weapons, and possibly their individual bravery and physical strength without engaging in overt conflict, but they cannot demonstrate that they *can* act as a group unless they *do* act as a group. Because there is thus always some uncertainty about whether collections of people can or will behave like groups of people when it begins to matter, and in particular when it is individually very risky to act for the collectivity, solidarity is a key player in group contention.

That solidarity—in the sense of members' willingness to make sacrifices for group welfare—can outweigh more traditional measures of strength has been repeatedly discovered in military conflict. The famous story of the Lost Battalion in World War I is one case. Toward the end of the war, a detachment of about six hundred American soldiers (not in fact a battalion but a collection of companies from four different battalions) broke through German lines in the Ardennes Forest only to find itself isolated and, when reinforcements failed to reach them, surrounded and drastically outnumbered by hostile forces. Short of ammunition and out of rations, and subjected to continuous machine-gun fire and artillery, including a deadly barrage from American forces using the wrong coordinates, the soldiers serving under

---

2. This claim is, I readily acknowledge, exactly parallel to Durkheim's argument against the empiricist account of knowledge—that abstract concepts such as space, time, and category could never be derived from concrete experience alone. Emile Durkheim, *The Elementary Forms of the Religious Life* (New York: Free, 1973).

Major. Charles Whittlesey nevertheless held their ground for five days until soldiers of the 308th Battalion finally broke through to relieve them. Only two hundred survived. Many more could have done so if they had been willing to desert or surrender.

Another well-known case is that of the 101st Airborne Division at Bastogne, also in the Ardennes Forest, during the Battle of the Bulge in 1944. Here, a small force of Allied soldiers with communication lines cut held their position against an enormous German counter-offensive involving more than one hundred thousand soldiers in a final effort to push back the Allied advance across northern Europe. In both instances, and others besides, small bands with limited resources prevailed against much larger numbers because individual members refused to desert their comrades—an option that remained available throughout the conflicts. And of course history offers numerous examples of peoples successfully defending their homelands against overwhelming invading forces.

The point is not that solidarity always outweighs other factors. In many cases numbers and resources are indeed determinative. Rather, the point is that these exceptional cases reveal the wide range of variation in group cohesion and furthermore the potential, usually unrealized, for human groups to act collectively. Variability in cohesion, and the impossibility of observing it except in its results, make it possible for social groups to surprise others and themselves in the course of conflict—violent and otherwise.

The tendency for groups to differ on the solidarity dimension, and the difficulty of establishing in advance just how cohesive rival collectivities are, together constitute a significant precondition for conflict. In this regard, uncertainty about relative cohesiveness plays a role in group struggles analogous to that of relational symmetry in the interpersonal strife examined in chapter 3. In the remainder of the present chapter I elaborate on this claim and offer evidence for its relevance in understanding why some conflicts that cross group boundaries remain interpersonal affairs whereas others become genuinely collective. Using systematic data concerning violence in a classic feuding society—a context in which received knowledge teaches us, incorrectly, that *all* conflicts are collective—I show that seemingly exotic phenomena such as "honor" and blood revenge can be explained as the result of competing efforts to maintain and signal group solidarity.

Collective Violence

The priority of the social group relative to the individual person is an article of faith for many social scientists, above all in sociology. All three of the theoretical descent groups in that discipline—functionalist, conflict, and institutional approaches—favor society- or group-level accounts instead of individualist accounts, inasmuch as they couch explanations in terms of value systems, class structures, organizational practices and forms, and so forth. In studies of social conflict, as with discussions of group domination, it is frequently assumed that when people see themselves as having a collective interest, they act in that interest.

Yet it happens quite frequently that members of groups with an apparent common interest do not act collectively to achieve it. Students of collective action often explain such failures with reference to the social dilemma inherent in cooperative social behavior—a dilemma resulting from the incentive each individual faces to let others contribute to collective goods from which all will benefit.[3] Observing that, despite temptations to shirk, people nonetheless sometimes succeed in acting collectively when doing so incurs significant risks, sociologists have painstakingly documented the processes by which groups of individuals manage to solve their free-rider problems. Chief among these are two mechanisms that generate solidarity and hence voluntary subordination of individual to group interests: Social influence, mediated by strong personal relations, by means of which people influence one another to act cooperatively, and the construction of interpretive frameworks, especially those involving collective identities, by means of which people see themselves as occupying similar social positions and having a common fate.[4]

The substance and logic of these views of collective action have

    3. Dennis Chong, *Collective Action and the Civil Rights Movement* (Berkeley: University of California Press, 1991); Russell Hardin, *One for All: The Logic of Group Conflict* (Princeton: Princeton University Press, 1995); Michael W. Macy, "Chains of Cooperation: Threshold Effects in Collective Action," *American Sociological Review* 56 (1991): 730–47; Michael W. Macy, "Backward-Looking Social Control," *American Sociological Review* 58 (1993): 819–36; Gerald R. Marwell, Pamela E. Oliver, and Ralph Prahl, "Social Networks and Collective Action: A Theory of the Critical Mass III," *American Journal of Sociology* 94 (1988): 502–34; Pamela E. Oliver and Gerald R. Marwell, *The Logic of Collective Action* (New York: Cambridge University Press, 1993).
    4. On the role of social networks, see Doug McAdam, "Recruitment to High Risk/Cost Activism: The Case of Freedom Summer," *American Journal of Sociology* 92, no. 1 (1986):

been most thoroughly developed and explored in the area of social protest, but the problem they address would seem to be generic to all forms of group conflict. Any instance of confrontation between collections of people—whether the boundary dividing them is one of class, ethnicity, clan, race, gender, or religion—involves in principle the possibility that group action will not occur because behavior will be dominated by individualistic motives. Yet outside the area of political and social protest, the literature concerning group conflict has had little to say about the collective action problem whose solution such conflict entails. Studies of the origins of racial, ethnic, nationalist, familistic, sectarian, or tribal conflict ordinarily adopt a supraindividual focus: The issue of interest is not typically how groups overcome internal obstacles to collective action (or, to say the same thing another way, how collections of people come to act as groups) but rather why members of distinct social groups see their interests as conflicting in the first place. The transition from group interest to group action is treated implicitly as unproblematic or as a functional response to conflict. Indeed, classic theoretical statements, notably that of Georg Simmel, usually portrayed intergroup tension as a basic source of internal solidarity. And of course it was one of the basic premises of Marxist and, later, syndicalist thinking that workers would learn to act as a class after repeated clashes with employers.

Outside of the protest literature, reasoning about group conflict

64–90; Roberto M. Fernandez and Doug McAdam, "Social Networks and Social Movements: Multiorganizational Fields and Recruitment to Mississippi Freedom Summer," *Sociological Forum* 3, no. 3 (1988): 357–82; Roger V. Gould, "Multiple Networks and Mobilization in the Paris Commune, 1871," *American Sociological Review* 56 (1991): 716–29; Roger V. Gould, "Trade Cohesion, Class Unity, and Urban Insurrection: Artisanal Activism in the Paris Commune," *American Journal of Sociology* 98 (1993): 721–54; Doug McAdam and Ronnelle Paulsen, "Specifying the Relationship between Social Ties and Activism," *American Journal of Sociology* 99, no. 3 (1993): 640–67. On collective identity, see Doug McAdam, *Political Process and the Development of Black Insurgency, 1930–1970* (Chicago: University of Chicago Press, 1982); Rick Fantasia, *Cultures of Solidarity* (Berkeley: University of California Press, 1988); Alberto Melucci, John Keane, and Paul Mier, eds., *Nomads of the Present* (Philadelphia: Temple University Press: 1989); Verta Taylor and Nancy Whittier, "Collective Identity in Social Movement Communities: Lesbian Feminist Mobilization," pp. 104–29 in Aldon Morris and Carol Mueller, eds., *Frontiers of Social Movement Theory* (New Haven: Yale University Press, 1992); Craig J. Calhoun, "'New Social Movements of the Early Nineteenth Century," pp. 173–215 in Mark Traugott, ed., *Repertoires and Cycles of Collective Action* (Durham, N.C.: Duke University Press, 1995); Roger V. Gould, *Insurgent Identities: Class, Community, and Protest in Paris from 1848 to the Commune* (Chicago: University of Chicago Press, 1995); Christopher K. Ansell, "Symbolic Networks: The Realignment of the French Working Class, 1887–1894," *American Journal of Sociology* 103 (1997): 359–90.

typically occurs as follows: A significant confrontation is observed in which people express and act on their hostility in terms that correspond to a socially salient group boundary. Analysts of the event note (for instance) that, in everyday life, members of the two groups compete for material benefits, residential space, or some other valued resource. This preexisting competition (or mere hatred, cultural misunderstanding, or whatever factor turns out to be the basis for hostility) therefore "explains" the violent outburst.

Because violent social confrontations attract attention—both in the popular press and in scholarly research—in proportion to their scale and severity, it is easy to disregard the conflicts that never escalate beyond a few persons or reach the point of violence at all. Yet these are generally far more common than are the conflicts that eventuate in significant mobilization.[5] Extant accounts of group conflict thus do their job too well: They make sense of the cases in which preexisting competition coincides with violent clashes between rival groups but are accordingly unable to explain why most confrontations do not lead to outbreaks of group violence. Studying only the instances in which tension does lead to group conflict leads to an underestimation of the obstacles to group unity—and, as it happens, of the importance of these obstacles to the process of conflict itself.

In this section I intend to demonstrate the significance of collective action problems for intergroup conflict beyond the domain of social protest. I offer evidence that groups of roughly equivalent status and strength come into conflict in ways that reveal the relevance of social dilemmas similar to those faced by subordinate groups in their confrontations with elites. Second, I show that the generality of the collective action problem itself has a direct and major consequence for the way conflict unfolds: The general awareness among contenders that putatively solidary groups may nonetheless fail to act together contributes to the likelihood of escalation to collective violence. In the course of a dispute, individuals call on allies as a way of demonstrating to their adversaries that they are not alone. But because people on both sides know that the other side's solidarity may unravel if the dispute intensifies, they will at least some of the time refuse to back down. The

5. James D. Fearon and David A. Laitin, "Explaining Interethnic Cooperation," *American Political Science Review* 90, no. 4 (1996): 715–35.

resulting escalation pits group against group rather than individual against individual, because allies of the original disputants must now show—to themselves, to adversaries, and to witnesses—that their initial display of solidarity was not hollow. Expressions of group solidarity are therefore double-edged: They may succeed in forestalling escalation, but they intensify the violence that occurs if they fail to do so.

Approaches to Group Conflict

No social process has attracted more theoretical attention than that of conflict among human groups. Nevertheless, attempts to explain the phenomenon continually return to three themes that can be succinctly termed *interest, identity,* and *social organization.* Accounts emphasizing interest observe that human communities value such resources as territory, capital, and access to markets and at times compete with other communities for the use of these resources. Group conflict, ranging from exclusion to war, thus occurs when migration, subsistence crisis, or shifts in relative strength persuade one community to encroach on another's resources or to preempt encroachment by the other.[6] Individualist versions of this sort of argument assert further that the very existence of such communities results from the fact that their members derive individual benefits from belonging: The Hobbesian problem of conflict between groups, in other words, arises only to the extent that it has been solved within groups.

Identity arguments concentrate on the idea that human beings are prone, at least some of the time, to see themselves and others as instantiations of categories (worker, Methodist, Uzbek, Southerner, woman) rather than as unique and autonomous persons.[7] According

6. Georg Simmel, *Conflict and the Web of Group Affiliations* (New York: Free, 1955); Anthony Oberschall, *Social Conflict and Social Movements* (New York: Prentice-Hall, 1978); Anthony Oberschall, *Social Movements: Ideologies, Interest, and Identities* (New York: Transaction, 1995); Susan Olzak, "Contemporary Ethnic Mobilization," *Annual Review of Sociology* 9 (1983): 355–74; Susan Olzak, *Ethnic Conflict and Competition* (Stanford: Stanford University Press, 1992).

7. Michael Hogg and Dominic Abrams, *Social Identifications: A Social Psychology of Intergroup Relations and Group Processes* (London: Routledge, 1988); Henri Tajfel, "Experiments in Intergroup Discrimination," *Scientific American* (November 1970): 96–102; Henri Tajfel, "Social Identity and Intergroup Behavior," *Social Science Information* 13 (1974): 65–93; John Turner and Howard Giles, *Intergroup Behavior* (Oxford: Basil Blackwell, 1981); Muzafer Sherif, *Group Conflict and Cooperation* (New York: St. Martin's, 1966).

to one version of this perspective, a basic psychological need for self-esteem leads people to attach positive value to the categories to which they belong and negative value to categories that do not apply to them; more generally, the point is that group membership may be constitutive of personal identity although groups are conventionally thought to be aggregations of persons. Particularly with regard to ethnicity and race, identity-based explanations attribute conflict to deep and venerable cultural differences (or at least beliefs about such differences) that foster misunderstanding, hostility, and resentment, often independent of any material basis for competition.[8]

Finally, arguments that invoke the concept of social organization draw attention to the normative arrangements and durable social relations that bind people into groups. This emphasis is most prevalent in studies of societies with weak or nonexistent states, where feuding is particularly common. In such societies, the absence of state institutions for peacekeeping and protection of property rights obliges people to organize themselves for mutual defense, most often in the form of kinship groups. In the typical social organization account of feuding societies, disputes, violence, and retribution are always collective because the institutional order obliges members of a kinship group to regard offenses against any member as offenses against all; moreover, it is the offender's group, rather than the offender individually, that bears responsibility. The standard response to an injury, therefore, is either a comparable injury inflicted on any member of the offender's clan or a collective payment to the victim's clan.[9] In the social organization ac-

8. Robert A. LeVine and Donald T. Campbell, *Ethnocentrism: Theories of Conflict, Ethnic Attitudes, and Group Behavior* (New York: Wiley, 1972); Donald L. Horowitz, *Ethnic Groups in Conflict* (Berkeley: University of California Press, 1985); Robert D. Kaplan, *Balkan Ghosts: A Journey through History* (New York: St. Martin's, 1993).

9. Jacob Black-Michaud, *Cohesive Force: Feud in the Mediterranean and the Middle East* (New York: St. Martin's, 1975); Christopher Boehm, *Blood Revenge: The Enactment and Management of Revenge in Montenegro and Other Tribal Societies* (Philadelphia: University of Pennsylvania Press, 1987); John King Campbell, *Honour, Family, and Patronage: A Study of Institutions and Moral Values in a Greek Mountain Community* (Oxford: Clarendon, 1964); Meyer Fortes, *The Dynamics of Clanship among the Tallens* (London: Oxford University Press, 1945); Max Gluckman, *Custom and Conflict in Africa* (Glencoe: Free Press, 1955); Margaret Hasluck, *The Unwritten Law in Albania* (Cambridge: Cambridge University Press, 1954); William Ian Miller, *Bloodtaking and Peacemaking: Feud, Law, and Society in Saga Iceland* (Chicago: University of Chicago Press, 1990); E. E. Evans-Pritchard, *The Nuer* (Oxford: Oxford University Press, 1940); Artun Unsal, *Tuer pour survivre: La Vendetta* (Paris: Editions L'Harmattan, 1990).

count, group conflict thus emerges deterministically from the web of relations governing social life, even when the triggering event involves two individuals.

It is the literature concerning traditional feuding societies that most often invokes social organization as the key factor in group conflict, but variants of the argument also appear in research concerning contemporary Western societies, especially in connection with ethnic conflict, organized crime, and urban gang warfare.[10] Although the routinized mechanisms for conducting feuds that are thought to characterize stateless societies typically do not exist in urban industrial settings, the social relations that tie people to their groups are nevertheless seen to make most conflicts collective, at least in principle.

The three kinds of accounts are not really rival theories because they are not mutually incompatible: Each could be capturing some aspect of group conflict. So it is best to see them as emphasizing three distinct factors—group interest, group identity, and social organization—that together make social life, and thus the conflicts that pervade it, collective. When all three factors are present, we should expect most disputes that cross group boundaries, including those that begin within dyads, to become group conflicts. Thus it should be considered surprising, from the standpoint of extant perspectives on social conflict, if individual disputes typically failed to escalate to the group level in social contexts where collectivism predominates.

Yet there is a good a priori reason to think that most conflicts, even in collectivist societies, will not become group conflicts. If it were true that people in such contexts had little choice about whether to see any given dispute as collective, the slightest altercation between any two persons from distinct groups would lead to a potentially devastating group war. This threat would presumably make violent disputes rare: If group interests thoroughly dominated social life, minor dyadic conflict would usually escalate to mutually disastrous collective conflict,

10. Diego Gambetta, "Mafia: The Price of Distrust," pp. 158–75 in Gambetta, ed., *Trust: The Making and Breaking of Cooperative Relations* (New York: Basil Blackwell, 1988); Diego Gambetta, *The Sicilian Mafia* (Cambridge: Harvard University Press, 1993); Martin S. Jankowski, *Islands in the Street: Gangs and American Urban Society* (Berkeley: University of California Press, 1991); Philippe Bourgois, *In Search of Respect: Selling Crack in El Barrio* (Berkeley: University of California Press, 1995).

and for this very reason people would avoid conflict even more assiduously than they do in individualistic societies. However, the existing evidence overwhelmingly suggests that there is more rather than less interpersonal violence in societies inhabited by self-protecting corporate groups[11]. Either people in such societies are remarkably and self-destructively imprudent, or collectivism is less than complete.

The most straightforward solution to this theoretical puzzle lies in recognizing that group solidarity is imperfect: Even when members of a lineage, tribe, or ethnic group have interests in common, customs that distinguish them symbolically from other groups, and social ties rooted in kinship or residence, they may also have individual interests that set them apart from fellow group members. The tension between group and individual welfare will be starkest when solidarity entails risking one's life for the group: All members will benefit if the group acts collectively in defense of its shared interests, but even moderately sensible members might hesitate before joining a possibly fatal fray. Given that disputants know this, expressions of group solidarity in the midst of a conflict may help avert escalation, but only if people are convinced that the expressions are sincere.

The following, then, summarizes the argument I shall defend in the present chapter. Individuals benefit from group life in part because membership offers protection against predation (along with more peaceable advantages, including affection and economic risk-spreading). Protection against the predatory actions of outsiders, however, is only as good as the perceived solidarity of the group, and the perception is contingent on solidary behavior. Expressions of support for one member by fellow group members will convince an outsider not to act aggressively against the threatened member to the extent that the support is seen as sincere: If members of a kinship group support each other in verbal disputes with others but consistently fail to sustain this support when disputes escalate to physical or lethal force, then their verbal behavior will not dissuade adversaries from escalating. Unless groups have a reputation for following through on solidarity ex-

---

11. See, e.g., Donald Black, *The Social Structure of Right and Wrong* (San Diego: Academic, 1993); Napoleon Chagnon, *Yanomamo: The Fierce People* (New York: Holt, Rinehart and Winston, 1983); Keith Otterbein, *Feuding and Warfare: Selected Works of Keith F. Otterbein* (London: Routledge, 1994).

pressed prior to violent conflict, such expressions of solidarity constitute "cheap talk" and will not convey information about what will happen after escalation.

My argument has four testable implications. First, among disputes that escalate to violence, collaborative use of violence should be
associated with expressions of unity prior to the first occurrence of violence. When group members act collectively in the early stage of a dispute, they communicate to their adversary their willingness to act collectively at the next, more dangerous stage. If escalation to violence
occurs anyway, group action at this stage should be more likely than in
cases where conflict at the first stage is purely dyadic: The pre-violence
assertion of group loyalty, combined with the failure of this assertion
to forestall escalation, places the group's reputation for solidarity at
stake. Conversely, disputes involving only two individuals before escalation should be more likely to remain dyadic once violence occurs because associates of the two disputants have implicitly declined to treat
the conflict as collective. In short, among disputes that eventually turn
violent, group action prior to violence should be positively correlated
with group participation in violence.

Second, and more notably, group contention prior to escalation
will also be associated with a higher likelihood that violence will include previously uninvolved associates of the disputants. If group action early in a dispute is a promise to act in concert if the situation
worsens, escalation of conflict places pressure on all available group
members—not only those who have already acted—to live up to the
promise. Therefore, when group contention has made an issue of reputations for solidarity, previously uninvolved kin should become involved in violence at a higher rate than when pre-violence contention
has remained dyadic. In other words, the inclusion of nondisputants
in violent conflict is not an automatic consequence of escalation but a
contingent response to group contention in the pre-violence stage.

Third, both types of collective violence should be most likely in
situations where group reputations for solidarity matter the most. If
one reason kin groups act collectively in conflicts is that doing so en-
hances the value of expressions of solidarity in future encounters, collaborative violence should occur most often between disputants with a
high likelihood of future interaction. Consequently, group violence
should be particularly likely when participants in opposing sides of a

conflict are already acquainted and thus have reason to believe they will interact again in the future.

Fourth, group participation in violence should be more rare when the boundaries between opposing sides in the conflict are less clear-cut. In particular, in societies organized principally by kinship, conflict pitting kin against one another should escalate less often to group violence, net of other factors, than conflicts in which the opposing sides have no kin connections. When a dispute divides two members of one family or clan, the potential allies of one party are also potential allies of the other, so any demonstration of solidarity with one side is offset by a commensurate show of distance from the other. Collective violence in conflicts among kin therefore conveys no information about overall group solidarity, and accordingly should occur less often in such conflicts than in conflicts between nonkin.

A Systematic Analysis of Corsican Violence

Chapter 3 has already introduced a handful of unhappy Corsican stories, but a bit more background seems worthwhile. Corsica is an island in the Mediterranean that, although neighbor to Sardinia, has been part of France almost continuously since its cession by Genoa in the late eighteenth century. Near the turn of the nineteenth century it became a department, the basic political unit of the nation since the revolution of 1789, with representation in the National Assembly and the same local political institutions as other departments. Linguistically, Corsica is closer to Italy than to France (the Corsican language is a dialect of Italian, although most inhabitants now mainly speak French). As with other Mediterranean islands, the economy has always been principally agrarian and pastoral, with tourism playing an increasingly important role beginning in the late twentieth century.

Nineteenth-century Corsica offers a valuable lens on group conflict because it fit the profile of what many anthropologists would call an "honor society."[12] Family attachments governed most aspects

12. See, e.g., John King Campbell, *Honour, Family, and Patronage;* Jean G. Peristiany, *Honor and Shame: The Values of Mediterranean Society* (Chicago: University of Chicago Press, 1966); J. Pitt-Rivers, *The Fate of Shechem, or the Politics of Sex* (Cambridge: Cambridge University Press, 1977); Jane Schneider, "Of Vigilance and Virgins: Honor, Shame, and Access to Resources in Mediterranean Societies," *Ethnology* 10 (1971): 1–24; Janet Abu-Lughod, *Rabat:*

of social life, and group prestige depended on the chastity of female members, in part because of its implications for building coalitions through marriage. Along with female chastity, group honor depended on male members' reputation for the capacity to defend the group's interests using violence.[13] Though now used in numerous languages, the word "vendetta" was originally Corsican.

The honor tradition, combined with the fact that most Corsican men bore both firearms and knives as a matter of course, produced an exceptional amount of violence throughout the 1800s. The annual homicide rate ranged from 17 to 80 per 100,000 inhabitants during this period, whereas for France as a whole the rate was consistently less than 1 per 100,000; in comparison, most contemporary Western societies experience homicide rates under 2 per 100,000; the largest U.S. cities have rates ranging roughly from 10 to 60 per 100,000 (U.S. Bureau of the Census 1996).

The disputes featured in the data are typical of those leading to homicidal violence anywhere, though tinged with the character of a pastoral-agrarian society in which honor plays a key role: Corsicans of the period killed one another because of card games, insults, property damage, boundary disputes, and verbal insults, but also, about 10 percent of the time, in revenge for past killings and, another 10 percent of the time, because of refusals to marry a "compromised" woman.

We can think of group conflict as having two distinct dimensions, both of which give violence or other kinds of struggles a collective character. One dimension is collaboration. When two or more people cooperate in a conflict with some third party, they have demonstrated their solidarity at least with respect to the incident in question. Collaboration in conflict can occur before matters escalate to the point of lethal violence, it can characterize the use of violence itself, or both (or neither). The implication of my thesis concerning the communicative

---

Urban Apartheid in Morocco (Princeton: Princeton University Press, 1980); David D. Gilmore, "Honor, Honesty, Shame: Male Status in Contemporary Andalusia," pp. 90–103 in Gilmore, ed., *Honor and Shame and the Unity of the Mediterranean* (Washington, D.C.: American Anthropological Association, 1987).

13. See, e.g., J. B. Marcaggi, *Fleuve de sang: Histoire d'une vendetta* (N.p.: Ajaccio Piazzola, 1993); Xavier Versini, *La vie quotidienne en Corse au temps de Mâerimâee* (Paris: Hachette, 1964); Francis Pomponi, *Histoire de la Corse* (Paris: Hachette, 1979); Stephen K. Wilson, *Feuding, Conflict, and Banditry in Nineteenth-Century Corsica* (Cambridge: Cambridge University Press, 1988).

intent of acts of solidarity is that, if a dispute becomes lethal, the violence is more likely to be collaborative when group contention of some kind has already occurred. If, on the other hand, contention has an exclusively one-on-one or dyadic character, then violence (if it occurs) should also be dyadic.

The second way in which conflict can have a group character involves *generalization* to nondisputants, that is, expansion of conflict to include people who have not actively taken a side but who are connected in some way to one of the parties. Generalized conflict, violent or otherwise, is rampant in struggles between large collectivities such as ethnic or racial groups. For instance, racial violence in the United States has frequently involved attacks on an available but uninvolved black person in "reprisal" for prior aggression against a white or attacks on a randomly selected white person in "reprisal" for injustices committed against blacks. Naturally, examples extend, in the United States and elsewhere, to almost any ethnic or sectarian boundary that has been the locus of group animosity. Attacks of this kind, directed against people whose only offense is membership in a group, are usually seen as thoughtless and essentially automatic expressions of rage. But they are in fact neither automatic nor incomprehensible, as I shall show in the case of revenge: They occur disproportionately when the precipitating event itself has a group character, lending plausibility to the idea of collective responsibility that generalization to nondisputants expresses.

In the cases of violence I examine here, "generalized violence" means that the incident included at least one person, either as a user or as a target of violence, who had not previously taken any action, verbal or physical, in the dispute. "Restricted violence" describes the logical alternative: incidents in which all users and targets of lethal force were already implicated at the time the dispute escalated to violence. Incorporating generalized conflict into this analysis permits a more stringent test of my argument because the only relevance a previously uninvolved person has is that he or she is tied to one of the disputants; by definition, the former has taken no action that might invite violence or indicate an intention to participate in it. Inclusion of nondisputants in violence is thus a stark indication that what may have begun as a dyadic conflict has become a group conflict in the eyes of at least one person. This outcome suggests that violence has a group character, then, not in the sense of action by multiple persons but rather in the sense of generalization of violence to include new members of a disputant's kin group. Naturally, it is logically possible, given the two definitions, for generalization to occur independent of whether collaborative violence occurs; empirically, however, the two phenomena are positively associated, reinforcing their interpretation as alternate measures of the collective nature of violence.

To lend these concepts some concreteness, consider the killing of Simon-Francesco Pasqualini in the village of Sorba Ocagana in July 1852. Giambattista Croce had purchased from Giulio Francesco Pasqualini the right to cultivate a section of the latter's property, called Filetto. On July 13, Pasqualini discovered that Croce was grazing one of his sheep on a portion of Filetto that he had not rented and instructed him to remove the animal. Croce refused, and Pasqualini stormed off, saying that he would go to court to recover the damages to his property.

A few hours later, Pasqualini's son, Simon-Francesco, arrived at Filetto and demanded that Croce respect his father's property rights. The two men nearly came to blows but were separated and deprived of their rifles by a number of men who had been drawn to the scene by the shouting. At that moment, Giambattista Croce's cousin, Anton-Francesco, ran up, seized one of the confiscated firearms, and aimed it at the younger Pasqualini, who was himself holding a small scythe. The bystanders intervened and again separated the two men, but just as matters seemed to have eased, Simon-Francesco Pasqualini walked back to the scene of the dispute, still holding his scythe, and was shot down by Anton-Francesco. He died a week later.[14]

In this dispute, escalation occurred when Anton-Francesco Croce arrived and aimed his cousin's rifle at Pasqualini. Inasmuch as Anton-Francesco had not been a disputant until that moment, his violent action on reaching the scene amounted to a generalization of the conflict. On the other hand, Pasqualini's actions up to that time had constituted collaborative contention: He was defending his father's interest in the land, not his own. It appears that Anton-Francesco's bold entry into the fray had at least something to do with the fact that his cousin had already been confronted by two Pasqualinis, one after the other. The Pasqualinis' cooperation during the nonlethal stage of the

14. Cour d'Assises de Bastia, 4th trimester, session of November 12, 1852.

Table 8 Association of Collaborative Violence with Prior Group Contention

Contention Prior to Onset of Violence	One-on-One Violence (%)	Collaborative Violence (%)	Total (%)
One-on-one contention	90.2	9.8	100.0
	(92)	(10)	(102)
Group contention	63.9	36.1	100.0
	(76)	(43)	(119)
Total	76.0	24.0	100.0
	(168)	(53)	(221)

Note: Figures in parentheses are base Ns for the adjacent percentages. "One-on-one" violence means that one individual attacked at least one other person, and at most two individuals used lethal force against each other. "Collaborative" violence means that multiple individuals attacked at least one other person.

Chi-squared = 20.89, d.f. = 1; $p < .001$

conflict made it into a group affair, putting implicit pressure on Croce to stand up for his cousin—although not necessarily, of course, to use lethal force in doing so.

This anecdote is, however, an anecdote—and my imputation of a connection between the Pasqualinis' collaboration on one side and the sudden intervention of a cousin on the other is, though plausible, hardly the only viable interpretation. Stronger evidence comes in the form of systematic patterns across all 221 incidents in the Corsican data. In the first place, only about one-quarter of all incidents involved collaborative violence—despite the popular (and scholarly) perception of Corsica and other Mediterranean honor societies as places governed by the "all for one and one for all" dictum. Most of the time, when deadly violence was afoot, Corsicans followed the principle of "one for one" instead. Moreover, in the moments *before* violence began, group contention occurred only slightly more than half of the time (that is, in 119 of 221 disputes). Group conflict was certainly not automatic at the pre-violence stage and was even less so after escalation. This pattern suggests at least two things: that the threat of collective violence (which is what I am suggesting group contention is) was not made lightly and that the disputants who made such threats only made good on them about half the time. Evidently Corsican disputants expressed solidarity in deadly matters more easily than they achieved it, even in a setting notorious for family feuds.

Those are univariate patterns, but these data contain important

Table 9 Association of Generalized Violence with Prior Group Contention

Contention prior to Onset of Violence	Restricted Violence (%)	Generalized Violence (%)	Total (%)
One-on-one contention	82.4	17.6	100.0
	(84)	(18)	(102)
Group contention	60.5	39.5	100.0
	(72)	(47)	(119)
Total	70.6	29.4	100.1
	(156)	(65)	(221)

Note: Figures in parentheses are base *N*s for the adjacent percentages. "Restricted violence" refers to incidents in which all users and targets of lethal force had already participated in contention prior to violence; "generalized" violence means that at least one person who had not participated in contention became either a user or target of lethal force.

Chi-squared = 12.63, d.f. = 1; $p < .001$

and relevant bivariate associations, too. As table 8 indicates, violence was more than three times more likely to be collaborative in incidents involving group contention: Collaborative use of violence occurred in more than one-third of disputes in which group contention occurred prior to escalation, compared with one in ten for disputes that involved only dyadic contention. Even if acts of solidarity prior to escalation were not a guarantee that violence itself would be collective, they clearly made collaboration in violence more likely.

Nearly the same story can be told about generalized violence. Again, as table 9 indicates, only in a minority of incidents—about 30 percent—was a nondisputant pulled into the violence. And again, this was significantly more likely to occur if some display of solidarity had taken place prior to escalation. This finding is a good deal more striking than the previous one, inasmuch as it cannot be explained as a matter of continuity in disputes. If two family members have stood together in an argument or in a shoving match, it might seem natural (although, as the data show, not automatic) for both to participate in the next, more violent, phase. But this argument cannot be made about the pattern in table 9. By construction, at least one group member involved in any case of generalized violence had taken no part in the dispute prior to that point. It would be difficult to find a purer example of the activation of group identities in conflict.

It is plain that group violence was the exception rather than the rule, even in one of the settings most closely associated with collective,

clan-based conflict. My explanation of this fact is, though counterintu-
itive, quite straightforward. Despite the advantages accruing to unified
collectivities, social groups cannot always achieve true solidarity. As a
result, displays of solidarity in the effort to intimidate an adversary do
not always work: Knowing that their rivals' unity may melt away as
danger mounts, adversaries are not always sufficiently intimidated,
making escalation the likely outcome. Disputants who have made representations of unity must now show that those representations were
genuine, with the consequence that violence is more likely to be collective when contention prior to escalation has included expressions
of solidarity. Solidarity displays do discourage escalation some of
the time, but at the price of deadlier group violence when such displays have failed as a deterrent. In short, it is because group solidarity
is weak, not because it is strong, that escalation to collective violence
occurs.

Revenge

Honor societies are renowned not only for the group violence to which
disputes often lead—albeit less frequently than is typically believed, as
I have shown—but also for the practice of blood revenge. As with collective conflict, institutionalized revenge-seeking in Mediterranean
and other feuding societies has frequently been explained as a culturally determined pattern: something that people in such settings do because they are taught by tradition that they are obligated to do it, that
others expect them to do it, and furthermore that they should expect
the same of others. In what might be called the cultural account of the
honor and revenge complex, the obligation to kill someone who is implicated in a prior act of aggression is a matter of social convention. It
is prescribed because dominant norms for understanding right and
wrong say it is—much as North American norms prescribe whistling
as a way to express approval for a public performance, whereas elsewhere it is a way of expressing scorn.

  There is a circularity in pure cultural accounts that is best avoided:
If we say that people do something because that is what people in their
culture do, we are in nearly the same pickle as the zoologist who says
that cheetahs eat meat because they are carnivores. It is true that cultural frameworks in societies in which revenge is institutionalized

lend legitimacy to the practice, but that does not tell us why revenge crops up so often as a legitimate response to aggression in stateless societies. As in the matter of group dominance, there has to be something outside of mere social convention that lends revenge both its stability in a given social context and its recurrent emergence across contexts, notably in arid, pastoral societies without centralized state authorities.

Social scientists interested in *explaining* the practice, as opposed to documenting or describing it, have most often seen it as a form of dispute resolution—a tool for settling conflicts in situations lacking a formalized, third-party justice system.[15] It is now commonly argued that the threat of revenge is a functional alternative to the threat of third-party punishment; according to this view, social groups, usually families of some kind, can deter rival groups from acts of aggression against their members by making it clear that the kin of someone killed during a dispute will punish the offender and possibly others in the offender's group. Even when blood payments are an accepted means of compensating kin of the deceased, the threat of violent revenge is present as a guarantee.[16] So far as this specific point is concerned, it is not necessary to choose between rationalist explanations, in which social actors more or less consciously converge on a system for managing conflict, and functionalist explanations, in which (to put it crudely) the social order as a whole selects a dispute-resolution mechanism that will contribute to its own stability. Regardless of the genesis of blood revenge as a practice, the expectation that it will follow a deadly attack deters aggression.

It is helpful, then, to see vendetta—violent retaliation for the death of a family member—as an extension of intergroup conflict along the lines I described in the previous section, and notably as a tactic for dis-

---

15. Allow me, on analytical grounds, to disregard the anachronism implied here: Although it is surely the case that revenge as a dispute-resolution technique predated formalized justice systems in most parts of the world, it has typically been the case that people operating with the former have ultimately, if reluctantly, seen the benefits of the latter. Revenge-based dispute resolution also routinely reemerges when states collapse. In that regard it is not unreasonable to see revenge-seeking as a response to the "absence" of courts, even in places where courts have never existed.

16. Black-Michaud, *Cohesive Force*; Boehm, *Blood Revenge*; Russell Hardin, *One for All: The Logic of Group Conflict* (Princeton: Princeton University Press, 1995); Hasluck, *Unwritten Law*; Miller, *Bloodtaking*.

playing solidarity when group cohesion is in doubt. If collaborative and generalized violence are means by which disputants demonstrate group solidarity in the course of conflict, retaliation for past aggression does the same thing after the fact. Vengeance is a way to express solidarity with the victim of past aggression, and the likelihood of its occurrence deters anyone who might hope to do away with a rival. Although this sort of solidarity display is perhaps made particularly poignant by the fact that the victim is in most cases not present to witness it, this fact only identifies more clearly who the intended audience is: first, the victim's adversaries; second, surviving kin who sense that their reputation as a cohesive group has been impugned; and third, any currently neutral parties who might harbor doubt regarding the unity of the victim's kin group.

Hence the close connection between "family honor" and the ability of a kin group to exact vengeance for the killing of one of its members. In any feuding society, from highland New Guinea to Montenegro, families that have not at least attempted to avenge a deceased member are seen as weak, dishonored, and worthy of scorn rather than respect. In both cultural and social organization accounts of honor, the link between dishonor and failure to pursue vengeance is a matter of convention: When a victim's sons or brothers decline to retaliate against the offender or someone connected to the offender, they are dishonored for the simple reason that they have failed to do what honor demands.

I contend that the link between revenge and group honor is more fundamental than mere convention. It results from the necessary association between group honor and group unity—the requirement that groups act collectively if they are to be socially real—and from the fact that vendetta is one of the strongest indicators of unity. Only a truly cohesive family group can push one of its members to risk death or imprisonment to avenge the killing of a relative. Revenge and honor are therefore connected by the fact that displays of solidarity, in the form of individual sacrifices for group welfare, are key determinants of dominance relations among groups.

If vendettas are displays of group unity, then it should be possible to observe patterns analogous to those I described above in connection with collective violence. In particular, retaliation should not be an automatic response to aggression, but rather should occur when the issue of group unity has become salient. So, just as collective violence turned out to be specifically associated with group contention, vengeance should in turn be associated with collective violence: When a violent attack makes group identity salient, the victim's kin group will be particularly likely to seek revenge—either to demonstrate that their solidarity equals that of the offending group or to sanction the offender's decision to escalate to the group level (for instance, by attacking a nondisputant) of a conflict that could have remained dyadic. Even in the latter case, retaliation constitutes a reply to the implicit contention that the original aggressor's group is more unified than that of the victim. Whenever a particular kind of violence is expected to invite a collective reply, the very fact of its occurrence expresses an expectation on the part of the assailants that the victim's kin will fail to respond as a group.

Again, a systematic examination of the circumstances under which nineteenth-century Corsicans sought revenge offers a critical test of my argument. In the first place, even in the society that provided European languages with the very term "vendetta," retaliatory violence was the exception rather than the rule: Of 165 lethal attacks appearing in court documents from 1851 to 1852, only 16, or 10 percent, led to a revenge attack in the ensuing fifteen years. (And, contrary to the popular notion, applied to Corsica as well as other societies, that feuds last for generations, most of the 16 revenge attacks occurred within a few months of the precipitating incident.) As with collective violence, vengeance was far from the automatic response to aggression that conventional descriptions of honor societies lead one to expect.

More important, incidents that provoked revenge attacks were systematically different from those that did not. Table 10 describes the extent to which various features of violent incidents affected the odds that a vendetta attack would follow. For example, the first row shows that the odds of a revenge attack roughly doubled with each additional participant in the original attack.[17]

Two factors contributed significantly to the likelihood of revenge: collaborative violence in the form of multiple assailants in the original incident, and generalized violence in the form of violence directed against a nondisputant. The impact of generalized violence was greater

17. These ratios are based on a logistic regression analysis of vendetta occurrence on incident characteristics. The full analysis appears in the appendix to this chapter.

Table 10 Aspects of Violent Incidents Leading to Vendettas

If incident involved . . .	. . . then odds of retaliation were multiplied by
An additional assailant	1.9*
(2 vs. 1, 3 vs. 2)	
Attack on a nondisputant	6.0*
Irregular trial	1.7
Kinship tie among disputants	1.2
Revenge for an earlier attack	1.6
Political conflict	6.4

Note: A ratio of 1.0 would indicate no impact on the odds of a vendetta. See appendix for full analysis.

*Statistically significant at $p < .05$

than that of collaborative violence: As table 10 shows, the odds of a vendetta were roughly six times greater, all else equal, when assailants in the original incident directed lethal force against someone who was related to a disputant but who had not taken part in the conflict. Other characteristics of violent incidents—notably whether the incident involved political conflict, revenge for an earlier attack, or efforts by an offender's family to influence the trial outcome—may also have contributed to the likelihood of revenge, as the odds ratios in table 10 indicate. Interestingly, these features are also interpretable as indicators of the collective character of conflict, but their estimated association with retaliation is not, in these data, statistically distinguishable from no association (see the appendix to this chapter for further details). The essential result is that vendettas were most likely carried out in response to violence with a group character.

Hand in hand with blood revenge, the theme of collective responsibility (to which I alluded earlier) runs through anthropological and historical descriptions of honor societies. It is often written that, in feuding contexts, enmity resulting from an act of aggression automatically extends beyond the offender to his entire kin group. Ethnographers writing about feuding in societies with segmentary kinship systems commonly claim that any member of an offender's lineage can become a target, aside from members excluded on the basis of an ascriptive trait such as sex or age. Ernest Gellner cites Berber tradition as holding that "if homicide takes place, the *ten* closest agnates [of the offender] are immediately at risk, because they are equally 'culpable'" (emphasis in original).[18] Reporting on feuds in Montenegro, Christopher Boehm asserts that "it was perfectly all right to kill the killer, his brother, or his father, or, if he had no father, then his son or some other male kinsman."[19] Napoleon Chagnon suggests that when the Yanomami conduct a revenge raid, they are likely to kill anyone from the offender's community, which is coextensive with a kin group.[20] Statements of this kind abound in the literature about feuding, although it is important to bear in mind that they almost always refer to what custom dictates, not to actual events.[21]

As with collective violence, the standard explanation for this supposed promiscuity in the way enmity is distributed is that, in such societies, groups take precedence over individuals as the repository of responsibility. People don't kill people; clans do. Inasmuch as the evidence from Corsica casts doubt on the idea that group violence is a necessary feature of conflict in "collectivist" societies, it should not be too surprising to find reasons to doubt the "group responsibility" idea as well. To be sure, Corsica is only one place, but, in the absence of systematic data on other places, it is a pretty good start.

Between 1840 and 1865, a total of fifty-nine vendetta attacks in Corsica left a documentary trace in the court records.[22] For fifty-eight

18. Ernest Gellner, "Trust, Cohesion, and the Social Order," pp. 142–57 in Diego Gambetta, ed., *Trust: Making and Breaking Cooperative Relations* (New York: Blackwell, 1988), p. 146.

19. Boehm, *Blood Revenge*, p. 58.

20. Chagnon, *Yanomamo.*

21. See Sally F. Moore, "Legal Liability and Evolutionary Interpretation: Some Aspects of Strict Liability, Self-Help and Collective Responsibility," pp. 51–108, and Rafael Karsten, "Blood Revenge and War Among the Jibaro Indians of Eastern Ecuador," pp. 303–26 in Max Gluckman, ed., *The Allocation of Responsibility* (Manchester: Manchester University Press, 1972); Hasluck, *Unwritten Law,* states that vengeance norms in some Albanian villages permitted the killing of any kinsman of a murderer, though only for a fixed period during which the avenger's blood was considered to be still "boiling." Karsten argues that Jibaro Indians take revenge on kin of an offender because "the individual forms an inseparable part of the whole; the members of the family are regarded as, so to speak, organically coherent with each other, so that one part stands for all and all for one" (p. 311). In *Albion's Seed: Four British Folkways in America* (New York: Oxford University Press, 1989), David H. Fischer, writing about the Appalachian region and the British isles, places great weight on the cultural legacy of "clan loyalty" in describing both the impact of dishonor and the burden of responsibility.

22. This number is considerably larger than the sixteen reported earlier, in part because it covers a broader period. In addition, the analysis of vendetta occurrence imposed more stringent requirements on the data insofar as it necessitated information not only on acts of retaliation but also on details of the precipitating incident.

Table 11 Kinship Structure of Corsican Vendettas

	Target's Tie to Offender			
Avenger's Tie to Victim	Ego	Nuclear Kin	Extended Kin	Total
Nuclear kin	**17**	**16**	3	36
	(47.2)	(44.4)	(8.3)	(62.1)
Extended kin	6	6	**10**	22
	(27.3)	(27.3)	(45.5)	(37.9)
Total	23	22	13	58
	(39.7)	(37.9)	(22.4)	(100.0)

Note: Percentages are in parentheses. Values exceeding chance levels are shown in boldface. For avenger relations, incidents in which all avengers were nuclear kin (including spouse) of the victim are classified as nuclear; those in which at least one relative outside the nuclear family participated are coded as "extended." The same criterion was used to classify vengeance targets. Chi-squared = 10.83, d.f. = 2; $p < .01$

of these, it is possible to identify the relation between avengers and the relatives they avenged, on one hand, and the relation between vendetta targets and the offenders in the original attack, on the other. Let us call the latter relation "ego" when the vendetta target was one of the original assailants, that is, when vengeance explicitly invoked the principle of individual responsibility. As the summary in table 11 shows, nineteenth-century Corsicans did not have all that much difficulty telling the difference between people who had killed their relatives and the relatives of those people. In 40 percent of these vendettas, avengers attacked the offender himself. (This should be "herself" in one instance. Lilla Lanfranchi shot her lover, Pietro Paolo DeSanti, because he reneged on his promise of marriage, and following her acquittal at trial was killed by the dead man's brother.) Considering the number of offenders who were in custody or in hiding (responding, obviously, to their status as primary targets for revenge), this figure reflects a strong bias on the part of avengers in favor of punishing people who had actually caused harm to their relatives.

At the same time, that leaves another 60 percent (thirty-five incidents) in which at least one of the vengeance targets was a relative of the original assailant or assailants. Note that, even here, the picture of collective responsibility has a distinctly radial rather than undifferentiated structure: Offenders' nuclear kin became targets for vengeance almost twice as often as more distant kin, despite the fact that the latter were by definition more numerous. Offenders were favored instead of their relatives as vengeance targets, and close relatives were favored rather than more distant ones.

It turns out that even these cases of what we might call "generalized vengeance," following the terminology introduced above, are not so easily interpreted as instances of collective responsibility—or at any rate, not in the ascriptive sense of guilt by mere kinship. Very often, when offenders' kin fell victim to vendettas, they were, though not directly guilty of violent acts, thoroughly implicated in the conflicts leading to violence or ensuing from it.

Consider the attack on Jacinto Battisti in 1850. Battisti commanded the Corsican *voltigeurs,* an army unit created to pursue bandits in the countryside.[23] His cousin, Dominico Dominici, had been arrested in 1847 for the murder of Pietro Paolo Vittini and sentenced to forced labor for life. Remarkably, the verdict was overturned by a superior court in Marseille, and Dominici was released. Three years later, Battisti was traveling in the countryside between the towns of Piazza and Santa Lucia when someone fired a rifle shot that passed close by one of his ears. Family members traveling with him said they spotted Giacomo-Felici Giocondi of Santa Lucia fleeing the scene.[24]

Giocondi was the cousin of Vittini, the man whose killing in 1847 had gone unpunished. So, in this vendetta, Giocondi sought revenge against the cousin of his cousin's killer. Despite appearances, however, this was no case of collective responsibility. Vittini's family blamed Battisti for having used his position and social connections to influence the court to acquit Dominici on appeal. In their eyes, he was therefore as much a collaborator in the killing of Pietro Paolo Vittini as if he had participated directly in the murder. Not that they were above such tactics themselves: Giocondi was himself acquitted, according to the reporting magistrate, as a result of assiduous lobbying of the jury on the part of the defendant's family. But, as is typical in feuds, actions that would be justified if undertaken by one's own side are crimes when committed by the other.

23. "Bandits," in this period, were not professional criminals but rather fugitives living in the hinterland, often with the help of relatives. Many of them were called *bandits d'honneur,* meaning that they were being pursued for a vengeance killing.

24. Cour d'Assises de Bastia, 1st trimester 1851, session 10.

In addition to revealing some subtleties in the way the French court system intertwined with Corsica's indigenous feuding practices, this case illustrates the danger in attributing generalized vengeance to an abstract conception of collective responsibility. In dozens of revenge cases, vendetta victims were much more than relatives of the offender: They were active participants in the offense, if not in its actual commission then in a variety of substantive acts of solidarity after the fact. One man was shot because he invited his son-in-law to live in his home after the latter's acquittal for murder, another because he regularly took food and water to a cousin who was evading arrest and retaliation by hiding in the mountains. Diana Peraldi of Corra was shot by Ignazio Piazza shortly after her brother had shot down Piazza's brother during a dispute about water rights. Both were rushing to the scene of the attack, Ignazio armed with a rifle. As Ignazio rushed past Diana, she unleashed a string of insults, calling him, among other things, a "coward." Already enraged by the attack on his brother, Ignazio turned in response to these words of provocation and shot Diana, mortally wounding her.

Admittedly, Diana Peraldi's display of solidarity with her brother was symbolic rather than substantive. Indeed, her own family saw her killing as an unnecessary generalization of conflict and later sought revenge. Nevertheless, in all of these cases the choice of revenge target was distinctly driven by behavior, not merely by a social convention assigning guilt to the entire set of offenders' kin. Retaliation was, as we saw earlier, spurred by attacks that made group membership salient. When vengeance was not visited on offenders themselves, it was also, it appears, directed particularly against group members who had closed ranks around the offenders. Vendettas therefore sanctioned collective action in two distinct ways: first, by punishing group violence itself, and second, by punishing displays of solidarity with offenders after the fact. Ironically, then, revenge served a purpose for contending families that was essentially the reverse of the role traditionally ascribed to it. Far from expressing the fundamentally collective character of life in honor societies, vengeance was a tool for *preventing* conflicts from becoming needlessly and dangerously collective. Knowing that they were subject to punishment if they extended help, kin of would-be aggressors had good reason to discourage violent acts, and kin of offenders had good reason to distance themselves from acts already committed.

The kinship structure of revenge drives this point home. As table 11 reveals, vendettas involving extended kin as avengers were disproportionately likely to involve extended kin of offenders as targets. When those seeking revenge were fathers, sons, or siblings of the original victim, the target of revenge was either the offender or his nuclear kin more than 90 percent of the time. But extended kin of the offender were targets in nearly half of the vendettas in which extended kin of the original victim participated. There was, in short, a close association between the kinds of kin ties invoked in the choice of vendetta target and the ties linking avengers to those avenged. The obvious inference is that aggrieved families mobilized kin for revenge in a way that displayed equivalent levels of solidarity to that displayed by offenders' families. The solidarity displayed in vendettas was calibrated to match the extent of cohesiveness already displayed by aggressors. It is not hard to see why. Any family failing to mobilize in response to collective action against itself would not only have failed to punish group-level aggression; it would, furthermore, have implicitly acknowledged the superior "groupness," and hence superior social rank, of its rivals.

It is conventional to explain collective conflict in terms of the existence of well-defined, solidary social groups. The idea is that human beings, organized into groups with a common interests—families, communities, ethnicities, and so forth—confront other groups whose interests compete with theirs. Or, leaving aside interests, it is often argued that cultural difference alone is enough to make groups into rivals.

There may indeed be some truth to the conventional view. Surely if social life were largely individualistic, with little higher-order organization of people into collectivities and hence no basis on which groups could consistently act collectively (either for private purposes or to combat other groups), group conflict would be a rare occurrence. Allegiances would shift along with motivations and opportunities, making it difficult to talk about groups at all. To borrow a concept from the study of organizations, collective action of any sort would involve spot contracts rather than identifiable "firms"—and, more important, would not happen terribly often.

This chapter has been dedicated to making the point that the same should hold for the other end of the individualism-collectivism scale— and that, by implication, most social life is not lived at either end. In a world made of highly cohesive, well-defined and disciplined collectivities, groups competing for wealth, land, or overall dominance would be able to size each other up in advance of outright conflict and work out accommodations that spared everyone the cost of violent resolution. To do this, however, rival groups would have to have accepted representatives who, moreover, would have to credibly promise their constituents' compliance with any agreement worked out in negotiation. It is for this latter reason that union discipline, for instance, is so crucial for labor negotiations: Unless union representatives can assure employers that the rank and file will adhere to an approved collective bargaining agreement, the parties have little reason to spend time working one out. The same goes for ethnic autonomy movements, relations between corporations and communities, and political factions.

In general, groups in competition face the fundamental problem that their unity is neither automatic nor easily gauged in advance of conflict. Musketeer pronouncements of the "all-for-one" kind are as readily falsified by behavior as they are issued by hopeful group members, and for this reason they are weak signals of a group's capacity to act together when it really matters. Sadly, as I have shown, it is the shakiness of social groups that pushes them into violent struggles with one another, as each side gambles that the other side's representations of solidarity will turn out to be hollow. On the other side of this coin, groups in contention try mightily to offer credible signals of their unity. At the beginning of the twenty-first century, suicide attacks have become the hallmark, in several parts of the world, of challenges to modern Western authorities and institutions. Other, less extreme forms of self-denial for a cause have long been used to signal unity, and of course the presentation of uniformity in dress and action is familiar to both armies and street gangs. Such maneuvers are more than expedient, efficient, or frightening to opponents. They are also tactics for displaying solidarity—the basic yet elusive ingredient in collective action.

On both the group and the individual levels, then, ambiguity about relative standing sets up a volatile situation. Individuals are more likely to press forward in disputes when their social tie fails to provide cues about rank; for their part, groups insist on testing each other's pretensions to superior unity when it is unclear which side will hold together more firmly. On both levels, furthermore, patterns in conflict reveal the underappreciated centrality of form, in the sense of what people do in disputes, relative to content—what the disputes are ostensibly "about." In the previous chapter, I showed that people (particularly those in unranked social relations) can end up attacking one another if someone tries to establish rank with the right set of words. In this chapter, I showed that groups can end up attacking each other because someone attempts to establish rank with an act of solidarity. In neither case does the dispute have to be about anything "important"—unless, as I propose, we recognize that social rank, by itself, is one of the most important issues of all.

METHODOLOGICAL APPENDIX

Source of the Data

Information about violent conflict is drawn from the records of the Cour d'Assises (court of assizes) of Bastia, which handled all cases of murder, attempted murder, and manslaughter for the department of Corsica. Because the population of the island was well-defined, stable, and small (roughly 200,000), and because the central authorities were determined to suppress violence in a region they regarded as troublesome and backward,[25] almost all instances of violent conflict led to a criminal trial.

Because of confidentiality restrictions, the most recent year for which data are available is 1893. Full transcripts of the trials no longer exist, but elaborate summaries of each case are preserved by the Ministry of Justice. Each summary contains detailed information about the defendant or defendants, a narrative of the events leading up to the incident, including past conflicts between the involved parties, and the outcome of the case. Yearly caseloads varied roughly between thirty and one hundred throughout the nineteenth century; although most

---

25. See J. B. Marcaggi, *Fleuve de sang: Histoire d'une vendetta* (N.p.: Ajaccio Piazzola, 1993); Stephen K. Wilson, *Feuding, Conflict, and Banditry in Nineteenth-Century Corsica* (Cambridge: Cambridge University Press, 1988); Gabriel Xavier Culioli, *Le complexe corse* (Paris: Gallimard, 1990).

of the cases handled by the Bastia court pertained to murder or attempted murder, a few involved burglary and a very few involved rape. Only cases involving the use of potentially lethal force (a firearm, cutting instrument, and in one case a beating with a heavy rock) were included in this study. In addition to 1893, all cases from 1851–52 and from 1865 were selected from the archival inventory, furnishing data from a range of historical and political contexts. Every case involving lethal or potentially lethal violence from these three time intervals was included in the sample, regardless of whether the incident led to a fatality or injury. Twenty-eight cases were dropped because the summaries provided insufficient information or because there was some doubt about the details of the incident. The resulting data set includes a total of 221 violent incidents in all, with thirty-two cases from 1865 and fifteen cases from 1893.

Outcome (Dependent) Measures

The outcome of interest, namely, whether violence had a group or a dyadic character, has two dimensions, which I have termed collaborative violence and generalized violence. Any incident in which more than one person on one side of a dispute employed lethal force (fired a weapon, lunged at someone with a knife or sharp instrument, or wielded a heavy object at a person's head) was coded as an instance of collaborative violence. Violence was also considered collaborative when one person audibly encouraged another to use a weapon, furnished someone with a weapon that the latter then used, or arranged for a third party to attack an adversary. (Five cases involving the latter sort of activity—essentially a contract killing—appear in the data.) The rationale for including these more indirect forms of group action is that individuals who participate in this way have materially contributed to violence, and moreover in so doing have borne some of the risk both of counterviolence and prosecution. The measure is dichotomous, with a value of 1 indicating collaborative violence and 0 indicating dyadic violence.

As noted in the main text, incidents are coded as including "generalized" violence if a nondisputant—someone who, until the moment of escalation to violence, had not taken part in the conflict—used lethal force or became a target of violence. New targets are treated the same way as new actors in coding because disputants might have acted preemptively against a nondisputant if they anticipated that the latter was about to join in violence.

Independent Measures

The relevant independent measures for the analysis are (1) whether group contention occurred prior to the first use of lethal force, (2) whether disputants knew one another prior to the dispute, (3) whether there was a kin tie between opposing sides in the incident, and (4) whether disputants belonged to groups with a history of conflict or competition. The variables are constructed as follows.

Group Contention. Any behavior mentioned in the trial summary that occurred prior to the outbreak of violence and could clearly be construed as taking sides in a dispute was noted. If more than one person on one side of a dispute had engaged in such behavior at any point before the first use of violence, this was recorded as group contention. For example, in one case from 1852, two youths from the town of Bastelica were arguing about a cap one had taken from the other. The elder brothers of the two intervened on behalf of their respective relatives, leading ultimately to a stabbing of one by the other. This event was coded as involving group contention (multiple disputants on both sides) but dyadic violence (only one person employing lethal force).

Disputes were thus exhaustively classified as having involved (1) purely dyadic contention (one person on each side) prior to violence, (2) asymmetric group contention (multiple persons on one side against a single person on the other), or (3) symmetric group contention. Actions that qualified as taking sides include voicing an opinion in favor of one party, insulting someone, issuing a demand, threatening some future action, striking someone with a hand or stick, seizing contested property, and filing a legal complaint. Actions not coded as taking a side included attempting to calm someone down, restraining someone engaged in a fistfight, informing one person about the actions of another, or arranging for a meeting to resolve differences. (An interesting detail is that there are no instances in which a disputant was restrained by a male family member. It seems probable that physical intervention of this kind was too likely to be misinterpreted by the opposing side to be helpful in preventing escalation. A much less likely but still possible interpretation is that restraint by an immediate family member always forestalled violence, thereby selecting such cases out of the data.)

Prior Tie. Disputants were coded as knowing one another either if the trial summary made it clear that this was so or if they lived in the same village. Since most communities had populations of a few hundred, it would have been nearly impossible for residents of the same village not to be acquainted. For residents of different communities, the threshold for inferring a social tie was low: disputants were coded as knowing one another if they if they had had business dealings, had been drinking or gambling together at the time of the incident, if they were engaged in a sexual rivalry, or if the document mentioned past interactions of any sort. Any tie between any two individuals on opposite sides of a dispute sufficed to qualify the dispute as occurring between acquaintances.

Kin Tie Between Disputants. Disputants were coded as connected by kinship only if specific reference to a kin tie appeared in the trial summary. Shared surname was not sufficient to establish kinship, given the considerable number of villages in Corsica with only one or two family names. Initially, consanguineal relationships were distinguished from relationships by marriage (see Daly and Wilson's [1988] discussion of this issue), but these were collapsed when investigation consistently failed to reveal a difference in their associations with the dependent variables. By construction, when opposing sides were coded as tied by kinship, they could not be coded as unacquainted.

Diffuse Group Conflict. In Corsican communities, as in many other face-to-face settings, recurrent conflict between the same sets of people was common, and in many cases such conflict was institutionalized in the form of political factions.[26] Trial summaries contain fre-

26. See Antoine Albitreccia, *La Corse: Son évolution au XIXe siècle et au debut du XXe siècle* (Paris: Presses Universitaires de France, 1942); Xavier Versini, *La vie quotidienne en Corse au temps de Mâerimâee* (Paris: Hachette, 1964); Francis Pomponi, *Histoire de la Corse* (Paris: Hachette, 1979); Wilson, *Feuding, Conflict, and Banditry in Nineteenth-Century Corsica.*

quent references to a history of conflictual (though not necessarily violent) relations between kin groups or between a particular family and an individual with whom they were on bad terms. Since new disputes occurring against the background of group conflict would be more likely to escalate to group violence, this sort of diffuse group conflict was coded as an indicator variable. Associations between group contention and the two outcome variables are thus estimated net of a background situation favoring collaborative or generalized violence.

Controls

Vendetta. Twenty-six of the 221 incidents were vendettas, murders or attempted murders committed in retaliation for a past killing. The analyses include an indicator variable for such incidents because of the high likelihood that these incidents exhibit a different pattern from that of disputes in which violence occurs for the first time. In particular, use of violence by a previously uninvolved individual was quite common in vendettas (39 percent of vendettas, as contrasted with 22 percent of other incidents) because vengeance was by definition the responsibility of someone other than the slain person; in some cases, too, the original killer was in custody or hiding, so the target of vengeance was also new to the conflict.

Presence of Other Group Members. Collaborative and generalized violence were potentially more likely when two or more members of a kin group were physically present at the moment violence began, simply because multiple group members would be available, either as actors or as targets. The regression models initially included a term for the presence of multiple persons on one side of the dispute and another for group presence on both sides. Various specifications showed that group presence was associated with a higher likelihood of collaborative and generalized violence whether group presence was mutual or asymmetric, but principally in the former case; hence the models reported here control for group presence on both sides.

Female Disputant. In light of the centrality to Corsican society of male dominance within families and of sexual purity, disputes involving only men and disputes involving at least one woman are likely to differ in the degree to which group solidarity is activated. In particular, spousal violence (of which there are several cases in the data) is a strong a priori candidate for a more dyadic outcome. Analyses therefore include an indicator variable reflecting involvement of a woman as disputant, user of violence, or target of violence.

Intervention by Third Party. Not surprisingly, many incidents of violence occurred after bystanders tried to separate disputants or, in the case of more drawn-out conflicts, local notables attempted to work out a compromise. It is possible that intervention of this kind could reduce the likelihood of collaborative or generalized violence, if only because it occasionally delayed escalation and thus gave people an opportunity to disperse. An indicator variable was therefore constructed that reflects whether any third party intervened prior to the first use of violence.

Analyses

The following tables report multivariate analyses of the bivariate associations reported in the main body of the foregoing chapter.

Table A.1 Logistic Regression of Collaborative Violence on Pre-violence Conflict Pattern

Variable	Model 1	Model 2	Model 3	Model 4	Model 5	Model 6
Independent variables						
Group contention prior to violence	1.65** (.38)	1.66** (.38)	1.75** (.40)	1.57** (.40)	1.34** (.42)	1.36** (.42)
Kinship tie linking disputants		−.26 (.42)	−.18 (.43)	−.18 (.45)	−.15 (.46)	−.14 (.47)
No prior tie between disputants		−.49 (.51)	−.55 (.52)	−.24 (.53)	−.44 (.55)	−.41 (.55)
Female disputant			−.43 (.38)	−.38 (.39)	−.39 (.40)	−.47 (.41)
Diffuse group conflict prior to dispute				1.20* (.48)	1.03* (.50)	1.00* (.51)
Vendetta				−.21 (.61)	.03 (.62)	−.07 (.64)
Two groups physically present					1.15** (.44)	1.26** (.46)
Third-party intervention						−.50 (.44)
Year: 1865						.01 (.51)
Year: 1893						.20 (.79)
Constant	−2.22	−2.10	−2.05	−2.26	−2.31	−2.17
−2*log-likelihood	221.13	219.95	218.61	210.45	203.57	202.08
Improvement chi-square (d.f.)	22.36** (1)	23.54** (3)	24.87** (4)	33.03** (6)	39.92** (7)	41.40** (10)

Note: N = 221. Standard errors are in parentheses.

⁺p < .10   *p < .05   **p < .01

Table A.2 Logistic Regression of Generalized Violence on Pre-violence Conflict Pattern

Variable	Model 1	Model 2	Model 3	Model 4	Model 5	Model 6
Independent variables						
Group contention prior to violence	1.11** (.32)	1.13** (.33)	1.17** (.34)	1.12** (.40)	.86* (.43)	.87* (.43)
Kinship tie linking disputants		−.87* (.42)	−.83+ (1.15)	−.63 (.49)	−.63 (.50)	−.60 (.51)
No prior tie between disputants		−.93+ (.50)	−.95+ (.50)	−.46 (.57)	−.66 (.59)	−.67 (.58)
Female disputant			−.19 (.36)	−.06 (.41)	−.22 (.42)	−.20 (.43)
Diffuse group conflict prior to dispute				1.59** (.48)	1.43** (.50)	1.43** (.50)
Vendetta				2.43** (.74)	2.52** (.75)	2.51** (.76)
Two groups physically present					1.42** (.51)	1.41** (.51)
Third-party intervention					−.95* (.45)	−.91* (.46)
Year: 1865						−.28 (.55)
Year: 1893						.21 (.81)
Constant	−1.54	−1.27	−1.24	−2.02	−1.76	−1.76
−2*log-likelihood	254.74	247.53	247.25	194.60	183.85	183.48
Improvement chi-square (d.f.)	13.02** (1)	20.24** (3)	20.51** (4)	73.16** (6)	83.92** (8)	84.28** (10)

Note: N = 221. Standard errors are in parentheses.
+$p < .10$ *$p < .05$ **$p < .01$

Table A.3 Likelihood of Vendetta Occurrence as a Function of Characteristics of Original Incident

Characteristics of original incident	Model 1	Model 2	Model 3	Model 4	Model 5	Model 6
Independent variables						
Number of assailants	.65*		.65*	.65*	.60*	.66*
	(.27)		(.29)	(.29)	(.30)	(.31)
Violence against nondisputant		2.12***	2.07***	2.07**	2.07**	1.79*
		(.56)	(.57)	(.62)	(.65)	(.76)
Fatal incident				−.04	−.05	−.11
				(.69)	(.69)	(.70)
Irregular trial outcome				.39	.40	.54
				(.58)	(.59)	(.61)
Female disputant					−.08	−.11
					(.66)	(.70)
Kinship tie between disputants					.21	.17
					(.75)	(.79)
Conflict types[a]:						
Material						.30
						(.83)
Sexual						−.10
						(1.29)
Political						1.86
						(1.18)
Vendetta						.45
						(.85)
Constant	−3.27	−2.87	−3.86	−3.94	−3.96	−4.36
−2*log-likelihood	101.72	93.70	89.48	89.03	88.95	86.62
Improvement chi–square (d.f.)	5.13*	13.15***	17.37***	17.82**	17.90**	20.23*
	(1)	(1)	(2)	(4)	(6)	(10)

Note: N = 174. Standard errors in parentheses.

[a]Reference category is "personal argument/other."

*p < .05   **p < .01   ***p < .001

CHAPTER 5

Conflict and Social Structure

Probably the most characteristic error people make when describing human behavior is to attribute the same kinds of properties to groups that ordinarily apply to individuals. Large corporations are said to be "civic-minded," "greedy," "arrogant," "honest," "short-sighted," or "prudent," although they comprise tens or hundreds of thousands of people who presumably vary on these dimensions. Ethnic groups, at least in the minds of their members or their rivals, are "industrious" or "lazy," "proud" or "humble," "honest" or "cunning," "reserved" or "emotional," "peace-loving" or "warlike." Although careful speakers or writers might specify that they use such terms in a statistical sense, to describe the average member of a category, awareness of this qualification and the limitations it should impose easily slips away. Equally important are errors that arise when we apply individual-level concepts to collectivities: there are many situations in which we might be tempted to talk about an organization's behavior as "arrogant" even though most of its members are as individuals modest and timid, just as there are situations in which a set of bold individuals can, because of internal disagreement, produce organizational behavior aptly termed "indecisive."

A common consequence of the casual mingling of individual and collective attributes is that explanations that might be satisfactory as accounts of individual behavior are transferred un-critically to group-level behavior. Explanations in the psychoanalytic vein, in which, for example, a nation's collective "guilt" about some past crime accounts for a "reaction-formation" of hostility against an ethnic minority or neighboring state, are widespread in historical, so-ciological, and journalistic writing.[1] More conventionally, as I observed in chapter 4, overt group conflict is routinely attributed to such feelings as "mutual distrust," "fear," or "resentment"—feelings that it is pre-sumably possible for group members to have but that collections of people cannot be said to experience, absent a statistical qualification (the typical member of group A resents the privileges members of B typically enjoy) or a redefinition of what a feeling is.

The same goes, as I have already pointed out, for the idea of inter-ests. Although some social scientists have been willing to recognize that the fact of a group's having a common interest does not ensure group action in pursuit of that interest, many scholars continue to treat the transition from group interest to group action as natural and unproblematic. Christian Serbs hate Bosnian Muslims, so the former join together in ethnic war against the latter. Rwandan Hutus resent Tutsi dominance, so when the opportunity arises they band together to slaughter Tutsis and establish Hutu rule. Men in work organiza-tions benefit collectively from practices that enhance their promotion chances relative to women, so they support such practices and make decisions perpetuating them. Women collectively suffer from these practices, so they devote time, energy, and money to activist causes aimed at eliminating them. Employers benefit collectively from legal arrangements that give them bargaining leverage vis-à-vis employees, so they combine their efforts—despite the fact that they are competi-tors in production and labor markets—to sustain such arrangements. Workers, of course, act collectively to undermine those same arrange-ments. If you think these are all reasonable inferences, you have prob-ably never been in a group of eight hungry people trying to choose a place to have dinner and walk there together.

It is not as if aggregation of individual traits into group attributes is always wrong: ten people who can each lift one hundred kilograms

1. A famous example is Raoul Hilberg, *Perpetrators Victims Bystanders: The Jewish Cata-strophe, 1933–1945* (New York: Harper Perennial, 1993).

will indeed be able to lift one thousand kilograms under the right conditions. The point is that the conditions matter: we commit the fallacy of composition unless we consider explicitly what it means to assemble what we know about individual group members into statements about groups. We will also be blind to many important aspects of group behavior if most of our statements about groups are essentially aggregations of statements about their members.

In chapter 4 I devoted sustained attention to a particular version of the gap between individual attributes and behavior, on one hand, and collective attributes and behavior, on the other. The implications go well beyond the negative lesson of acknowledging that, because of the collective action problem, groups sometimes fail to act in their collective interest (assuming they can even establish what that is). Much more important is the discovery that this very fact—that people engaged in conflict cannot always count on their fellow group members to act collectively—itself shapes what people organized into rival groups do. The evidence suggests that competing groups have an overriding concern with fostering the perception that they are solidary—that their internal cohesion enables them to overcome the social dilemma that stands between group interest and group action. When reputations for solidarity permit clear and stable comparisons of opposing groups, relations between them will also be stable and in particular will subordinate one collectivity to the other. When these comparisons are cloudy, on the other hand, conflict, in particular group conflict, is a likely outcome. Hence the sensitivity of Corsican disputants to the details of their struggles that conveyed messages about the relative cohesiveness of their respective groups: notably, whether family members acted in concert or alone; whether they acted against disputants only or disputants' kin as well; and precisely how distant participants in conflict were, in kinship terms, from the relatives they aided or avenged. These details mattered because solidarity was—and is, in many other contexts—the key ingredient of success in group conflicts, making representations about solidarity a key aspect of such conflicts.

Recognizing and correctly interpreting this fact required prior recognition that groups are not always able to act in a unified way—and moreover that group members are acutely aware of the limits on their unity. We can learn a lot more about the nature of group conflict, in other words, if we decline to accept at face value the claims group representatives make about how unified they are. In fact, it may be precisely when group solidarity is most fragile that group members make the most grandiose representations of unity and commitment. At any rate, the central lesson is that the coincidence of collective action with collective interest is something people have to work at, and the varying rates of success in that endeavor both drive group conflict and determine dominance relations among collectivities.

In light of the conceptual and behavioral distance between individuals and groups, this chapter and the next have two connected aims. The first concerns a move outward, so to speak, from the seemingly circumscribed conflicts on which I have concentrated to large-scale patterns and events that impinge on and produce such conflicts. I shall show how networks of social relations link even society-wide processes to interactions among individuals. Conflict ramifies through social networks to produce disruptions far from the source. This phenomenon depends on the fact that dominance relations, like other dyadic relations, regularly interlock with other relations to form social networks. Such interlockings often exert a stabilizing effect, but, as I will demonstrate, they can also magnify the impact of a disruption occurring in one part of a large network by transporting it into other, more peripheral regions. This previously unnoticed fact concretely relates the dyadic struggles for interpersonal rank discussed and examined in the first part of this book to the group contests analyzed in chapter 4.

If the present chapter engages in a move outward from the level of the individual, the next and final chapter entails a move inward. I shall propose that the agnosticism I have directed toward group unity—an agnosticism that sees unity as contingent and enacted rather than fixed and automatic—be applied as well to an entity whose coherence I have implicitly portrayed as self-evident: the individual person.

Propagation of Conflict in Social Structures

Scholars who study patterns in social networks or their effects have tended to concentrate on small-scale settings: private organizations, activist groups, state agencies, and neighborhoods. Occasionally the scale expands to encompass clusters of such units: industries, social movement arenas, domains of policy activity, and cities. But the impression remains that network analysts investigate processes that don't extend terribly far. Social scientists interested in "big" questions or "big" phenomena, such as the origins of capitalism or the rise and collapse of nation-states, are apt to see networks of social relations as features of the social landscape that are too localized to attract their interest. They are after bigger game.

This restricted view of the import of structured social ties is misleading. Just as "big game" form part of an elaborate set of interdependencies—in which the elimination or expansion of a single insect species can alter the flora of a region, shrinking the population of plants or small animals on which the big game subsist—large-scale social processes are always tied to, and indeed are made of, small and localized interactions. They have no choice but to take place in local contexts. Every social phenomenon we know about, from cultivation techniques to systems of law to world religions encompassing a billion or more people, endures, expands, and evolves by passing from actual, living people to other actual, living people—or vanishes by not doing so.

To put the point the other way around, terms such as "technology," "democracy," "environmentalism," and "Islam" are useful heuristics in talking broadly about social transformations or continuities, but they nevertheless refer to abstractions, not things. As abstractions, they are necessarily empty of causal significance. Environmentalism did not bring about a shift in the way producers produce or the way consumers consume; it was actual people, espousing principles that the term "environmentalism" summarizes, who did so. Calvinism did not appear in Europe and change the way merchants and producers organized their enterprises. Rather, Calvin and other Reformation pastors persuaded their disciples and parishioners to think and act differently about their relation to God and to worldly activity (or perhaps discovered that their followers were ready to be so persuaded); these parishioners and disciples did the same with their associates, and so forth, with implications for the power of the Roman Catholic Church, for the autonomy of regional princes, and for European economic development.

The shorthand way to summarize that process is to say that Protestantism changed the political and economic landscape of sixteenth- and seventeenth-century Europe. But as often happens, reliance on shorthand expressions is a good idea only so long as we keep in mind that that is what they are. When one starts to see Protestantism or capitalism as things that act in the world (or for that matter, Europe as something acted on), rather than as ways to identify common features in the concrete actions of myriad individuals engaged (albeit interdependently) in worship or production, one has lost sight of how things work. It is the same mistake as thinking that the statement "The Great Depression swept across the globe" means that a cloudlike entity called a Depression migrated from country to country, sapping the strength of the world's economies—when in fact it means that a process of contraction beginning in some economies induced contraction in others, by virtue of their many interdependencies.

All of that ought to be obvious, even if we need to give ourselves a reminder now and then. What is perhaps not obvious is that the dependence of big processes on actual people and their actual behavior has systematic implications for social life and for how we ought to make sense of it. In the realm of conflict, one major implication is that (just as company failures trigger failures in other enterprises by depriving them of customers) a struggle for rank in one relation, however it is resolved, can set off further struggles in neighboring relations, triggering yet other struggles, and so forth. If this implication were borne out, it would offer a way to talk about big processes that keeps their connection to concrete social interaction salient. I shall presently offer some novel evidence supporting the proposition, but for the moment I wish to emphasize some of the broader inferences that follow from this way of thinking and refer to existing scholarship that lends these inferences credence.

Consider again the case of the Reformation: if it is reasonable to say that Protestantism led to conflict across much of northern Europe, it is only because particular notables and particular clerics embraced the Reformed Church in their own communities and challenged the authority of the pope through his local representatives. The large-scale story of the Reformation consequently occurred in a different way in every community, shaped by existing local alliances and rivalries.

Yet the dependence of macroscopic phenomena on microscopic patterns implies a good deal more than that big processes come in local varieties. It means in addition that the big picture is at least as much a product of the thousands of local pictures as the latter are a product of the former. Yet this reciprocity is usually missed. Because writers in the human sciences are constrained by genre considerations, they usually offer either syntheses or monographs—casting stories such as that of the Reformation either in a broad national or continental form that acknowledges local variation but portrays it as a matter of departures from the grand theme, or in a highly focused community-level form that treats the larger context as a fixed background. The background, however, is merely an aggregation of other local stories. It is only "fixed," that is, independent of local variation, in the statistical sense that no one locality exerts a very big influence on the macroscopic process. Collectively, however, all there is a collection of localities, tied to each other by the even smaller-scale phenomena of migration, mercantile and occupational travel, and face-to-face social relations.

The emergence of centralized nation-states furnishes an even crisper example of the way social relations refract macroscopic processes into local contexts. This process is a particularly fitting locus for such a demonstration insofar as the aggregation of multiple settings into the large-scale organizations we now call territorial states seems by definition to be a matter of *creating* such linkages in places that presumably lacked them. Yet the evidence strongly indicates that centralizers built their states not on new foundations but on preexisting social structures, in the sense of interlocking—that is, not entirely localized—systems of patronage and influence. In England, to take one prominent example, the half-century civil war that eventuated in a constitutional monarchy derived its sectarian character from the fact that ambitious gentry had begun in the 1500s to use local control over church positions as a means to assemble political clienteles and to attach themselves to extralocal patrons.[2] Had the patronage resources available to ambitious gentry been more diverse and less church-centered, the bloody seventeenth-century struggle between king and parliament might not have become a struggle between Catholics and Protestants. There might well have been a civil war, but the way patron-client relations would have sorted participants into opposing sides might not have been plausibly characterized in sectarian terms. In this case of state formation, then, confessional conflict cannot be described

2. Peter S. Bearman, *Relations into Rhetorics: Local Elite Social Structure in Norfolk, England, 1540–1640* (New Brunswick: Rutgers University Press, 1993). See also Perez Zagorin, *The Court and the County* (New York: Atheneum, 1970).

as a society-wide phenomenon sweeping through localities; it was instead a product of the way elite social ties were locally structured.

Prior research of my own concerning the first major standoff in the creation of the federal apparatus of the United States of America revealed something similar. Imposition in 1794 of the very first federal tax, an excise levied on whiskey production, precipitated a revolt in western Pennsylvania known as the Whiskey Rebellion. Although the concrete grievance was taxation and the economic hardship it would inflict on small-scale distillers who consumed their product rather than selling it, the rebellion's leaders were wealthy members of the western Pennsylvania political elite on whom the financial impact was minor.

Not surprisingly, the insurrection's leaders cast their resistance to the excise in terms of democratic, anti-centralist political principles rather than narrow financial interest—and, indeed, elite participation in tax resistance was uncorrelated with ownership of a still or other in-dices of economic position. It was correlated, instead, with elite mem-bers' position in the patronage structure encompassing public offices in western Pennsylvania. Notables with patronage links to the three federal officials in the region (two members of the House and a U.S. senator) sided with the U.S. government; so did notables whose cli-ents—men whom they had sponsored for public office—had no fed-eral ties. In contrast, elite members whose clients also had patronage ties to federal officeholders spearheaded the insurrection. To put it crudely, elites whose local political standing would be enhanced or unaffected by an expansion of federal authority opposed the revolt or stood on the sidelines; elites whose clients had an opportunity to shift their allegiance to the clients of newly powerful federal officials, or to federal officials themselves, became leaders of the rebellion. The "big" process of federal statebuilding generated local conflict by reallocating political advantage according to a pattern laid down by preexisting po-litical relationships.[3] By the same token, the centralizing process could only proceed because most localities included some people who could see the advantage of cultivating their clientelistic relations with state-builders at the center. This is a story played out whenever ambitious

---

3. Roger V. Gould, "Patron-Client Ties, State Centralization, and the Whiskey Rebel-lion," *American Journal of Sociology* 102 (1996): 400–429.

people—in small towns, in national polities, in large and small organizations, and in intellectual fields—perceive shifts in the quality or reliability of the relations available to them or to potential rivals.

I stated above that the interlocking of such relations implied something like a ripple effect in social conflict as a disruption in one relation changes the terms, or at any rate diminishes the stability, of social ties adjacent to the initial disruption. It should be easy to imagine how this rippling might operate. Everyone has experienced the tension that results when two people find themselves in conflict and turn to mutual friends for moral support. If mutual friends choose opposing sides, relations previously free of conflict are jeopardized, and in a way that may implicate even more relations. Most people have also witnessed the disruption that ensues when the departure of a key person from a business, a church, a family, or any other kind of social group creates a vacancy to which more than one person aspires. In processes of this sort, social conflict can propagate, like a sound wave, through chains of social relations.

The obvious question, given my assertion that social networks have an impact at a larger scale than is usually thought, is what the range of such conflict waves might be. Answering this question in a definitive way would be a major enterprise, since it would entail detailed information not only about conflicts in many places at once but also about the chains of social relations through which such conflicts might be transmitted. Concentrating on a localized and small population might introduce too many confounding factors in the form of events producing multiple conflicts in close temporal proximity.

There is nevertheless suggestive evidence for the existence of conflict waves on a significant scale. Barring an obvious alternative mechanism, it is reasonable to infer that they are mediated by concrete social relations—making the issue of how social networks are structured consequential at the level of nation-states, not just communities, organizations, or industries. The figure below depicts the time-series for the annual homicide rate in Corsica over the course of the nineteenth and early twentieth centuries; about 220 of the homicides that underlie the figure were examined in chapter 4. Even without a smoothed curve, it is easy to spot an overall trend downward during the hundred years covered by the graph. From rates in the first third of the nineteenth century that exceed those of the most violent U.S. cities

Corsican Homicide Rate, 1835–1914 (yearly homicides per 100,000)

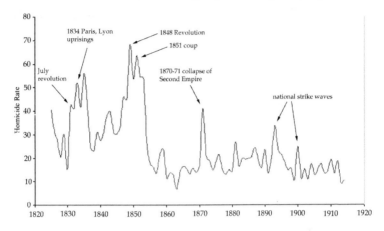

in the late twentieth and early twenty-first centuries, Corsica's homicide rate declined by 1910 to a level that, although much higher than that of contemporary European nations, is comparable to the present overall rate for the United States. Evidently, the increasingly visible presence of the criminal justice system imported from the metropole lowered rates of violence overall during this period.

More significant than long-term trends are the obvious spikes in the homicide rate that, although larger in the first half of the century, continued to occur until the early 1900s. What is most remarkable about this figure is the coincidence of the largest spikes (defined, roughly speaking, as large but short-lived increases over preceding years) with major transitions in French national politics. The frequency of homicides in Corsica increased dramatically when the Bourbon monarchy fell in 1830; when uprisings in major mainland cities in 1834 threatened the fledgling Orleanist monarchy; when the latter was replaced by the French Second Republic in 1848, and when the Republic was abolished by Louis Bonaparte's coup in 1851; and when Bonaparte's Second Empire collapsed in 1870.

It might seem natural to account for this pattern by postulating that regime transitions in Paris prompted political competition in Corsica, whose towns and villages were obliged to elect new officials each time France underwent a change of government. And indeed, some of the island's bloody feuds—collective conflicts in which multiple revenge attacks occurred over the course of a year or more—began when political transitions altered the balance of local influence between rival families and their adherents.

Violence occasionally broke out at voting sites, notably when members of one faction suspected their rivals of tampering with the ballot box—not always an unreasonable suspicion, inasmuch as the town official in charge of the ballot box frequently belonged to one or another of the dominant families. Lethal conflict could also occur after an election shifted local hierarchies by weakening the position of a dominant individual or faction, in much the same way that the expansion of federal authority in the Whiskey Rebellion fostered conflict about the altered clientelistic prospects of political notables.

Yet flare-ups of this kind could not by themselves produce the spikes in homicide rates observed in the figure. In fact, of the 221 homicides for which I have collected detailed information—and these included incidents tried in 1849, 1851, and 1852, the years most likely to reflect increased political violence—only 7 can be classified as violence between rival political factions. The overwhelming majority of the homicides in these politically tumultuous years, and in other periods as well, fit the familiar profile: conflicts about land, unpaid debts, sexual rivalry, unkept promises of marriage, and verbal affronts. Lethal violence increased during years of political upheaval, but most of it was not visibly a part of those upheavals.

The reason for this association, I contend, is that the local shifts in social rank that political transitions brought about impinged on other relations within families and among neighbors connected to these shifts, increasing the likelihood of strife in these adjacent relations as well. Any relation whose terms are thrown into question by shifts in the status, influence, or social network position of one or both parties becomes more like the symmetric tie that chapter 3 showed was more vulnerable to lethal escalation of disputes. Villages, towns, or regions that experience a sudden upsurge in the prevalence of undefined relations should also experience an increase in the incidence of violent conflict. That is what the spikes in Corsican homicide rates in 1830, 1834, 1848–51, and so forth represent.

To be sure, the majority of the ripples triggered by disruptions of social rank led to nothing more than tension or perhaps fisticuffs, but given the large number of social ties linked by one or two steps to any given dyad, even a modest increase in the likelihood of violence in each of these ties would be sufficient to produce the spikes seen in the figure. If overall social welfare is the outcome of interest, the parallel increase in nonlethal conflicts, likely to be far more numerous than homicides, might prove to be an even more significant byproduct of political transformation.

Corsica is undoubtedly an unusual place, for many of the same reasons that make it a worthwhile setting for examining social conflict. As it turns out, however, there is good reason to believe that the propagation of waves of conflict through social networks occurs more generally. Again, although it would be nice to be able to track particular examples, there are built-in obstacles to such a strategy. Any effort to follow the network path from one conflict to prior disputes in other relations would be subject to the criticism that applies to any causal account constructed retrospectively: because conflict of some sort occurs regularly, and because relations typically interlock with others, it will *always* be possible to find antecedent conflicts in relations close to the focal conflict. A more disciplined demonstration, a test that, even if it is more indirect, could in principle undermine the argument, is desirable.

National figures for homicide rates and political transitions offer an appropriate basis for such a demonstration. The data in question necessarily come from the twentieth century, because it was only then that states began to record national crime statistics, including homicide rates, in a reliable and intertemporally consistent way. At the same time, only a few nation-states with reliable data-collecting agencies also experienced sufficient political instability in the twentieth century to permit a comparison of stable with unstable periods. France and Italy, each of which went through multiple regime changes well into the twentieth century, are the best examples. Finland experienced fewer moments of upheaval but nonetheless went through two periods of shifting political arrangements—the late 1920s and early 1930s, when conservatives responded to the growing influence of Communists and Social Democrats by mounting an effort to exclude them from politics, and immediately after liberation in 1945. Most other candidate nations were either too stable, like the United States and the United Kingdom, or, like India, Portugal, and Germany, experienced

Table 12 Regression of Homicide Rate on Regime Change, Moving Average, and Year: France, 1931–71

Variable	Coefficient	s.e.	t
Regime change	.24	.10	2.35*
Two-year moving average	.79	.12	6.61**
Year	−.004	.004	−1.11
Constant	8.32		

$*p < .05$ $**p < .01$

Table 13 Regression of Homicide Rate on Regime Change, Moving Average, and Year: Italy, 1900–71

Variable	Coefficient	s.e.	t
Regime change	3.47	1.21	2.87**
Two-year moving average	.35	.14	2.51*
Year	−.07	.02	−3.16**
Constant	147.80		

$*p < .05$ $**p < .01$

Table 14 Regression of Homicide Rate on Regime Change, Moving Average, and Year: Finland, 1917–70

Variable	Coefficient	s.e.	t
Regime change	1.19	.53	2.25*
Two-year moving average	.73	.07	9.80**
Year	−.03	.009	−3.23**
Constant	68.05		

$*p < .05$ $**p < .01$

instability so severe that data are not comparable or consistently available across time periods.

Using the longest continuous time-series available jointly for the two variables, tables 12, 13, and 14 report the associations between homicide rates and political instability in France between 1931 and 1971, for Italy from 1900 to 1971, and for Finland from 1917 to 1970. The indicator of instability comes from the large-scale, cross-national database on democracy and authoritarianism compiled by Ted Gurr and colleagues.[4] Any year coded as involving constitutional uncertainty (such as 1958 in France), or in which either of the indices for levels of democracy and levels of authoritarianism changed by more than a single point, is recorded as a period of political instability. Because there is a long-term downward trend in homicide rates, even given the upward movement that began in many Western nations in the 1950s, it is necessary to account for the overall association with time. In addition, given that the outcome of interest is short-term increases in violence, the analyses control for the moving two-year average.

In all three countries, regime changes were significantly associated with short-term increases in measured homicide rates. The magnitude of the association is largest in Italy, owing to a higher baseline rate and larger overall fluctuations in the first half of the century (the period of greatest instability, during which Mussolini seized political control with the promise of restoring order). Nonetheless, the patterns are consistent with that illustrated in the figure for Corsica: on a national level, more people were murdered in years of political transition—even when, as in France in 1958 and 1968, the political instability itself was not particularly violent but instead took the form of constitutional change.

Although it is difficult to find detailed evidence that such increases in lethal violence can be traced to national political events through lengthy chains of disrupted social ties, it is reasonable to seek an explanation of the association in this mechanism. It is, first of all, more plausible than the ready alternatives. The heightened level of lethal violence observed during moments of regime transition cannot fairly be called "civil war," that is, political violence directly tied to the transition: Finland and France were disrupted at several points in the twentieth century, but nothing approaching the widespread political violence of the nineteenth century took place. Italy did experience major domestic disturbances, including vengeance attacks on Fascists, just after the fall of Mussolini and during the Allied occupation—but

    4. Keith Jaggers and Ted Robert Gurr, "Polity III: Regime Change and Political Authority, 1800–1994 (Computer file). 2nd ICPSR version. Boulder, Colorado: Keith Jaggers/College Park, Maryland: Ted Robert Gurr (producers), 1995. Ann Arbor, Mich.: Interuniversity Consortium for Political and Social Research (distributor), 1996.

the total number of recorded homicides in this period exceeded fifteen thousand, far more than such disturbances produced.

Nor can increased violence be viewed as evidence of a relaxation of state control of civilian behavior. It is unlikely that large numbers of would-be killers await periods of relaxed policing to commit their acts of aggression: most murders occur in the heat of the moment, so to speak, making them more immune than other crimes to fluctuations in the likelihood of legal sanction. More important, the measure of political instability employed here indexes authoritarian shifts about as often as shifts toward democracy, and moreover includes a considerable number of cases of constitutional revision—periods in which the state was not weakened, as in coups or civil wars, but was undergoing self-induced and legal transformation. It is particularly hard to account for heightened rates of violent conflict in these moments without recognizing the influence constituent assemblies and other peaceful transitions can have on the stability of clientelistic, hierarchical social ties—and on ties connected, at one remove or several, to those ties. Finally, further analysis shows that the rate of assault is related to political instability in a way that resembles the association found for homicide, whereas rates of property crime do not exhibit this association. If relaxed legal control were the main reason for increased rates of violent interpersonal conflict, property crimes, which are more opportunistic than attacks on persons, ought to have a stronger association with regime change, not a weaker one.[5]

Conclusion

One of the most powerful rhetorical maneuvers in which social scientists have engaged since at least the mid-1800s is to expose institutions that putatively benefit all of society as the means by which one segment of society keeps another segment under control. Marx applied this interpretation to markets (notably the market for labor) as well as to liberal ideologies and academic discourse representing markets as natural; Marxian social scientists have applied it to legal arrangements that disproportionately aid property holders (often under the guise of "en-

5. Lawrence Cohen and Marcus Felson, "Social Change and Crime Rate Trends: A Routine Activity Approach." *American Sociological Review* 44 (1979): 588–608.

couraging investment") and to institutions that disproportionately incarcerate those without property. Although the dimensions used to define the relevant segments have become more numerous—from bourgeois and proletariat to light-skinned and dark-skinned, male and female, and many other sorts of powerful and powerless—the overall theme has remained central to social science, at least the part of it devoted to criticism of the social order. From markets to marriage rules to mental ability tests, all manner of practices and institutions touted as valuable for all are vulnerable to reframing as valuable for a few at the expense of many.[6]

The corollary to this critique of dominant institutions—governments, churches, private enterprises, social service agencies, hospitals, and so on—is the reframing of practices termed "deviant" by such institutions as *resistance*. Styles of clothing or speech deemed inappropriate by elites are reinterpreted as symbolic rejection of the dominance of those elites or of the rules they impose; worker absenteeism, shirking, and even secretly mocking the boss become covert means of labor militancy, and vandalism, property crime, and sometimes assault and murder can be understood as organized revolution or rebellion rather than as "disorder" or "riot."[7] Once the institutions regulating behavior are exposed as political, in the sense of furthering particular rather than universal aims, behavior exhibited in defiance of

6. See Georg Ruche and Otto Kirchheimer, *Punishment and Social Structure* (New York: Columbia University Press, 1939); E. Schattschneider, *The Semi-Sovereign People: A Realist's View of Democracy in America* (New York: International Thomson, 1997); Frances Fox Piven and Richard Cloward, *Regulating the Poor* (New York: Vintage, 1993); Thomas Scheff, *Bloody Revenge: Emotions, Nationalism, and War* (Universe.com. 2000); G. W. Domhoff, *Who Rules America: Power and Politics* (New York: McGraw-Hill, 2001); Linda Gordon, *Pitied but Not Entitled* (Cambridge: Belknap Press of Harvard University Press, 1995); Catharine E. MacKinnon, *Toward a Feminist Theory of the State* (Cambridge: Harvard University Press, 1991).

7. Richard Hebdige, *Subculture: The Meaning of Style* (London: Routledge, 1981); E. P. Thompson, *The Making of the English Working Class* (New York: Random House, 1963); William H. Sewell Jr., *Work and Revolution in France: The Language of Labor from the Old Regime to 1848* (New York: Cambridge University Press, 1980); James C. Scott, *Weapons of the Weak* (New Haven: Yale University Press, 1987); Alain Cottereau, "The Distinctiveness of Working-Class Cultures in France, 1848–1900," in Ira Katznelson and Aristide Zolberg, eds, *Working-Class Formation* (Princeton: Princeton University Press, 1986); Philippe Bourgois, *In Search of Respect: Selling Crack in El Barrio* (New York: Cambridge University Press, 1995); Mark Baldassare, *The Los Angeles Riot* (1994); Charles Tilly, Louise Tilly, and Richard Tilly, *The Rebellious Century* (Cambridge: Harvard University Press, 1975); John Merriman, *The Margins of City Life* (Oxford: Oxford University Press, 1997).

regulations becomes political as well. In the United States, this view has received poignant and forceful support from a now widely recognized pattern: in the period following World War II, crime rates rose in unison with the expansion of civil rights activism and a wide range of other kinds of protest. For much of the postwar period, the graph of protest events by year is nearly interchangeable with the graph of overall crime rates, with both rising steadily from the mid 1950s through the 1960s and peaking some time in the early 1970s. Where the political right has tended to make sense of this correspondence by depicting protest as lawlessness, the left, and with it a sizeable segment of social science, has been more prone to depict lawlessness as protest.

Given the explicitly evaluative agenda underlying this reinterpretation, it would be surprising to see physical violence in the context of interpersonal conflict benefiting from the heightened legitimacy that accrues to "deviant" behavior reclassified as political dissent by social scientists. Yet a major scientific embarrassment results from what I imagine would be the common claim that, although nonstandard dress styles and musical preferences, disorderly behavior, petty theft, and even vandalism are defensible expressions of resistance to oppressive conditions, physical violence and homicide are not. The embarrassment results from the fact, documented in the previous section, that measured rates of criminal homicide and criminal assault appear to be *more* closely associated with moments of political transition than are measured property crimes. I suspect that adherents of the deviance-as-dissent view would be uncomfortable with the realization that actions causing grievous bodily harm (most often against members of the same social group as the person doing the action) express political dissatisfaction more faithfully than the more forgivable transgressions we have become accustomed to calling resistance.

My task in this conclusion is therefore made somewhat easier by the fact that the aim of this chapter is not to tell a comforting or politically desirable story but rather a scientifically defensible story, one that makes sense in a logically coherent way of empirical patterns in social conflict. And the story that appears most defensible in scientific terms is not that deviance is actually protest, nor is it that protest is simply dressed-up deviance. It is that *both* protest and other kinds of conflict occur with greater frequency when social relations are disrupted and the disruption is transmitted to neighboring relations. Shifts in the political order, including not only revolts and coups but reformulations of the polity undertaken by legal means, set in motion further shifts that in many instances lead to conflict in previously stable configurations of social relations. We might reasonably see such conflicts as reflecting protest, and in particular protest in pursuit of social equality, if the instigator of conflict resists domination but does not seek to invert it. The same could be said for conflict in which a clearly dominant actor violently suppresses a bid for equality, as at Amritsar in 1926 or at Birmingham in 1963. But such cases do not exhaust the set of conflicts set in motion by disruptions in interconnected systems of social rank. That set includes the large number of interpersonal conflicts, some of them lethal, in which both parties would prefer to end up in a superior social position. It would be fairer to see these conflicts as contests for rank than as battles about equality.

Reframing disorderly behavior, unconventional opinions, and outright rebellion as political dissent or as self-conscious assaults on inequality is no doubt scientifically defensible in many instances. Moreover, whether "dissent" is the best interpretation is often independent of how violent the action is, even if the popularity of the action does depend on the extent of violence. Nonviolent civil rights demonstrations are more popular, and generally arouse more sympathy in third parties, than guerrilla insurgencies financed with ransom kidnappings and mobilized using forcible recruitment of teenagers; yet there is no scientific principle on which to base a claim that the former is more like "resistance and the latter is more like crime. That is a moral, not a theoretical, judgment.

A theoretical distinction worth making is that between conflict in which one party aims to challenge hierarchy as such and conflict in which both parties aim to achieve a superior rank while making no objection to the persistence of a hierarchical order. The difference, if you like, is that in the former case the structure of social relations is under attack whereas in the latter case the parties to conflict are only fighting about who will occupy which position in a structure that will remain hierarchical. It is not yet possible to say, however, what determines which of these two types of conflict will predominate when extant arrangements are disrupted by political events, major demographic shifts, economic transitions, or other exogenous triggers.[8] The many challenges to monarchical authority and to forced servitude during the long nineteenth century produced democratizing trends (at the price of sometimes heavy casualties) in much of western Europe and North America, but the same challenges stimulated authoritarian tendencies, whether in the name of elites or the masses, in much of South and Central America and in central and eastern Europe. To the extent that we understand why democracy prevailed in some instances and murderous dictatorships in others, the answers have more to do with the constellation of forces and the set of coalitions possible once transition had begun than with the way extant hierarchies came under challenge in the first place, or even with the kinds of agendas challengers publicly espoused at the outset.

Similarly, the many challenges to repressive hierarchies in the late 1900s divided fairly evenly into transitions to pluralistic democracies, on one hand, and to genocidal regimes, on the other. It is hard to say why the overthrow of white rule in South Africa occurred because of legislation whereas the overthrow of Tutsi rule in Rwanda was achieved by organized mass slaughter, just as it is not obvious why the fall of state socialism in eastern Europe led to autocracies in such places as Kazakhstan, Afghanistan, and Georgia and parliamentary regimes in the Czech Republic, Poland, and Russia (with a lot of intermediate cases besides).

In short, we do not know very much about the circumstances under which the ouster of a dominant group will be followed by an egalitarian structure or merely an inversion of ranks. Accounting for these divergent political outcomes has not, however, been my purpose in this chapter or in this book. Instead, it has been to identify a feature common to instability in general, whether on the level of large nations undergoing major transitions or of small groups of people whose social standing relative to one another is in doubt. Independent of the

---

8. It is worth distinguishing between political events that are reasonably termed exogenous, such as the sudden death of a charismatic leader, and those that are endogenous to the process of conflict, such as assassinations, coups, urban revolts, antiauthoritarian religious movements, and so forth. The latter must be seen as part of the propagation of conflict waves I have described, although they may be situated at an early point in that process; the former are best understood as the epicenter of the process.

goals of challengers or indeed of the form things will take after the dust settles, we can be confident that the fact of the challenge will bring about a whole population of new conflicts. These new conflicts can be both large and small, both integral to the initial disruption and far removed from it—and they are in many cases connected to recognizably "big" events only by chains of social ties that lash people's fates to the fates of others they may never have met.

[CHAPTER 6]

Honor and the Individual

Just as the cohesiveness of a group cannot be uncritically assumed, no matter what pretensions to solidarity its members
have, the coherence of an individual across time and across
domains of interaction turns out, on careful scrutiny, to be
variable as well. Some people are scattered over time, in the
sense that they do things they later regret, make commitments to themselves and to others that they soon abandon or
forget, switch allegiances at a moment's notice, and disregard
inconsistencies in their beliefs or behavior. Such people are
analogous to groups that lack social cohesion. They are collections of momentary selves that, because they inhabit the
same body, are strung into a single self by social convention;
yet each momentary self behaves like a distinct person who
pursues his or her own well-being at the expense of other
selves in the sequence. If such people had a patron saint, she
might be Holly Golightly.

Other people are made of selves that are strongly linked
across time and across domains of interaction. They think
about and are influenced by the long-term consequences of
their actions, not simply immediate ones. They decline to
make commitments that they know will be impossible to
fulfill and conversely feel constrained by commitments they
have made in the past. Unlike temporally disconnected people,

they are uncomfortable expressing contradictory opinions from one conversation to the next and tend to see greater virtue in behavioral consistency than in spontaneity (which they are more likely to call "caprice"). Their patron saint might be John Calvin, if he were not already taken, or it might be Benjamin Franklin, if he had in fact lived the life he prescribed. Perhaps he is Atticus Finch. Atticus Finches would most likely portray the Golightlies as "childish," and the latter might retort that the Finches are "bores." These are of course extreme cases, drawn to capture the affinity among a variety of ways in which present, future, and past selves relate to one another. Ordinary people vary between these two theoretical extremes, and most are probably in the middle.

Now, the fact that individuals vary in coherence, although usually not described in those terms, is obvious in areas about which common sense has a great deal to say. Everyone knows, for example, that for some people a promise made is a promise kept, whereas for others a promise made implies little about future behavior. Imagine that I am known as a responsible person. When I say on Wednesday that I will arrive promptly at eight on Friday, those who know me expect that I will in fact arrive at the appointed hour. Implicitly, they believe that at seven on Friday, I will feel bound by the commitment I made two days earlier. If they were to think about it further, they might conclude that I keep my promises because I am sensitive to the consequences I will face in the future if I break them. I care about past commitments because I care about how living up to them will influence my future—that is, how it will affect future versions of me. Or I might care about them merely because I am dedicated to thinking of myself as a reliable person. Probably it is a bit of both.

Imagine, on the other hand, that I have a reputation as someone who frequently fails to come through. When I promise to arrive at eight, those whom I have routinely disappointed before know not to count on me; they sense that, at seven on Friday, I will pay less heed to Wednesday's promise than to the pressing desire for an additional two hours of sleep—a desire intensified by my decision, Thursday evening, to stay up late rather than prepare for an early morning. Implicitly, when my associates discount my promise, they do so because of at least three beliefs about me: first, that I have made a facile commitment on Wednesday without thinking much about Friday; second, that when I wake up on Friday I will not think very hard about commitments I made on Wednesday; and third, that when I decide whether to get up I will assign much more weight to how it feels, right then, to be getting up, than to the more distant implications of not keeping the eight o'clock appointment.[1] At each moment, I am assumed to make choices without much regard for choices made earlier or for consequences to be incurred later.

Such beliefs about the way people are influenced by their own past actions and by the consequences of such actions reveal that the commonsense notion of reliability is a special case of the broader and less accessible phenomenon with which I began this chapter: that of variation in the degree to which individuals' actions and utterances cohere over time, or the degree to which they resemble Golightlies or Finches. Social scientists, especially economists, conventionally portray this variation as a matter of people's attitudes toward or interest in the future—as a question, that is, of how much weight different people assign to the future in relation to the present. I propose an alternative and broader framework, in which what varies is the pattern and strength of the ties linking past and present incarnations of a given person to one another (as well as to other people). In this framework, keeping a promise can be as much a matter of loyalty to past pronouncements as it is a matter of concern for the future reputational rewards accruing to someone who keeps his or her word. Seeing individuals as successions of selves with variable network structures, I shall show, makes it possible to place such diverse phenomena as revenge, honor, forgiveness, dominance, loyalty, and peacemaking into a single theoretical system. Much of the difference between honor societies, which value impulsive acts and vengeance, and urbanized modern societies, which putatively encourage prudence and forgiveness, amounts to a difference in models of how individuals are sup-

---

1. In truth, if I already have a reputation as an unreliable person, the consequences of going back to sleep are diminished. One might conclude that even a forward-looking person would stay in bed in such circumstances. But if redemption is possible, the forward-looking person will behave differently from the present-oriented person: he or she will respond to the benefits to be had by defying everyone's expectation, whereas someone who dwells in the present will be unmoved by such distant inducements.

posed to cohere over time. Revenge-seeking and impulsive, violent responses to insult require that individuals look backward, notably to past wrongs, and that they substantially disregard their personal well-being in the future; prudence and peacemaking demand, in contrast, that wronged persons abandon the past and embrace the future. These are, I contend, alternative social prescriptions for assembling successive moments of experience into an individual person—a person seen here not as an undifferentiated unit but as a social network, varying in structure and cohesiveness, of momentarily existing selves.

In chapter 4 I wrote about the notion of honor mostly with reference to group rivalries and therefore said a good deal more about group honor than about individual honor. But we know that individual-level notions of honor and honorable action have been equally salient in traditional societies as have group-level notions—even when, as I have suggested, group honor consists precisely of the subordination of individual interests and desires to group welfare. In Tokugawa Japan, a samurai could do nothing more noble than to sacrifice his life for his lord, as the forty-seven *ronin* taught. Yet samurai honor, like honor elsewhere, consisted also of innumerable personal traits: bravery, military prowess, asceticism, even cleanliness.

Let us set aside the commonly asserted idea that honor consists also in demonstrating concern about one's own reputation as honorable. This amounts to saying that maintaining personal honor requires making others aware of one's desire to maintain it. Such a second-order principle—honor demands that one protect one's honor—is entirely parasitic on the first-order principles I just noted, which focus on specific behaviors and personal traits, because all of these traits are already defined in terms of public perceptions. Adding levels gratuitously confuses matters; we might as well say, for instance, that honor also demands demonstrations of concern for whether one's demonstrations of concern about honor have been appreciated.

So individual honor, across dozens of settings in which scholars have seen fit to apply the term to local standards for how people should act, requires a set of public behaviors that together create a certain image of a person. The behaviors in question, moreover, do not vary arbitrarily from one society to another. If they did, "honor" would mean nothing more than "the respect people earn by doing the things other people approve of." But the concept has more cross-cultural content than that: It *always* requires courage, for instance. It is true that, in most traditional honor settings, women's behavior, in the form of obedience to husbands and fathers, chastity, modesty, and so forth, is tightly linked to group honor with no expectation of bravery.[2] This fact in no way militates against my assertion, however: When group honor requires women to be chaste and loyal but not brave, it is only men who are thought capable of being honorable as individuals.

Courage, naturally, means that the honorable person (or honorable man, in the traditional honor setting; I shall return to the question of gender-specificity below) can face a deadly threat, and by implication lesser threats, without flinching or fleeing. It is common to think of duels as contests in which rivals try to kill each other, but this is entirely wrong. To be sure, duels have led to many deaths, but the truly victorious duelist, at least since the time when pistols became the weapon of choice, was the one who calmly allowed himself to be fired on and then, facing a frightened opponent, gallantly discharged his weapon into the air.[3] Even in Corsica, where, as I pointed out in chapter 2, there was no particular shame in ambushing one's opponent, it was common for a young man in a moment of anger to challenge his adversary by saying, "Why don't we go outside so we can measure ourselves against each other?" Marksmanship or skill with a stiletto was not the issue: In more than a thousand nineteenth-century trial documents, I have not once encountered a Corsican boasting of his (or her) *technical* ability to cause harm. The question, as with the more formalized contests that obsessed European nobles and gentry in the American South, was who had more courage—who was more indifferent to the threat of grievous harm. The same is true, day in and day out, of swaggering male adolescents, and occasionally older men, the world over;

2. Jane Schneider, "Of Vigilance and Virgins: Honor, Shame, and Access to Resources in Mediterranean Societies," *Ethnology* 10 (1971): 1–24; Anton Blok, *The Mafia of a Sicilian Village, 1860–1960: A Study of Violent Peasant Entrepreneurs* (New York: Harper, 1974); Janet Abu-Lughod, *Rabat: Urban Apartheid in Morocco* (Princeton: Princeton University Press, 1980).

3. Kevin MacAleer, *Dueling* (Princeton: Princeton University Press, 1994); Bertram Wyatt-Brown, *Southern Honor: Ethics and Behavior in the Old South* (New York: Oxford University Press, 1982); Robert A. Nye, *Masculinity and Male Codes of Honor in Modern France* (New York: Oxford University Press, 1993).

and it has often been true, at least in the American gang context, of young women as well.[4] In honor settings, winning contests of courage is the primary means of achieving dominance. Although we don't think of it this way, indifference to harm is simply indifference to the well-being of one's future selves. Caution is the reverse: a strong reluctance to court danger in the present because of the impact it will have on each future momentary version of one's person. What inhabitants of honor societies call "fear" or "cowardice" can be seen as devotion to the stream of future incarnations of oneself. Those of us who have been taught to wear seatbelts, look both ways before crossing the street, and save for retirement like to think of it as "prudence," but it is the same thing. Call it caution or cowardice; either way, it is a matter of subordinating one's interest in the present—which may be to win a contest of wills, to avoid effort, or to spend money—to the collective interest one's successor selves have in existing, in having functioning limbs, and so forth.

This is not to say that the contentious honorific individual lives only in the present, as would a Golightly. It is well known that both men and women in honor settings are highly sensitive to verbal insults. More important, they *remember* insults, and bear grudges about them, for a long time. In one of the more dramatic demonstrations of this aspect of personal honor, Richard Nisbet and Dov Cohen showed that college students from the southern United States were about twice as likely as northerners to say they would be angry for a month or more if a friend were to insult them. Strikingly, there was not much difference between northerners and southerners in their reports of how long they would remain angry about being punched.[5] Honor requires in particular that people nurse memories of symbolic affronts, the effect of which is to prolong the period during which the affronted person continues to want redress—hence increasing the likelihood of some kind of retaliation. This is not to say that persons of honor would *not* be angry a month later about being struck, especially in public; the

4. For examples of "acting tough" among female adolescents, see Gerald R. Suttles, *The Social Order of the Slum* (Chicago: University of Chicago Press, 1967); Ruth Horowitz and Gary Schwartz, "Honor, Normative Ambiguity, and Gang Violence," *American Sociological Review* 39, no. 2 (1974): 238–51; Anne Campbell, *Girls in the Gang* (New York: Blackwell, 1986).

5. Richard E. Nisbet and Dov Cohen, *Culture of Honor: The Psychology of Violence in the South* (Boulder, Colo.: Westview, 1996).

point, rather, is that in this respect they are not quite so different from members of societies in which respect and honor play a less central role.[6]

Much as bravery implies indifference to the desires of future selves, obsession with the righting of past wrongs signifies a strong devotion to past selves. Those of us who cannot remain incensed about something done to us more than a few days ago are likely to say that it is important to be forward-looking and to let bygones be bygones. Leaving aside the fact that it is usually those who have *committed* the wrong who espouse this putatively civilized, future-oriented (and in such cases self-serving) view, what is significant about it is its explicit discounting of the demand past selves might make to be compensated for wrongs they have suffered. Turning the other cheek means turning one's back on the right that one's predecessor selves have to be avenged—much as a young Corsican man's failure to avenge his father or brother constituted, in the eyes of other family members and of the community at large, a renunciation of his social tie to the deceased.

Taken together, these expectations about how men in honor societies ought to behave amount to a model of how momentary selves should be connected to each other across time. Think of each connection as implying a bond of solidarity between selves at different moments. Sensitivity to insult dictates strong connections from the present self to past selves, albeit connections that become weaker as selves recede. To say that an honor-obsessed individual is as angry a month after a verbal slight as the rest of us might be after a day is also to say that he is more loyal to his predecessor selves than we are. At the moment it is delivered, the symbolic affront might be no more painful to the man of honor than to the peaceable modern urbanite; it is simply that the sting of the insult passes quickly for the latter but lingers for days, even weeks, for the former—because his subsequent selves are so closely tied to the version of himself who actually experienced it. We could depict this difference as a contrast between, on one hand, a present self strongly tied to its predecessors and weakly connected to its successors, and, on the other, a present self weakly tied to the past and

---

6. It seems likely that the North-South difference would reappear if the time scale were stretched, that is, if subjects were asked whether they would be angry for a year about being punched.

strongly tied to a long string of future selves. Keep in mind that these are prescriptive models—ideas about how people ought to behave, depending on what society they inhabit. That neither is easy to achieve in practice is demonstrated by the energy devoted in each model's respective setting to *making* people live up to it. There are not many social settings in which individuals have to be pushed to live in the present (that is, to attach all available loyalty to one's present self and one or two adjacent selves) because people already have a strong tendency to do so.

Neither the honor model, with its obsessive emphasis on loyalty to past selves and disregard for the future, nor the modern consequentialist model, with its fascination for future selves—some of them decades away—and disdain for past ones, corresponds to a natural human tendency. Instead, each asks people to structure the connections among their sequentially occurring selves in a highly asymmetric way. Let us suppose that at any one moment a person has a fixed amount of regard available for distribution across past selves, future selves, and possibly other people. If so, then the intense connection people in honor settings feel for their past selves must come at someone's expense. There are two candidate classes of selves who might pay the price: other people and future versions of oneself. Now, it is a commonplace that social relations in modern, market-based contexts are more tenuous, and strong connections fewer in number, than in traditional honor settings. Even allowing for the limits to family unity on which I dwelt in chapter 4, it is still the case that inhabitants of feuding societies are more closely tied to others, notably extended kin, than are modern urbanites. It follows that the honorable individual's devotion to past selves is offset by a weakened connection to future ones. The man of honor, at least in principle, sacrifices his future selves on behalf of past versions of himself and on behalf of past, present, and future incarnations of his kin.

Symmetrically, women in these settings are expected to care most about future versions of themselves and of their families. Many of the women cut down in the course of family feuds, in Corsica as in other honor societies, had placed themselves between disputing men. Like priests in Catholic Mediterranean settings, and like holy men in other feuding contexts, female members of rival clans often found themselves in the role of peacemakers: people who put the interests of the entire community ahead of the particularist concern of angry men with vengeance for past offenses.[7]

In short, the strong commitment to redressing past wrongs and the indifference to the future displayed by adult men in honor settings are two sides of the same coin. So, naturally, are the commitment to the future and willingness to forgive the past that modern contexts routinely demand of everyone (and that feuding contexts demand of women and spiritual figures). From primary schools to corporate workplaces, people in authority teach their subordinates—children or adults who are acting like children—to put aside their differences, dispense with their grudges, and play or work together in pursuit of future harmony. Much of the time, they do not even try to justify this forward-looking agenda in terms of the well-being of all: Outside of religious teaching, it is often thought sufficient to appeal to each person's enlightened self-interest rather than to anyone's desire, considered weak and unreliable in market societies, to further the collective good.[8]

7. On the role of holy men in peacemaking, see E. E. Evans-Pritchard, *The Nuer* (Oxford: Oxford University Press, 1940); Ernest Gellner, "Trust, Cohesion, and the Social Order," pp. 142–57 in Diego Gambetta, ed., *Trust: Making and Breaking Cooperative Relations* (New York: Blackwell, 1988); Stephen K. Wilson, *Feuding, Conflict, and Banditry in Nineteenth-Century Corsica* (Cambridge: Cambridge University Press, 1988). Oddly, the most famous account of a Corsican vendetta, Prosper Mérimée's *Colomba* (Paris: Fayard, 1999), portrays the murdered man's daughter, the title character, as the key actor in the feud—goading and even tricking her brother Orso into firing the fatal shots that end the novella. Although women occasionally played a part in instigating violence in actual Corsican feuds—in Venzolasca in the early 1850s, for instance, the matriarch of the Lanfranchi clan helped provoke her rivals by saying, "their bullets don't penetrate"—they were much more likely to try to stop violence, or at any rate to stay out of it.

8. Hence the strong tendency among many scholars and social critics is to discount the claims to altruism on the part of people who do good. The standard trope is to show that the person who claims to have done something good has in reality been pursuing a private interest. So, the Union fought the Civil War against secessionist states not to rescue southern blacks from slavery but instead to make them available as wage-laborers for northern industrialists. The Communist Parties of the Soviet Union, China, and elsewhere collectivized industry and agriculture not because they wanted to achieve socialist equality but because they were power-hungry oligarchs. The United States helped rebuild Japan and Germany after World War II not to be kind but to set up a global economic system that would ensure its own international dominance. Andrew Carnegie donated millions of dollars to build libraries not because he wished to enlighten the masses but because he wanted them to remain docile. Populist leaders claim to represent common folk not because they care about common folk but because they think they can build successful careers by manipulating a large constituency. All of these arguments, from both left and right, rely on the plausibility of the idea that people typically help themselves before helping others and help others only to the degree that it is good for them.

I propose that, if somehow left to their own devices, people would gravitate to neither of these extremes. Nor (after infancy) would they gravitate naturally to the extreme intertemporal dissociation characteristic of Golightlies or the exceptional integration, symmetric with respect to past and present and smoothly spread across time, of Finches. The most probable "natural" network of intertemporal loyalties is one that ties present selves to nearby past and future ones, in a roughly symmetric structure. It is typically quite a challenge to convince children to be patient, even when doing so will increase the enjoyment of whatever they are waiting for: From their point of view, the person who will benefit from dessert postponed until after dinner might as well be someone else. Fortunately for adults, children are also, symmetrically, unable to remain upset about things for more than a few moments. The links among children's momentary selves are bunched pretty tightly around the present self, with essentially no connection to distant ones in either direction. Socialization, in particular that of children, endeavors to mold selves into a network that is stretched more smoothly across time, and usually in one direction more than the other.

We can see the effects of socialization in favor or one model or another, and the limited success of any given model, in the characteristic failures from which they suffer and in the common solutions people adopt to address such failures. Failed socialization in the rationalist, consequentialist model typically means a shortfall in the number of future selves to which the present self is loyal or in the strength of these loyalties. As a result, Western states impose forced savings programs to protect people from their own present-oriented spending habits. They control the availability of drugs that make people live in the present, such as narcotics, and liberally permit consumption of drugs that make people productive and functional—that is, interested in working rather than loafing. They penalize people who bypass legal channels for settling disputes in order to achieve more immediate gratification of their desire for redress. An effectively socialized person would bear less of a grudge *and* see the superiority of legal means to self-help.

Defenses against weak attachments to future selves go further. Laws oblige people to attend school, buy liability insurance, wear seatbelts, and don motorcycle helmets—all to counteract the tendency to care more about one's present self than the well-being of future selves or that of anyone else. Firms offer advantages to clients who lock in to purchases early and in bulk and (relatively speaking) penalize those who buy at the last minute in quantities suited to immediate consumption. In a world populated only by perfectly integrated, future-oriented people, none of these inducements would be necessary: People would go to school, save money, drive safely, and buy ahead of time, all by themselves. To the degree that they do not, real-world behavior in the market-based world appears to be guided by a network of intertemporal selves that involves thick loyalties to selves in the near future and thin loyalties to more distant ones.

I have already noted that the characteristic failure in honor settings is excessive devotion to future selves, at the expense both of past selves and of kin groups who would collectively benefit from the courage displayed by a member. Accordingly, aggrieved groups are often obliged to put considerable pressure on the one or two members selected for the task of vengeance. Sanctions range from cajoling to outright ostracism; in Corsica, kin of a victim might go to the length of publicly committing other family members to the pursuit of revenge—as when Santo Santini dipped his hand in the blood of his fallen son and smeared it on his youngest son's face, shouting, "If I die, remember that you must avenge your brother!" Five years later, father and both surviving sons did exactly that, although their bullets missed their intended target and struck his children instead.[9] It is said that Corsican men plotting revenge would stop shaving, the beard serving both as a signal to others that the matter was not settled and as a constant reminder to its wearer that he had not yet achieved his objective.

It is illuminating to consider, finally, the behaviors that express willful refusal to abide by societal expectations concerning the linkage of selves over time. In honor societies, refusal to subscribe to the preferred network structure would take the form of excessive regard for one's present and future and insufficient attention to kin or to one's past. Inasmuch as this sort of deviance typically does not run afoul of the law, people who live this way appear in documentary records, at least those of the courthouse, only as victims or bystanders. They tend to lose contests for rank, along with the respect of bystanders; so, nat-

---

9. Cour d'Assises de Bastia, sessions of 26 February 1856 and 15 December 1856.

urally, they turn inward and try to display indifference—possibly heartfelt—to the scorn they earn on the part of those more wedded to the traditional honor model.[10]

In modern bureaucratic settings, rebels look uncannily like the ideal honorable man in traditional settings. Consider the behaviors with which young people reject the effort of the mainstream to socialize them: they avoid school, indulge in drugs, alcohol, and cigarettes (the more toxic, the better), drive recklessly, and assume a range of risks most people would find unacceptable. These acts of rebellion are not chosen at random: Each one, in a different way, demonstrates the rebel's refusal to consider the well-being of future incarnations of himself or herself. Prominent tattoos and other permanent body mutilations are perhaps the most telling of these acts, in that they express something momentarily important to the rebel that must be borne by all of his or her successors regardless of their preferences. No doubt the mere shock value of such practices adds to their appeal, but what makes them shocking to others is the same thing that attracts rebels to them: They signal utter disregard for, even exaggerated hostility toward, future selves. Mere violation of norms is not sufficient to establish a behavior as rebellious; deviance must take the specific form of subordinating future selves absolutely to the whims of the present one.[11] No adolescent ever rebelled against her parents by overinvesting in bonds.

In short, it seems that honor societies and modern market-based societies are not qualitatively different, however distinct they might appear on the surface. This is true in two senses. First, both settings harbor people who diverge from the normative structure tying sequential selves to one another. Honor societies have their share of diligent, cautious people who try to stay out of trouble and worry about the future—they just don't earn as much respect as their bolder brethren. Modern societies have any number of prideful, grudge-bearing, impulsive people—but those people (apart from the ones who become Marines or successful athletes) are more likely to wind up in prison or in occu-

---

10. David Gilmore offers a sensitive portrait of just such a rebel, whom he encountered during his fieldwork in Andalusia: a gentle man who liked to cook and spend time with his wife and children. Gilmore, *Manhood in the Making* (New Haven: Yale University Press, 1990).

11. "No Future" was the title (and refrain) of a single by the Sex Pistols, one of the most impressive commercial successes associated with the punk "movement" of the 1970s and 1980s.

pations with limited authority and rewards. Although different societies mold people into different kinds of sequential selves, their raw
material is not all that malleable.

The second and more important connection between honor settings and contemporary market settings stems from the fact that the
models they offer occupy points on a single continuum. The main
difference, I have argued, is in which direction the loyalties tying sequential selves together flow: principally backward toward past selves
and "sideways" toward an extended set of kin, or principally forward
toward future selves and sideways to a very limited number of close associates. Other configurations are surely possible, although it might be
difficult for them to persist as social structures. Fully functioning societies of Golightlies, say, are probably hard to find.[12]

There is, then, a third sense in which the ideal types of honor societies and modern societies are more alike than different. It seems
likely that, in either setting, people would have enormous difficulty
sorting themselves into stably ranked social positions if everyone lived
up to the normative sequential self model to an equal degree. In honorific competition, life would not be sustainable if nobody ever backed
down and accepted defeat. (Consider the modern world's honorific
game of Chicken, in which two drivers race toward each other, each
one hoping the other will swerve first. Both live only if someone loses,
although of course the winner is better off than the loser.) Although
the evidence in this book has concentrated on the cases in which
people did not back down, the point is that these contests were *supposed*
to end with one person deferring to the other (something that we know
happens every day), possibly setting the stage for a stable hierarchical
relation.

The reason heterogeneity in the way selves are structured is also a
fundamental ingredient in modern settings is less grim, perhaps, but
no less important. As I observed in chapter 2, most people spend most
of their waking hours laboring in hierarchical organizations, varying
in size of course from a dozen or so to hundreds of thousands. Outside
of work, things often look much the same, in voluntary associations,
churches, and school boards, all of which have roles differentiated with
respect to authority. These organizations, especially but not exclusively

12. Aside from southern California, perhaps.

large corporations, offer their members a peculiar bargain: Accept your current subordinate position eagerly or at least with dignity, follow directions dutifully and perhaps beyond, and you shall eventually be rewarded with a new position in which you may ask the same of others (while your new superiors continue to do the same with you). In other words, organizations extract work from people—those, at least, who see themselves as having careers as opposed to jobs—by asking them to accept low-ranking positions in the present in return for the promise of higher rank, and accompanying rank-related rewards, later on. They succeed only to the extent that there is a steady supply of people willing to make this trade, out of commitment to the well-being of successor selves ten or more years into the future.

Naturally, the trade also depends on there being a reasonable likelihood of future advancement. In low-wage jobs with transparently little prospect for advancement, subordination depends instead on the employees' immediate need for pay. Employers are for some reason puzzled when such employees fail to show a willingness to do extra work or to cheerfully accept scoldings and other forms of symbolic degradation; in contrast, senior partners in law and accounting firms, high-level managers in large companies, and senior members of many other career-based organizations are frequently delighted to see how much humiliation their underlings seem willing to accept. Not surprisingly, years of such treatment often make newly promoted people eager to recoup the losses in pride they have suffered as subordinates, perpetuating the pattern.

The problem is that not everyone can be promoted, even if shortsighted managers (and before them, kings) sometimes try to achieve this by manufacturing titles to accommodate the demand for advancement. Some people have to learn that their efforts have fallen short, that they turned out not to have "what it takes" to merit further advancement—or at least that others receiving bigger or faster promotions displayed more of it. Organizational leaders have to be able to point to some qualities that vary across personnel if they are to keep the exchange going. At the same time, those qualities have to be hard to define or measure, or else it would be obvious in advance who was going to win the contest. Forward-looking selves will only accept subordination in the present in return for possibly superior rank for their successor selves if it is plausible, but not certain, that their efforts will result in advancement. For the bargain to sustain itself, people must vary in their ability to absorb years of demeaning treatment on behalf of future, higher-ranking selves.

In this regard, then, there is a noteworthy difference between honor societies and most of our urbanized, modern world.[13] In the former, people achieve superior social rank by successfully extracting immediate and public deference from their rivals—which they can do only by displaying greater courage, which is to say superior indifference to their future selves. In the latter, the situation is reversed. Much of the time, the greatest rewards and highest social rank accrue to those who, out of devotion to their future selves, successfully suppress their desire for superior rank so as to attract the favor of those who currently hold it. Those who fail—they are usually branded by superiors as having "an attitude"—are the ones for whom this long-term exchange is unbearable.

In the early nineteenth century, Alexis de Tocqueville—an aristocrat entirely comfortable with hierarchy and with his own position in it—thought he found in the American people a love of equality surpassing that of any other society. Somehow he missed a crucial detail. Americans, like anyone else, then and now, prefer equality to subordination, but many, perhaps most, would find a situation in which others were subordinate *to them* even more satisfactory. The idea of equality, of a society without rank, is much more a compromise solution—an insistence that, if I can't be king, then no one else can either—than it is a fulfillment of a noble dream. If that were not so, then many tens of thousands of people would grow old instead of being cut down for making a disparaging remark or going to prison for avenging the remark. And an even larger number of people, many hundreds of millions, would make other people's lives happier by not looking for opportunities to make such remarks, to put people down, to make others, individuals and groups, feel foolish or weak or small. But the desire for superior rank is strong, and so they do.

13. I have already noted that youth in poor urban neighborhoods in North America and Europe inhabit a setting much like honor contexts.

Abu-Lughod, Janet. *Rabat: Urban Apartheid in Morocco*. Princeton: Princeton University Press, 1980.

Albitreccia, Antoine. *La Corse: Son évolution au XIXe siècle et au debut du XXe siècle*. Paris: Presses Universitaires de France, 1942.

Ansell, Christopher K. "Symbolic Networks: The Realignment of the French Working Class, 1887–1894." *American Journal of Sociology* 103 (1997): 359–90.

Baldassare, Mark. *The Los Angeles Riot: Lessons for the Future*. Boulder, Colo.: Westview, 1994.

Bales, Robert F., Fred Strodtbeck, T. M. Mills, and Mary E. Roseborough. "Channels of Communication in Small Groups." *American Sociological Review* 16 (1951): 461–68.

Bearman, Peter S. *Relations into Rhetorics: Local Elite Social Structure in Norfolk, England, 1540–1640*. New Brunswick. N.J.: Rutgers University Press, 1993.

Beattie, J. H. M. "Homicide and Suicide in Bunyoro." In *African Homicide and Suicide*, edited by Paul Bohannan, 130–53. Princeton: Princeton University Press, 1960.

Benedict, Ruth. *The Chrysanthemum and the Sword: Patterns of Japanese Culture*. Boston: Houghton-Mifflin, 1946.

Berger, Joseph, M. Hamit Fisek, Robert Z. Norman, and Morris Zelditch Jr. *Status Characteristics and Social Interaction: An Expectation States Approach*. New York: Elsevier, 1977.

Black, Donald. *The Social Structure of Right and Wrong*. San Diego: Academic, 1993.

Black-Michaud, Jacob. *Cohesive Force: Feud in the Mediterranean and the Middle East.* New York: St. Martin's, 1975.

Bloch, Marc. *Feudal Society.* 1940; reprint, Chicago: University of Chicago Press, 1961.

———. *Slavery and Serfdom in the Middle Ages.* Berkeley: University of California Press, 1975.

Bloch, Maurice. "The Long Term and the Short Term: The Economic and Political Significance of the Morality of Kinship." In *The Character of Kinship,* edited by Jack Goody, 75–87. Cambridge: Cambridge University Press.

Blok, Anton. *The Mafia of a Sicilian Village, 1860–1960: A Study of Violent Peasant Entrepreneurs.* New York: Harper, 1974.

Boehm, Christopher. *Blood Revenge: The Enactment and Management of Revenge in Montenegro and Other Tribal Societies.* Philadelphia: University of Pennsylvania Press, 1987.

Bohannan, Paul. "Homicide among the Tiv of Central Nigeria." In *African Homicide and Suicide,* edited by Paul Bohannan, 30–64. Princeton: Princeton University Press, 1960.

Bourdieu, Pierre. "The Sentiment of Honor in Kabyle Society." In *Honor and Shame: The Values of Mediterranean Society,* edited by Jean G. Peristiany, 191–242. Chicago: University of Chicago Press, 1966.

Bourgois, Philippe. *In Search of Respect: Selling Crack in El Barrio.* Berkeley: University of California Press, 1995.

Burling, Robbins. "Maximization Theories and the Study of Economic Anthropology." *American Anthropologist* 64 (1962): 802–21.

Calhoun, Craig J. " 'New Social Movements' of the Early Nineteenth Century." In *Repertoires and Cycles of Collective Action,* edited by Mark Traugott, 173–215. Durham, N.C.: Duke University Press, 1995.

Campbell, Anne. *The Girls in the Gang.* New York: Blackwell, 1984.

Campbell, John King. *Honour, Family, and Patronage: A Study of Institutions and Moral Values in a Greek Mountain Community.* Oxford: Clarendon, 1964.

Caplow, Theodore. "Rule Enforcement without Visible Means: Christmas Gift Giving in Middletown." *American Journal of Sociology* 89 (1984): 1306–23.

Carson, Clayborne. *In Struggle: SNCC and the Black Awakening of the 1960s.* Cambridge: Harvard University Press, 1981.

Chagnon, Napoleon. *Yanomamo: The Fierce People.* New York: Holt, Rinehart and Winston, 1983.

Chong, Dennis. *Collective Action and the Civil Rights Movement.* Berkeley: University of California Press, 1991.

Coase, Ronald H. *The Nature of the Firm: Origins, Evolution, and Development.* New York: Oxford University Press, 1991.

Cohen, Lawrence, and Marcus Felson. "Social Change and Crime Rate Trends: A Routine Activity Approach." *American Sociological Review* 44 (1979): 588–608.

Coleman, James S. *The Adolescent Society: The Social Life of the Teenager and Its Impact on Education*. New York: Free, 1961.

Collier, Jane F. *Marriage and Inequality in Classless Societies*. Stanford: Stanford University Press, 1988.

Cook, Scott. "The 'Anti-market' Mentality Re-examined: A Further Critique of the Substantive Approach to Economic Anthropology." *Southwest Journal of Anthropology* 25 (1969): 378–406.

Cottereau, Alain. "The Distinctiveness of Working-Class Cultures in France, 1848–1900." In *Working-Class Formation*, edited by Ira Katznelson and Aristide Zolberg. Princeton. Princeton University Press. 1986.

Cour d'Assises de Bastia, 1st trimester, session 10, 1851.

Cour d'Assises de Bastia, 4th trimester, session of November 12, 1852.

Culioli, Gabriel Xavier. *Le complexe corse*. Paris: Gallimard, 1990.

Dalton, George. "Economic Theory and Primitive Society." *American Anthropologist* 63 (1961): 1–25.

———. "Primitive Money." *American Anthropologist* 67 (1965): 44–65.

Daly, Martin, and Margo Wilson. *Homicide*. Chicago: Aldine de Gruyter, 1988.

Darnton, Robert. *The Great Cat Massacre and Other Episodes in French Cultural History*. New York: Random House, 1985.

Darwin, Charles. *The Expression of the Emotions in Man and Animal*. 3d ed. New York: Oxford University Press, 1998.

Dentan, Robert K. *The Semai: A Nonviolent People of Malaya*. New York: Holt, Rinehart and Winston, 1979.

de Waal, Frans. *Chimpanzee Politics*. Baltimore. Johns Hopkins University Press. 2000.

———. *Peacemaking Among Primates*. Cambridge: Harvard University Press: 1990

Domhoff, G. W. *Who Rules America: Power and Politics*. 4th ed. New York: McGraw-Hill, 2001.

Duesenberry, James. *Business Cycles and Economic Growth*. New York: Greenwood, 1958.

Dumont, Louis. *Homo Hierarchicus: The Caste System and Its Implications*. Chicago: University of Chicago Press, 1967.

Durkheim, Emile. *The Elementary Forms of the Religious Life*. 1912; reprint, New York: Free, 1973.

Elias, Norbert. *The Civilizing Process*. 1939; reprint, Oxford: Blackwell, 1994.

Evans, Sarah. *Personal Politics: The Roots of Women's Liberation in the Civil Rights Movement and the New Left*. New York: Random House, 1980.

Evans-Pritchard, E. E. *The Nuer*. Oxford: Oxford University Press, 1940.

Fantasia, Rick. *Cultures of Solidarity*. Berkeley: University of California Press, 1988.

Fearon, James D., and David A. Laitin. "Explaining Interethnic Cooperation." *American Political Science Review* 90, no. 4 (1996): 715–35.

Fernandez, Roberto M., and Doug McAdam. "Social Networks and Social Move-
    ments: Multiorganizational Fields and Recruitment to Mississippi Freedom
    Summer." *Sociological Forum* 3, no. 3 (1988): 357–82.

Fischer, David H. *Albion's Seed: Four British Folkways in America.* New York: Oxford
    University Press, 1989.

Flanagan, James G. "Hierarchy in Simple 'Egalitarian' Societies." *Annual Review of
    Anthropology* 18 (1989): 245–66.

Fortes, Meyer. *The Dynamics of Clanship among the Tallens.* London: Oxford Univer-
    sity Press, 1945.

Foucault, Michel. *Discipline and Punish: The Birth of the Prison.* New York: Vintage, 1995.

Frank, Robert. *Choosing the Right Pond.* Cambridge: Harvard University Press, 1985.

Friedell, Morris. "Organizations as Semilattices." *American Sociological Review* 32
    (1967): 46–54.

Gambetta, Diego. "Mafia: The Price of Distrust." In *Trust: The Making and Breaking
    of Cooperative Relations,* edited by Diego Gambetta, 158–75. New York: Black-
    well, 1988.

———. *The Sicilian Mafia.* Cambridge: Harvard University Press, 1993.

———, ed. *Trust: Making and Breaking Cooperative Relations.* New York: Blackwell,
    1988.

Gellner, Ernest. "Trust, Cohesion, and the Social Order." In *Trust: Making and Break-
    ing Cooperative Relations,* edited by Diego Gambetta, 142–57. New York: Black-
    well, 1988.

Genovese, Eugene D. *Roll, Jordan, Roll: The World the Slaves Made.* New York: Vin-
    tage, 1972.

Gilmore, David D. "Honor, Honesty, Shame: Male Status in Contemporary Andalu-
    sia." In *Honor and Shame and the Unity of the Mediterranean,* edited by David D.
    Gilmore, 90–103. Washington, D.C.: American Anthropological Association,
    1987.

———. *Manhood in the Making: Cultural Concepts of Masculinity.* New Haven: Yale
    University Press, 1990.

Ginat, Joseph. *Blood Disputes among Bedouin and Rural Arabs in Israel: Revenge, Medi-
    ation, Outcasts, and Family Honor.* Pittsburgh: University of Pittsburgh Press,
    1987.

Given, James Buchanan. *Society and Homicide in Thirteenth-Century England.* Stan-
    ford: Stanford University Press, 1977.

Gluckman, Max. *Custom and Conflict in Africa.* Glencoe, Ill.: Free Press, 1955.

———, ed. *The Allocation of Responsibility.* Manchester: Manchester University
    Press, 1972.

Godelier, Maurice. *La Production des grands hommes: Pouvoir et domination masculine
    chez les Baruya en Nouvelle-Guinée.* Paris: Fayard, 1982.

———, ed. *Un domaine contesté: l'anthropologie économique.* Paris: Mouton, 1974.

Goodman, Nelson. *Ways of Worldmaking.* 1954; reprint, Indianapolis: Hackett, 1977.

Gordon, Linda. *Pitied but Not Entitled: Single Mothers and the History of Welfare*. Cambridge: Belknap Press of Harvard University Press, 1995.

Gould, Roger V. *Insurgent Identities: Class, Community, and Protest in Paris from 1848 to the Commune*. Chicago: University of Chicago Press, 1995.

———. "Multiple Networks and Mobilization in the Paris Commune, 1871." *American Sociological Review* 56 (1991): 716–29.

———. "Patron-Client Ties, State Centralization, and the Whiskey Rebellion." *American Journal of Sociology* 102 (1996): 400–429.

———. "Trade Cohesion, Class Unity, and Urban Insurrection: Artisanal Activism in the Paris Commune." *American Journal of Sociology* 98 (1993): 721–54.

Greenberg, James B. *Blood Ties: Life and Violence in Rural Mexico*. Tucson: University of Arizona Press, 1989.

Greenberg, Kenneth S. "The Nose, the Lie, and the Duel in the Antebellum South." *American Historical Review* 95 (1990): 57–74.

Hallpike, Christopher R. *Bloodshed and Vengeance in the Papuan Mountains*. Oxford: Clarendon, 1977.

Hardin, Russell. *One for All: The Logic of Group Conflict*. Princeton: Princeton University Press, 1995.

Hare, A. Paul. *Handbook of Small Group Research*. New York: Free, 1962.

Hare, A. Paul, Edgar F. Borgatta, and Robert F. Bales, eds. *Small Groups: Studies in Social Interaction*. New York: Knopf, 1966.

Hasluck, Margaret. *The Unwritten Law in Albania*. Cambridge: Cambridge University Press, 1954.

Hebdige, Richard. *Subculture: The Meaning of Style*. London: Routledge: 1981.

Herzfeld, Michael. *The Poetics of Manhood: Contest and Identity in a Cretan Mountain Village*. Princeton: Princeton University Press, 1985.

Hilberg, Raoul. *Perpetrators Victims Bystanders: The Jewish Catastrophe, 1933–1945*. New York: Harper Perennial, 1993.

Hogg, Michael, and Dominic Abrams. *Social Identifications: A Social Psychology of Intergroup Relations and Group Processes*. London: Routledge, 1988,

Homans, George C. *Social Behavior: Its Elementary Forms*. New York: Harcourt, Brace, and World, 1961.

Horowitz, Donald L. *Ethnic Groups in Conflict*. Berkeley: University of California Press, 1985.

Horowitz, Ruth. *Honor and the American Dream: Culture and Identity in a Chicano Community*. New Brunswick, N.J.: Rutgers University Press, 1983.

Horowitz, Ruth, and Gary Schwartz. "Honor, Normative Ambiguity, and Gang Violence." *American Sociological Review* 39, no. 2 (1974): 238–51.

Ikegami, Eiko. *The Taming of the Samurai: Honorific Individualism and the Making of Modern Japan*. Cambridge: Harvard University Press, 1995.

Jaggers, Keith J., and Ted Robert Gurr. "Polity III: Regime Change and Political Authority, 1800–1994." (Computer file.) Boulder, Colo., 1995.

———. "Polity III: Regime Change and Political Authority, 1800–1994." 2nd ICPSR version. Ann Arbor, Mich.: Interuniversity Consortium for Political and Social Research, 1996.

Jankowski, Martin S. *Islands in the Street: Gangs and American Urban Society.* Berkeley: University of California Press, 1991.

Kanter, Rosabeth Moss. *Men and Women of the Corporation.* New York: Basic, 1993.

Kaplan, David. "The Formal-Substantive Controversy in Economic Anthropology." *Southwestern Journal of Anthropology* 24 (1968): 228–51.

Kaplan, Robert D. *Balkan Ghosts: A Journey through History.* New York: St. Martin's, 1993.

Karsten, Rafael. "Blood Revenge and War among the Jibaro Indians of Eastern Ecuador." In *The Allocation of Responsibility,* edited by Max Gluckman, 303–26. Manchester: Manchester University Press, 1972.

Katznelson, Ira, and Aristide Zolberg, eds. *Working-Class Formation.* Princeton: Princeton University Press, 1986.

Knauft, Bruce M. "Reconsidering Violence in Simple Human Societies: Homicide among the Gebusi of New Guinea." *Current Anthropology* 28 (1987): 457–500.

Kressel, Gideon M. "Sororicide/Filiacide: Homicide for Family Honour." *Current Anthropology* 22 (1981): 141–58.

La Fontaine, Jean. "Homicide and Suicide among the Gisu." In *African Homicide and Suicide,* edited by Paul Bohannan, 94–129. Princeton: Princeton University Press, 1960.

Leacock, Eleanor. "Women's Status in Egalitarian Society: Implications for Social Evolution." *Current Anthropology* 19 (1982): 247–76.

LeClair, Edward E. "Economic Theory and Economic Anthropology." *American Anthropologist* 64 (1962): 1179–1203.

LeVine, Robert A., and Donald T. Campbell. *Ethnocentrism: Theories of Conflict, Ethnic Attitudes, and Group Behavior.* New York: Wiley, 1972.

Lipuma, Edward, Moishe Postone, and Craig Calhoun, eds. *Bourdieu: Critical Perspectives.* Chicago: University of Chicago Press, 1993.

Lorenz, Konrad. *On Aggression.* New York: Harvest, 1974.

MacAleer, Kevin. *Dueling.* Princeton: Princeton University Press, 1994.

MacKinnon, Catharine E. *Toward a Feminist Theory of the State.* Cambridge: Harvard University Press, 1991.

Macy, Michael W. "Backward-Looking Social Control." *American Sociological Review* 58 (1993): 819–36.

———. "Chains of Cooperation: Threshold Effects in Collective Action." *American Sociological Review* 56 (1991): 730–47.

Malinowski, Bronislaw. *Argonauts of the Western Pacific.* New York: Waveland, 1994.

Marcaggi, J. B. *Fleuve de sang: Histoire d'une vendetta.* 1898; reprint, n.p.: Ajaccio Piazzola, 1993.

Marcuse, Herbert. *One-Dimensional Man: Studies in Ideology of Advanced Industrial Society*. Boston: Beacon, 1992.

Marriott, McKim. *Caste Ranking and Community Structure in Five Regions of India and Pakistan*. Poona, India: Deccan College Building Centenary and Silver Jubilee Institute, 1965.

Marwell, Gerald R, Pamela E. Oliver, and Ralph Prahl. "Social Networks and Collective Action: A Theory of the Critical Mass III." *American Journal of Sociology* 94 (1988): 502–34.

Mayer, Adrian C. *Caste and Kinship in Central India: A Village and Its Region*. Berkeley: University of California Press, 1970.

Mazur, Allan. "A Biosocial Model of Status in Face-to-Face Primate Groups." *Social Forces* 64 (1985): 377–402.

McAdam, Doug. *Freedom Summer*. New York: Random House, 1993.

———. *Political Process and the Development of Black Insurgency, 1930–1970*. Chicago: University of Chicago Press, 1982.

———. "Recruitment to High Risk/Cost Activism: The Case of Freedom Summer." *American Journal of Sociology* 92, no. 1 (1986): 64–90.

McAdam, Doug, and Ronnelle Paulsen. "Specifying the Relationship between Social Ties and Activism." *American Journal of Sociology* 99, no. 3 (1993): 640–67.

Melucci, Alberto, John Keane, and Paul Mier, eds. *Nomads of the Present: Social Movements and Individual Needs in Contemporary Society*. Philadelphia: Temple University Press, 1989.

Mérimée, Prosper. *Colomba et Autres Nouvelles*. Paris: Fayard. 1999.

Merriman, John. *The Margins of City Life: Explorations on the French Urban Frontier, 1815–1851*. Oxford: Oxford University Press, 1997.

Miller, William Ian. *Bloodtaking and Peacemaking: Feud, Law, and Society in Saga Iceland*. Chicago: University of Chicago Press, 1990.

Milner, Murray. *Status and Sacredness: A General Theory of Status Relations and an Analysis of Indian Culture*. Oxford: Oxford University Press, 1994.

Molm, Linda. *Coercive Power in Social Exchange*. New York: Cambridge University Press. 1997.

Moore, Sally F. "Legal Liability and Evolutionary Interpretation: Some Aspects of Strict Liability, Self-Help and Collective Responsibility." In *The Allocation of Responsibility*, edited by Max Gluckman, 51–108. Manchester: Manchester University Press, 1972.

Moreno, Jacob L. *Who Shall Survive? Foundations of Sociometry, Group Psychotherapy, and Sociodrama*. Beacon, N.Y.: Beacon House, 1953.

Morris, Aldon, and Carol Mueller, eds. *Frontiers of Social Movement Theory*. New Haven: Yale University Press, 1992.

Nash, Manning. *Primitive and Peasant Economic Systems*. San Francisco: Chandler, 1967.

Newcomb, Theodore. *The Acquaintance Process*. New York: Holt, Rinehart and Winston, 1961.

Nisbet, Richard E., and Dov Cohen. *Culture of Honor: The Psychology of Violence in the South.* Boulder, Colo.: Westview, 1996.

Nye, Robert A. *Masculinity and Male Codes of Honor in Modern France.* New York: Oxford University Press, 1993.

Oberschall, Anthony. *Social Conflict and Social Movements.* New York. Prentice-Hall, 1973.

———. *Social Movements: Ideologies, Interest, and Identities.* New York. Transaction, 1995.

Oliver, Pamela E., and Gerald R. Marwell. *The Logic of Collective Action.* New York: Cambridge University Press, 1993.

Olzak, Susan. "Contemporary Ethnic Mobilization." *Annual Review of Sociology* 9 (1983): 355–74.

———. *Ethnic Conflict and Competition.* Stanford: Stanford University Press, 1992.

Omark, Donald R., F. F. Strayer, and Daniel G. Freedman, eds. *Dominance Relations: An Ethological View of Human Conflict and Social Interaction.* New York: Garland STPM, 1980.

Ortner, Sherry. "Is Female to Male as Nature Is to Culture?" In *Woman, Culture, and Society,* edited by Michelle Z. Rosaldo and Louise Lamphere, 67–88. Stanford: Stanford University Press, 1974.

Otterbein, Keith. *The Evolution of War: A Cross-Cultural Study.* Human Area Relations Files. 1989.

———. *Feuding and Warfare: Selected Works of Keith F. Otterbein.* London. Routeledge. 1994.

Patterson, Orlando. *Slavery and Social Death: A Comparative Study.* Cambridge: Harvard University Press, 1982.

———. *The Sociology of Slavery: An Analysis of the Origins, Development, and Structure of Negro Slave Society in Jamaica.* London: MacGibbon and Kee, 1967.

Peristiany, Jean G. *Honor and Shame: The Values of Mediterranean Society.* Chicago: University of Chicago Press, 1966.

Peters, Emry. "Some Structural Aspects of the Feud among the Camel-Herding Bedouin of Cyrenaica." *Africa* 37 (1967): 261–82.

Pitt-Rivers, J. *The Fate of Shechem, or the Politics of Sex.* Cambridge: Cambridge University Press, 1977.

Piven, Frances Fox, and Richard Cloward. *Regulating the Poor: The Functions of Public Welfare.* 2d ed. New York: Vintage, 1993.

Polanyi, Karl, C. M. Arensberg, and H. W. Pearson, eds. *Trade and Market in the Early Empires.* Glencoe, Ill.: Free Press, 1957.

Polletta, Francesca. *Freedom Is an Endless Meeting: Democracy in American Social Movements.* Chicago: University of Chicago Press, 2002.

Pomponi, Francis. *Histoire de la Corse.* Paris: Hachette, 1979.

Price, Richard, ed. *Maroon Societies: Rebel Slave Communities in the Americas.* Baltimore: Johns Hopkins University Press, 1979.

Putnam, Hilary. *Reason, Truth, and History.* Cambridge: Cambridge University Press, 1981.

Ridgeway, Cecilia. "Nonverbal Behavior Dominance and the Distribution of Status in Task Groups." *American Sociological* Review 52 (1987): 683–94.

Ridgeway, Cecilia, and David Diekema. "Dominance and Collective Hierarchy Formation in Male and Female Task Groups." *American Sociological Review* 54 (1989): 79–93.

Rivers, W. H. R. *Kinship and Social Organization.* 1914; reprint, London: Athlone, 1968.

Romanucci-Ross, Lola. *Conflict, Violence, and Morality in a Mexican Village.* Chicago: University of Chicago Press, 1986.

Rosaldo, Michelle Z. *Knowledge and Passion: Ilongot Notions of Self and Social Life.* Cambridge: Cambridge University Press, 1980.

———. "Woman, Culture, and Society: A Theoretical Overview." In *Woman, Culture, and Society,* edited by Michelle Z. Rosaldo and Louise Lamphere. Stanford: Stanford University Press, 1974.

Rosaldo, Michelle Z., and Louise Lamphere, eds., *Woman, Culture, and Society.* Stanford: Stanford University Press, 1974.

Rosaldo, Renato. *Ilongot Headhunting, 1883–1974.* Stanford: Stanford University Press, 1980.

Rosenfeld, Richard. St. Louis Homicide Project, Washington University of St. Louis.

Ruche, Georg, and Otto Kirchheimer. *Punishment and Social Structure.* New York: Columbia University Press, 1939.

Sahlins, Marshall. "On the Sociology of Primitive Exchange." In *The Relevance of Models for Social Anthropology,* edited by Michael Banton, 139–236. London: Tavistock, 1965.

———. *Stone-Age Economics.* Chicago: Aldine-Atherton, 1967.

Schattschneider, E. E. *The Semi-Sovereign People: A Realist's View of Democracy in America.* New York: International Thomson, 1997.

Scheff, Thomas. *Bloody Revenge: Emotions, Nationalism, and War.* Universe.com. 2000.

Schneider, Jane. "Of Vigilance and Virgins: Honor, Shame, and Access to Resources in Mediterranean Societies." *Ethnology* 10 (1971): 1–24.

Schwartz, Barry. *Vertical Classification.* Chicago: University of Chicago Press, 1981.

Scott, James C. *Weapons of the Weak: Everyday Forms of Peasant Resistance.* New Haven: Yale University Press, 1987.

Searle, John. *Intentionality: An Essay in the Philosophy of Mind.* Cambridge: Cambridge University Press, 1983.

Sewell, William H. Jr. *Work and Revolution in France: The Language of Labor from the Old Regime to 1848.* New York: Cambridge University Press, 1980.

Sherif, Muzafer. *Group Conflict and Cooperation.* New York: St. Martin's, 1966.

———. *Social Interaction: Process and Products.* Chicago: Aldine, 1967.

Simmel, Georg .*Conflict and the Web of Group Affiliations*. 1923; reprint, New York: Free, 1955.

Stampp, Kenneth. *The Peculiar Institution: Slavery in the Antebellum South*. 1956; reprint, New York: Vintage, 1989.

Stewart, Frank Henderson. *Honor*. Chicago: University of Chicago Press, 1994.

Strathern, Marilyn. *The Gender of the Gift: Problems with Women and Problems with Society in Melanesia*. Berkeley: University of California Press, 1990.

Suttles, Gerald R. *The Social Order of the Slum*. Chicago: University of Chicago Press, 1967.

Tajfel, Henri. "Experiments in Intergroup Discrimination." *Scientific American* (November 1970): 96–102.

———. "Social Identity and Intergroup Behavior." *Social Science Information* 13 (1974): 65–93.

Taylor, Verta, and Nancy Whittier. "Collective Identity in Social Movement Communities: Lesbian Feminist Mobilization." In *Frontiers of Social Movement Theory*, edited by Aldon Morris and Carol Mueller, 104–29. New Haven: Yale University Press, 1992.

Thomas, Elizabeth Marshall. *The Harmless People*. New York: Vintage, 1959.

Thompson, E. P. *The Making of the English Working Class*. New York: Random House, 1963.

Tilly, Charles, Louise Tilly, and Richard Tilly. *The Rebellious Century*. Cambridge: Harvard University Press, 1975.

Tinbergen, Nikolaas. *Social Behavior in Animals*. London: Chapman and Hall, 1953.

Traugott, Mark, ed. *Repertoires and Cycles of Collective Action*. Durham, N.C.: Duke University Press, 1995.

Turner, John, and Howard Giles. *Intergroup Behavior*. Oxford: Blackwell, 1981.

United States Bureau of the Census. 1996.

Unsal, Artun. *Tuer pour survivre: La Vendetta*. Paris: Editions L'Harmattan, 1990.

Varma, Sushil C. *The Bhil Kills*. Delhi: Kunji, 1978.

Verrier, Elwin. *Maria Murder and Suicide*. Bombay: Geoffrey Cumberlege/Oxford University Press, 1943.

Versini, Xavier. *La vie quotidienne en Corse au temps de Mâerimâee*. Paris: Hachette, 1964.

Voorhies, B. "Possible Social Factors in the Exchange System of the Prehistoric Maya." *American Antiquarian* 38 (1973): 486–89.

Webb, Malcolm C. "Exchange Networks: Prehistory." *Annual Review of Anthropology* 3 (1974): 357–83.

Weber, Max. *Economy and Society*, trans. H. H. Gerth and C. W. Mills. Berkeley: University of California Press, 1980.

Whyte, William F. *Street Corner Society: The Social Structure of an Italian Slum*. Chicago: University of Chicago Press, 1993.

Wikan, Unni. "Shame and Honor: A Contestable Pair." *Man* 19 (1984): 635–52.

Wilbanks, William. *Murder in Miami.*New York: University Press of America, 1984.

Williamson, Oliver. *The Economic Institutions of Capitalism.* New York: Free, 1987.

Wilson, Stephen K. *Feuding, Conflict, and Banditry in Nineteenth-Century Corsica.* Cambridge: Cambridge University Press, 1988.

Wyatt-Brown, Bertram. *Southern Honor: Ethics and Behavior in the Old South.* New York: Oxford University Press, 1982.

Zablocki, Benjamin. *The Joyful Community.* Chicago: University of Chicago Press, 1980.

Zagorin, Perez. *The Court and the County.* New York: Atheneum, 1970.

Note: *Italicized page numbers indicate figures.*

academia: competition in, 19n. 16; incentive system in, 12–13n. 11; rewards in, 20–22. *See also specific disciplines (e.g., sociology)*
acquaintances, 71–72, 86, 140
agency, use of term, 3
Albania, revenge attacks in, 131n. 21
Althusser, Louis, 107
altruism, 175n. 8
animal behavior, 27–28
anthropology: biases in, 59n. 18; dominance defined in, 30–31; on economic behaviors, 13–14; "not on Easter Island" phenomenon, 12–13n. 11
apology, efficacy of, 77n. 7
asymmetrical relations: concept of, 70–71; in constructing various selves, 174; in control vs. well-being, 50–51; family relationships as, 68–69, 72; friendships as, 48–49, 51–53; homicides due to substantive matters linked to, 69–70, 85; homicides less likely in, 87–93, *97;* in intentional communities, 22n. 18; in in-

terpersonal influence, 46–49; marriage as, 88; master/slave relations as, 41–42, 108. *See also* bureaucratic organizations; exit option

bandits, 133
Bantu tribes, 95
Bean, Roy, 23
Benedict, Ruth, 11n. 10
Berber people, 130–31
Bhil tribe, 90–91, *92, 97,* 99
Bison-Horn Maria tribe, 100
Black, Donald, xv
blood revenge. *See* vendettas
Boehm, Christopher, 131
Bohannan, Paul, 95, 102
bureaucratic organizations: acceptance of hierarchy in, 179–81; competition in, 18–21; efficiency in, 21–22; employment relations in, 42–43, 62, 70; explicit status cues in, 70–72; honor societies compared with, 17–18, 20–23; third-party adjudication in, 62. *See also* academia; nation-states; schools

conflict institutionalized in, 140–
41; revenge attacks due to conflict
in, 130
populism, 175n. 8
principle, anger based in, 52. *See also*
honor
protest: in political transitions, 162–66;
value of, even in failure, 37n. 6
Protestant Reformation, 151–54
psychology: on dominance, 28–31; on
group characteristics, 148; on identity categories, 116

race: as identity category, 116; inequality
based on, 34–35
racial violence, 122
regime collapse, violence in response
to, 63
religious societies, 23
resistance, definition of, 162–63. *See also*
protest
resources, cultural vs. material, 7–8. *See
also* motivations
responsibility: collective, 130–34; individual, 168–69
revenge. *See* vendettas
Roman empire, 109
rural areas, symmetric-asymmetric relation homicides in, 90–93

same-sex couples, 88n. 11
schools, 46–48
seniority, 20
Sex Pistols (group), 178n. 11
sexual relationships, 88, 98
Simmel, Georg, 88, 113
social rank: asymmetries in, 46–49; attempts to suppress, 22n. 18; competition for, 17–21, 181; compo-
nents of, 45–46; as critical issue,
137; disruptions in, 63–65, 157–58,
160–66; emergence of, 22–25; examples of murders due to affronts
against, 78–82; limits of, 179;

metaphorical representation of,
11; relations inconsistent with, 66.
See also elites; hierarchy
social relations: ambiguous vs. clear
cues on, 60–61, 69–72; collective
identities as conceptual devices in,
33n. 4, 50; conflict as intrinsic to,
38; disruptions in, 63–65, 157–58,
160–66; domination in stable vs.
unstable types of, 61–63, 66; hierarchies' emergence in, 22–23; interlocking nature of, 150, 161–66;
interpersonal violence in context
of, 5; local-level specifics in, 152–
55; symbolic harm in context of,
55–57. *See also* asymmetrical relations; symmetrical relations
social sciences: "big" questions in, 151–
53; concepts useful in, 40–41,
90n. 13; conflict approaches in,
37–38; on crime, 4–5; differences
as focus of, 9–13; dominance
defined in, 30–36; as focused on
custom (not events), 131; formalists vs. substantivists in, 14–15; on
honor and blood societies, 7–9,
127, 130–31; on individual interests, 169; natural sciences compared with, 15–16n. 14; on social
order, 161–62; theory in, 65,
101n. 24; thick vs. thin concepts
in, 28–30, 50, 106. *See also* anthropology; history; Marxist theory;
methodology; political science; sociology
social status. *See* social rank
social structures: concept of, 61; conflict
propagated in, 152, 155–61; as continuum, 135–36; human vs. nonhuman, 60n. 19; individual vs.
group attributes in, 147–50; interlocking nature of, 150, 161–66;
local-level specifics in, 152–55;
research on, 150–51

senseless/reasonable divide in, 1–3; systematic analysis of Corsican, 120–26; terminology in discussing, 17; trivial motivations in, 2–7, 12, 51, 54–55, 73–78. *See also* group conflict; homicide; interpersonal conflict

Weber, Marx, 17n. 15
Whiskey Rebellion, 154–55
Whittlesey, Charles, 111
Whyte, William F., 61n. 20
Williamson, Oliver, 43n. 11
witchcraft, 83–84n. 10, 99–102

women: as acting tough, 172; coding of, as disputants, 141–42; excluded from honor concept, 171; in honor societies vs. urbanized modern areas, 174–75; in patriarchal systems, 108–9
World War I, military solidarity in, 110–11
World War II, rebuilding after, 175n. 8

Yanomami people, 59n. 18, 131
youth: hierarchies of, 23, 46–48; in urban areas, 6–7, 23, 172